MEMPHIS BEAT

MEMPHIS BEAT

The Lives and Times of America's

MUSICAL CROSSROADS

Larry Nager

St. Martin's Press ♏ New York

Grateful acknowledgement is due to the following for the use of photographs in
this book: The Memphis *Commercial Appeal*; Fantasy Records; Sam Phillips
Collection. The photographs of Jerry Lee Lewis with the Memphis Horns, Carl
Perkins with Paul McCartney, Isaac Hayes and Albert King, and Billy Lee Riley
with Bob Dylan are © Karen Pulfer Focht. Used by permission.

Design by Leah S. Carlson

Library of Congress Cataloging-in-Publication Data

Nager, Larry.
    Memphis beat: the lives and times of America's musical crossroads /
Larry Nager. —1st ed.
        p.   cm.
    Includes bibliographical references (p. 247) and index.
    ISBN 0–312–15587–5
    1. Popular music — Tennessee — Memphis — History and criticism.
I. Title.
ML3477.8.M46N34   1998
781.64'09768'19 — dc21   97–47305
                                                          CIP
                                                          MN

First edition: June 1998

10   9   8   7   6   5   4   3   2   1

To my parents, Ralph and Shirley, for teaching me the importance of the past.
To my wife, Rosanna, for keeping me in the present.
To my children, Alex and Emma, for showing me the future.
To Jody and Diana Stephens, for giving us our first home and our first friends in Memphis.
To the late Lionel Linder, for getting this whole thing started.
To the musicians of Memphis, for finding the soul of the city and sharing it with the rest of us.

CONTENTS

FOREWORD

You have in your hand a volume that contains not just history of the most valued sort: there are, in addition, signs of a Revival in the revelations contained herein.

To me this book offers a panoply of Memphis music in all its unique glory—and of the great Southern influence, black and white, it had on music and the vast human experience the world over.

Larry Nager's illuminations of the people front- and backstage, on and off the "record," are filled with insight into the power of the human spirit, through trials and tribulations, uplifting joys and downtrodden miseries, as it can only be revealed in the language of song and in the spirit that these grassroots revelators shared of themselves.

Shake hands with each of them, as you enjoy this emotional introduction to the framers of our musical Constitution, these purveyors of a ticket to a Free Music World no longer obscured by bigotry or "oversight."

Larry, you have given us a great read. Your love for and devotion to that which you know and believe in so much have been weighed herein, and have not been found wanting.

Sam Phillips

▲▲▲ ▲▲▲▲▲▲▲ ▲▲▲▲ ▲▲▲▲▲ ▲▲▲ ▲▲ ▲▲▲▲▲

ACKNOWLEDGMENTS

▼▼▼▼▼▼ ▼▼ ▼▼ ▼▼▼▼▼ ▼▼▼▼ ▼▼▼▼ ▼▼ ▼▼▼▼▼ ▼▼▼

This book would not be possible without the help of hundreds
of people in Memphis and the Delta. Despite the stereotype of
Southerners mistrusting outsiders, I found almost none of that.
Perhaps it was just the openness of the music community, but
from my first days in Memphis, when my wife and I rented our
apartment from our future dear friends, Big Star drummer Jody
Stephens and his wife Diana, to our last going-away party a little
more than four years later, I met some of the finest, most generous
people I've ever known.

Sam Phillips and his sons Knox and Jerry were among the
first members of the music community to welcome me to town,
and their helpfulness and giving spirits never flagged. They provided invaluable information on everyone from Dewey Phillips to
Furry Lewis. The Thomas Family—Rufus, Marvell, Carla, and
Vanesse—helped give a fuller portrait of Memphis and the Beale
community and aided me in countless stories. Andrew Love and
Wayne Jackson (the Memphis Horns), David Porter, and Isaac
Hayes all provided detailed background, not just about what went
on at Stax, but in the community at large through the 1960s and
1970s. I also owe a debt of gratitude to Judy Peiser and the Center
for Southern Folklore on Beale; Bill Ferris and the Center for the
Study of Southern Culture at Ole Miss; the Delta Blues Museum
in Clarksdale; Ernest Withers, who has documented the city for
half a century; Jim and Mary Lindsey Dickinson, who know
where the bodies are buried and aren't afraid to tell; Peter Guralnick and the late Robert Palmer, for sharing their love of music and
writing; Dr. Dave Evans, both for his blues scholarship and for
letting me sit in with his Last Chance Jug Band; Ellen Mitchell,
who makes the best fried chicken I've ever tasted; the folks at Sun

Studio; Roland Janes and the rest of the folks at Sam Phillips Studio; Willie Mitchell and his family; Memphis NARAS head Jon Hornyak; Mid-South Concerts' Bob Kelley, for always keeping things interesting; music savants Dick Waterman, Dennis Brooks, David Less, and Dudley Radcliff; Terri Hinte from Fantasy Records; writer/musician Rick Clark; promoter Jay Sheffield, writer Robert Gordon; the staff at WEVL; James Williams and Irwin Sheft for their wealth of jazz knowledge; *Bluespeak* editor Norm Shaw, for carrying all those records; Ken Neil and Dennis Freeland at the *Memphis Flyer*; Sid and Steve Selvidge and Bruce VanWyngarten for those Second Street String Band sessions; Rod & Hank's Vintage Guitars; John Montague and the Memphis Music Museum; Pat Tigrett, for loving Memphis music on her own grand scale; John Elkington, for believing in Beale Street when almost no one else did; Amy Culbertson, my first editor; former *Commercial Appeal* music writer Walter Dawson; current *Commercial Appeal* music writer Bill Ellis; *Commercial Appeal* entertainment editor Jon Sparks, a great editor and a better friend; Cal Morgan, my editor at St. Martin's, who knows more about Memphis music than most Memphians; photographer/historian Ernest Withers; and Cincinnati photographer Michael Wilson, for making me presentable. Karen Focht, Larry Coyne, and Claude Jones of the *Commercial Appeal*'s photo department provided patient assistance in gathering the photos. And thanks to everyone else I've momentarily forgotten, but will surely remember when I wake up at 4:00 A.M.

Many of the people who aided and abetted this in various ways have since passed on: Luther Allison, Carl Perkins, Albert King, Charlie Rich, Jimmy Rogers, Lee Baker, Junior Kimbrough, Booker T. Laury, George Paul Eldridge, Jim Kingsley, and *Commercial Appeal* editor Lionel Linder, the man who hired me and helped get this thing started.

Finally, my deepest thanks go out to all the musicians of Memphis, past, present, and future, for finding the soul of this city and sharing it with the rest of us.

▲▲▲▲▲▲▲▲▲▲▲▲▲▲▲▲▲▲▲▲▲▲▲▲▲▲▲▲▲▲

INTRODUCTION

▼▼▼▼▼▼▼▼▼▼▼▼▼▼▼▼▼▼▼▼▼▼▼▼▼▼▼▼▼▼

We live in an age when everything is possible and nothing is real. Millions of us band together in virtual communities, E-mailing strangers through our home computers, working at jobs that fail to satisfy us, entertained by electronic gadgets that keep us disconnected from each other and ourselves. Meanwhile, outside our cubicles, the malling of America continues, as the country loses its diverse regional identities and every place comes more and more to look, feel, taste, smell, and sound just like every place else.

All that standardization has come at a cost—the sense of emptiness, of alienation, of rootlessness that so many of us feel. We combat that by trying to buy a history, hoping to gain some sense of connectedness to something bigger, older, more enduring than ourselves, something in which we might find our true reflection. This search takes on many forms, from spiritual quests to collections of folk art. Ethnic foods, gourmet coffees, Cuban cigars, log homes, world music—all those trends are, at their core, attempts to make some sense out of our high-tech, low-impact culture, to attain some feeling of uniqueness in a world gone bland.

For many of us, that quest for authentic experience leads to music. Not the manufactured hits and custom-made pop fads on today's charts, but something more enduring, the blues, jazz, gospel, and rock and roll that exploded out of the South in the middle of this century. Trace those sounds back to the source, and all roads lead to Memphis and the Mississippi Delta. Memphis is arguably the most musical city on the planet; again and again, revolutionary sounds have emerged from its streets to change the way the world, sang, danced, played guitar, and lived.

In the modern search for the genuine, the distinctive regional identity still found in Memphis and the Delta has become all the more rare and precious. The music that has come out of this area owes almost nothing to the music industry centers of the East and West Coasts. Instead it's born from local traditions, from music communities with roots going back to slavery times, when field hands entertained themselves and their owners after the sun went down.

Memphis first gained a reputation as a music center back in W. C. Handy's day, almost one hundred years ago. In a city that was half black and half white, where social segregation was the rule but cultural integration was a fact of life, the primary colors of American music forever blended. Black and white, rural and urban, the haves and have-nots came together to create a tradition that became a dream for generations to come, a path for younger musicians to follow. And follow it they did.

I was born just a few miles from Handy's house—the one he died in, that is, in Yonkers, New York. And yet, a thousand miles away from the Mississippi, I too was raised on Memphis music, playing washboard in Memphis-inspired jug bands when I was barely a teenager and listening to the Delta blues–influenced sounds of the Rolling Stones, Canned Heat, Led Zeppelin, and other blues-rock bands on the then-new FM radio stations.

Like thousands of others, I was curious about where all that music came from, and tracing its roots led me back, again and again, to this "metropolis on the American Nile." In 1982, after kicking around the Midwest and Southeast in bluegrass and jug bands and blues groups, I began writing about music for newspapers and magazines. In 1991, the music reporter job came open at the *Commercial Appeal* in Memphis and off we went, my wife Rosanna and myself.

I was amazed at what I found, how little had changed since the

days I'd read about. But the music seemed intertwined in ways
that didn't fit all the books I'd read. I realized that no one had ever
written a book about Memphis music purely as Memphis music.
And it *was* a distinct music, despite its incredible diversity: the
same cultural forces that worked on the blues of Memphis Minnie
acted on the jazz of Phineas Newborn Jr. and the rockabilly of
Elvis. Memphis music, I came to see, was in many ways the same
story over and over again.

I'd never seen a place so uniquely itself as Memphis. There's
simply nowhere else like it. The entire city seems to move to its
own rhythm, one that's just a bit behind the beat. You can hear it
in the ramshackle blues of the Memphis Jug Band and in the
southern soul of Stax and Hi. You can even see it in the way people in Memphis drive. No one here stops for yellow lights, and
even red lights are fair game for the first couple seconds. But everybody follows that rhythm, so folks at the red lights know to hesitate
a few seconds after the green appears.

That's Memphis, laid-back, taking its own sweet time, breathing to its own Mississippi rhythm. The heartbeat of the city, and
the music this city has made for more than one hundred years, has
shaped and continues to shape the world.

That's the Memphis beat—just far enough behind to be ahead
of everyone else.

This book tries to tell that story, combining the hundreds of
original interviews I conducted while at the *Commercial Appeal*
with period newspaper accounts, every related book I could find,
and the thousands of recordings of Memphis music from every
era that I've enjoyed through the years. I hope my perspective—
that of an outsider who lived and worked in the music community
on a daily basis; of a former professional musician, a student of an-
thropology, a practicing journalist, and a lifelong music lover—has
allowed me to do some justice to the story of the Memphis beat.

It's an amazing story, woven through with surprising harmonies
and counterrhythms. And it's not finished yet.

1

▼▼▼▼▼▼▼▼▼▼▼▼▼▼▼▼▼▼▼▼▼▼▼▼▼▼▼

Conquistadores, Frontier Folk, and Fiddlers

Hernando de Soto was the first European to get the blues in the Mississippi Delta. Unlike the tourists who come to Memphis and the Mid-South today, though, that's not what the old conquistador was looking for.

It was around 1541, a little more than four hundred years before Elvis hit town, that de Soto found his way to the banks of the Mississippi, a few miles downriver of the fourth Chickasaw bluff, the future site of Memphis. De Soto was hoping for the sort of reception he'd found in Peru with his old boss Francisco Pizarro. But instead of easily conquered Incas and wealthy cities filled with gold, de Soto and his troops found only hostile, Catholicism-resistant Chickasaw and other local tribes. Disheartened, the Spaniards quickly built four rafts, escaped across the river, and headed west.

Back then, the future home of the blues was still just a happy hunting ground. Bear, panther, and deer roamed the muddy banks of the Mississippi and on up to what would one day be Union Avenue, Beale Street, and other Memphis landmarks. While the Spanish seemed interested only in gold and converts, other European nations were less single-minded. The rich fur trade, combined with the river bluffs offering protection from the Mississippi's frequent flooding (as well as military assaults), drew the attention of England and France over the next couple of centuries. The area became a battleground in the French and British wars of the eighteenth century. To tip the balance, local tribes of Chickasaw were supplied with English guns.

At that point, it seemed a toss-up whether the region would wind up British or French. Even the Spanish were waiting in the wings, sequestered reasonably nearby in Florida and Mexico. With the enormous wealth pouring out of the Spanish colonies in South and Central America, there was at first little threat from that quarter. That would change, however, as Spain's mounting European war debts soon outweighed what little South American gold eluded the English pirates sailing the Caribbean shipping lanes.

During the first third of the eighteenth century, the conflict over what was then North America's western frontier came down to the British and French. Thanks to the Chickasaw's hostility toward the latter, the odds weighed in England's favor, even though French forts dotted the Mississippi downriver of Memphis at Biloxi, Natchez, and other sites. The Chickasaw Bluffs that later became Memphis proved strategically vital to their namesake tribes, who used them as vantage points from which to wage guerrilla warfare.

In 1739, Jean-Baptiste Le Moyne, sieur de Bienville, the French governor of Louisiana, discovered just how effective those bluffs could be when he attempted to expand his holdings with a pathetically unsuccessful campaign against the Chickasaw. Despite his superior weapons and sizable army, Bienville waited too long to launch his attack, remaining in the fort his men had constructed, Fort Asuncion. By then his forces of Frenchmen, African Americans, and Indians of other tribes were decimated, the Europeans by disease, the rest by desertion. It wasn't much of a fight, but Bienville's halfhearted, unsuccessful campaign has the distinction of being the first documented historical event on the site of what became modern Memphis.

The British eventually won out in the Memphis area, while the French consolidated their holdings downriver in New Orleans, which may explain why it's much easier to get a glass of iced tea in Memphis today than a demitasse of café au lait. More to the point of our story, the British victory cleared the way for the slave-labor plantation system that had proven so profitable for the English in Virginia, the Carolinas, and the rich sugarcane fields of the Caribbean islands.

But for the rest of the eighteenth century the region produced more conflict than cotton. Spain, by then debt-ridden, made repeated claims. In 1795, Don Manuel Gayoso de Lemos, the Spanish governor of Louisiana, perhaps figuring the newly independent nation had its hands full elsewhere, tried to move in on America's western frontier. He bought a section of the lower bluffs from France for thirty thousand dollars and built a fort there. President George Washington responded quickly, however, calling the purchase "an unwarranted aggression." Facing potential attack from the young country, Gayoso's garrison in 1797 burned their fort and crossed the river to build Fort Esperanza. Later known as Hopefield, the Arkansas settlement would develop a reputation for rowdiness and lawlessness that outstripped even its wild and woolly neighbor across the river.

Fort Esperanza remained worrisome to the British settlement, but by that point the south bluffs had firmly become part of the western American frontier and were well on their way to becoming Memphis.

Like many men of that era, Gayoso remains a part of Memphis life today in the form of a street name. In his case, history became notoriety: Gayoso Street, which runs parallel between Beale and Union, became home to some of the city's more opulent brothels in the late nineteenth and early twentieth centuries. Employing light-skinned black women, the Gayoso Street whorehouses, like similar establishments in New Orleans, catered exclusively to a well-to-do white clientele. Many a prominent Memphian, waiting to go upstairs, first developed a taste for the blues and ragtime he heard on those whorehouse pianos played by itinerant musicians from the Gilded Age onward.

If the history of New Orleans is any indication, it would prob-

ably have been much better for the region's slaves had the French
or the Spanish won out in the Delta. One of the early rationales for
slavery was that it was a way for good Christians to bring their re-
ligion to the idol-worshiping African. As Protestant Anglo-Saxon
slaveowners forced Christianity on their slaves, they banned drums
and anything else that smacked of the old tribal religions and folk-
ways.

News of the bloody slave rebellions in the Caribbean cemented
the region's ban against drums, which were believed to be a form
of slave telegraph. By contrast, in New Orleans's Congo Square,
Sunday afternoon slave drumming exhibitions and dances were officially sanctioned and became a long-standing tradition enjoyed
by blacks and whites alike. Despite the ban, though, drumming did
survive in remote parts of the Delta in the form of fife-and-drum
bands. The traditional British marching bands (familiar to us
through Revolutionary War iconography) became, in the nineteenth century, a venue for slave musicians to preserve African
traditions within the bounds of acceptable "white" music. Fife-
and-drum bands continue to be heard today in parts of the Delta
and the Mississippi hill country outside Memphis; along with the
field hollers and work songs of that period, they constitute a direct
link with black southerners' African heritage.

By 1819, British claims to its former colony had forever been severed by the War of 1812. America was busily attending to the business of building a new nation when Generals Andrew Jackson and
James Winchester, in partnership with retired Tennessee Supreme
Court chief justice John Overton, founded the city of Memphis.

Overton and Jackson had been working toward that moment
since they'd first acquired the site in the 1790s from the estate of
John Rice, who was killed by Indians in central Tennessee. Overton got the 5,000-acre tract for $500, $2,000 less than the late Mr.
Rice had paid for it. With political connections in mind, he sold
a half share to his friend Jackson for a mere $100. That was a good
start, but it wasn't until 1818, when the Chickasaw ceded almost

7 million additional acres for around $300,000, that Memphis became more than a pipe dream.

It wasn't out of chronic generosity or a shared death wish that the Chickasaw gave up their land, of course. As far back as 1802, trading posts had been set up in the area for the purpose of running the Indians so heavily into debt that they would be forced to sell their land. That bit of strategy came from Thomas Jefferson and would be revived years later in a slightly altered form in the plantation-sharecropper system. The plantation store would re-place the trading post, as recently freed African Americans, lacking land, traded their newfound freedom for seed, tools, and other ne-cessities, spending themselves and often their descendants back into virtual slavery.

In many ways, Memphis in its early years possessed a more lib-eral racial attitude than it would exhibit from the Civil War on-ward. So liberal, in fact, that the first first lady of Memphis was a black woman. In 1826, following incorporation, Marcus Winches-ter, son of Memphis's cofounder, was elected the town's first mayor. His wife, Lucille Lenora, was described in historical ac-counts as "a beautiful French quadroon." The couple had married in Louisiana, where, unlike Tennessee, racial intermarriage was legal. The marriage caused some talk — hypocritically enough, as many white male Memphians had black mistresses. Nonetheless, Winchester managed to be reelected, a situation that would have been unimaginable even twenty years later, as racial lines began to be more rigidly drawn. His successor, Isaac Rawlings, also had a black wife, but his marriage, a common-law arrangement, was deemed more acceptable.

In its early years Memphis had to contend with a variety of rival settlements in the area. In 1824, the Shelby County seat was set ten miles east of Memphis on the Wolf River in the town of Raleigh. An exodus of the more refined settlers followed, as Memphis was already earning its reputation as a wide-open frontier river town. Most Memphis houses at the time were little more than rough log cabins. Bears would occasionally wander into the "city" from the surrounding woods, roaming streets filled with holes so deep that as late as 1843 a team of oxen drowned after falling into one.

"A tough and uninviting hole overrun by the scum of the river": That is how historian Gerald M. Capers described the Memphis of 1820–40 in his classic *Biography of a River Town*. "And proud of it," he might well have added. Memphis was working overtime to make a name for itself as a sprawling, brawling, hard-drinking, hard-living river settlement. The first Memphis brothel opened in 1830, but years before that prostitutes were already freelancing up and down the muddy streets. Whiskey sold for twenty-five cents a gallon and was even served outside religious camp meetings, which, like most activities in early Memphis, tended to be rowdy affairs. For those who needed an excuse, there were sound medical reasons for preferring whiskey to the local water, which was pulled out of the unsavory Wolf River that snaked through the settlement.

There was whiskey. There were women. And in Memphis, from the start, there was music. The earliest "Memphis sound" was provided by itinerant fiddlers and banjo players sawing and plunking tunes like "Zip Coon" (better known today as "Turkey in the Straw"), "The Eighth of January" (commemorating the War of 1812's Battle of New Orleans, it topped the pop charts 150 years later as "The Battle of New Orleans," with lyrics by Ozark folk singer Jimmie Driftwood), "Old Dan Tucker," "Arkansas Traveler," and "Boatman." The tunes were similar to the reels played by British and Irish fiddlers, rhythmic dance pieces consisting of two parts, repeated in an AABB fashion. The regional differences that would later develop in American fiddle music had yet to take shape, but the African influence, with its greater emphasis on supple, syncopated rhythms, was already beginning to enter the music.

One ingredient was missing, though. Today it's the center of just about every rock, country, and blues band, but the guitar was almost never heard in those early ensembles. In fact, while fairly common in the Spanish colonies of South America, it was rarely seen anywhere in North America until 1833, when German immigrant Christian Friedrich Martin arrived in New York to establish one of the very first guitar-making shops in the country. Martin, a carpenter, had made boxes in his native Germany in which makers of fine violins shipped their instruments. Crafting those crates, he came up with the idea of a box that made music as well as contained it. And though Elvis leading the rock revolution with his leather-bound C. F. Martin D-18 "box" was 120 years and a whole universe away, Martin's instinct was true: He created a new instrument for a new country. But change came slowly, and the violin continued as king of the instruments. For the rest of the nineteenth century the guitar remained primarily a status symbol of the rich, found in fashionable drawing rooms where its delicate catgut strings were primly plucked by the lily-white fingers of cultured young ladies.

For the raucous dancing of the sort favored by those old-time Memphians, all that was needed was a single fiddle player with a bowing arm liberally lubricated by the local home brew. More proper folk considered dancing a tool of the devil, but even they would have admitted it was relatively wholesome and considerably less lethal than the river folk's other pastimes. Those early Memphians spent many a night beating their feet in the Mississippi mud to rowdy frontier jigs and reels, and they were still hot-stepping when W. C. Handy hit town at the turn of the century. "Memphis has always been a grand dance town, one of the hottest of the hot," he would write in his autobiography.

Despite its rough beginnings, Memphis was headed to much greater things, and as the nation grew, the Bluff City kept pace. The Mississippi was becoming a more important route of travel and commerce. The flatboat gave way to the steamboat, with the first packet line between Memphis and New Orleans starting in 1834. With the coming of the railroads, Memphis achieved a powerful position as the trade center between St. Louis and New Orleans. In 1840, when the population numbered 1,800, Memphis began calling itself a city; twenty years later it was home to 22,623, and had overtaken Nashville as the largest city in Tennessee.

That same period saw the growth of a uniquely American form of theater: the minstrel show. Many of the dance tunes that set feet to stepping in Memphis's early years were first popularized in the day's minstrel revues, fast becoming the country's most popular form of theatrical entertainment. After the War of 1812, when the States had once and for all beaten the British, Americans were eager to distance themselves from their European roots. Distinctively American forms of culture and entertainment began to develop. Soon the American stage became overrun with such uniquely native stock characters as the New England Yankee and the Noble Red Man. The African minstrel was not far behind.

There had been blackface performers as far back as the eighteenth century, but most of them made little attempt to re-create authentic black style in dialogue or music. That would soon change. In 1822, English performer Charles Matthews traveled through America collecting African American dialects, stories, songs, and malaprops to use in his productions. He would later tell of attending a performance of *Hamlet* by the African Theater Company. During the play's famous soliloquy, Matthews recalled, the audience of freedmen misinterpreted the phrase "by opposing" as "by opossum" and, preferring American fiddle music to Shakespeare, began raucously calling for "Possum up a Gum Tree," a dance tune still played by American fiddlers.

By 1830, minstrelsy had taken on a distinctly authentic flavor. The humor remained condescending at best and flagrantly racist at worst, but many of the tunes performed on the stage came from folk tradition (and others, just as surely, would become part of tradition years after their minstrel debut). One performer, Thomas D. Rice, adapted a hobbling "jig-walk" dance he'd learned in 1828 from an old crippled slave. Rice's "Jim Crow" became such a popular minstrel act that it later entered daily speech in the term for segregation legislation — "Jim Crow" laws.

In those early days, blackface performers such as Rice worked as singles, usually with traveling circuses and the like. But the 1840s saw blackface entertainment become a full-fledged craze, and the shows expanded to meet the demand. In 1842, four men — one of them Dan Emmett, who introduced the anthem "Dixie," — formed the Virginia Minstrels, banding together in hopes of surviving the economic recession then battering the entertainment business. Though the quartet broke up the following year during a successful tour of England, they would inspire hundreds of similar minstrel troupes. The minstrel shows were most successful in the urban centers of the East and in Europe, places where genuine African American musicians were rare and sufficiently exotic to draw large audiences.

Many minstrels also toured the South. Between 1845 and 1860, at least one minstrel troupe a year performed in Memphis, according to Robert C. Toll's history of the minstrel movement, *Blacking Up*. But minstrelsy wasn't the only entertainment enjoyed by antebellum Memphians. The November 1, 1844, issue of the *Appeal*, the precursor of the city's modern daily newspaper, the *Commercial Appeal*, advertised: "To the ladies in particular . . . a new splendid lot of Music" offered by E. W. Rowlett. To play that sheet music, the merchant also offered pianos, violins, flutes, harps, and guitars for sale. Lessons on those instruments were being offered by "Mrs. Johnson, late of Boston," in her school for young ladies. And Mrs. Johnson's wasn't the only palace of higher learning in Memphis. The Collegiate Institute of Memphis offered two departments, "one for each of the sexes." Memphians then were enjoying a variety of pastimes, from horse racing on the Central Course to the Vaux Hall Gardens resort, which advertised that "a good band of music . . . will be in attendance." Restaurants and hotels were sprouting up, as the newly opened Delmonico's offered "Epicurean delights" at thirty-seven cents a meal. Within a few years there would be touring troupes appearing at Crisp's Gaiety Theatre or the Old Memphis Theatre. Famed opera diva Jenny

Lind sang in Memphis in 1851, and Shakespearean actors like Edwin Booth and James Hackett regularly made stops in the Bluff City.

Although minstrelsy helped create and perpetuate the familiar racial stereotype of the lazy, simpleminded black man, the fiddle and banjo tunes performed in the shows were some of the first examples of the black-white musical interaction in American music, and today it's impossible to pin down the origins of many tunes as either African or Anglo. Many of the minstrels' jigs, hornpipes, and reels had roots in the Celtic traditions of Ireland, Scotland, and England, but the unique changes in rhythm found in their American versions may well have come from slave musicians, whose more sophisticated sense of syncopation came from the polyrhythmic traditions of West Africa, where most American slaves had originated.

Slave musicians had long been a part of American music. Minstrel pioneer Matthews wrote of a conversation with another touring European, a Norwegian violinist named Ole Bull, who appeared in Memphis in 1856. Bull told him how, at one of his performances in New Orleans, "a nigger fiddler" had stolen the show. W. C. Handy's uncle Whit Walker was both a former slave and a fiddler. For plantation slaves fiddling was a source of extra income, better food, and higher status. In *Lay My Burden Down: A Folk History of Slavery*, one of the former slaves interviewed tells of "Old John Drayton . . . the smartest of all the niggers on the master's place. Old John play for all the dances on the plantation. He fair make the fiddle talk. When Master give a dance he always call 'pon John." The tradition continued well into the twentieth century; for many country blues musicians, including Mississippians Bo Chatmon (also known as Bo Carter) and Big Bill Broonzy, the fiddle was part of their earliest musical training.

The banjo traces its roots to West Africa, though similar instruments can be found in China, Japan, and the Mideast as well. It was minstrel musician J. W. Sweeney, however, who is said to have added the shortened fifth string, creating the instrument familiar to bluegrass fans today. And it's in bluegrass that many of the minstrel-slave tunes survive. Until shortly before his death in 1996, Bill Monroe, the eighty-four-year-old Father of Bluegrass, closed every Grand Ole Opry performance with the old minstrel piece "Watermelon on the Vine."

Middle Tennessee, the area around Nashville, remained a hotbed of that sort of musical black-white interaction well into the twentieth century. DeFord Bailey was an African American harmonica soloist who performed on the Opry from 1927 to 1941. Bailey, who inspired Opry founder and former *Commercial Appeal* columnist George D. Hay to name the program *The Grand Ole Opry*, also played banjo, possessing a repertoire that ranged from minstrel and square dance tunes to blues.

In 1942 and 1946, the Library of Congress recorded two black string bands from Middle Tennessee: the duo of fiddler Frank Patterson and singer-banjoist Nathan Frazier, and a trio consisting of fiddler John Lusk, banjoist Murph Gribble, and guitarist Albert York. Lusk's grandfather had been a slave fiddler in New Orleans who no doubt had played many of the same tunes that had stolen the Norwegian Ole Bull's thunder more than a century earlier. A 1989 Rounder Records reissue of those recordings reveals the tight interplay between Frazier and Patterson, highlighted by banjoist Frazier's dynamic doubling of fiddler Patterson's melody lines. Their repertoire included that old War of 1812 favorite "Eighth of January," the minstrel tune "Dan Tucker," and the folk tune "Bile Them Cabbage Down." The music would be immediately recognizable to anyone familiar with old-timey country music, but this isn't exactly hillbilly music: Though Frazier plays a tautly rhythmic clawhammer style, instead of the high, nasal mountaineer's vocal style, he sings in an unusually deep, resonant voice. The fiddle-banjo-guitar trio led by Lusk, while less instrumentally accomplished, played a rarer set of tunes, including one from slavery times, "Pateroller'll Catch You." Also known as "Run Nigger Run," it exhorts a runaway slave to escape the plantation owner's patrol that's after him. Both bands called their style of music "breakdown," a term used by American fiddlers, both black and white, in referring to up-tempo dance tunes.

Signs of such interplay have turned up as far afield as Belize, the Central American nation formerly known as British Honduras. There the descendants of black slaves who had come from Jamaica, Barbados, and Bermuda developed a style of music they called "brukdon," obviously a derivative of "breakdown." An album of "brukdon" recordings from the seventies and eighties, released in 1994 on the Corason label, includes Brad Pattico & Co.'s "Boil Di Cabbage Don," a variant of the familiar American breakdown, "Bile Dem Cabbage Down." Did it come to Belize from the common stock of fiddle tunes created in the nineteenth century by slave musicians? It seems likely.

There remains very little direct record of this early black-white crossover in America, however, as black string bands were rarely recorded by the commercial record companies early in the century. The reason had nothing to do with the quality of the music; black country musicians simply didn't fit the racially based catalog divisions. In the twenties and thirties recordings by African Americans were routinely placed in the "race" series; rural white musicians were listed in the "old-time songs" or "hillbilly" sections. By some, the division was taken as seriously as any of the other "Jim Crow" laws; early recordings by some blues singers even had "colored" etched into the shellac. In 1928, when the white blues and ragtime duo Austin and Lee Allen were mistakenly placed in Columbia Records' "race" section, the Franklin, Tennessee, natives sued their record company for $250,000. Yet it was hardly a random error; musically the Allen Brothers' records fit the "race" section far more than some of the countrified material put out by such black string bands as the Mississippi Sheiks.

Around 1903, a Mississippi string band much like the Sheiks is credited by W. C. Handy with inspiring his conversion to "our native music," turning him into "an *American* composer [italics his]." Handy and his conventional, well-schooled dance band were in the Delta town of Cleveland, Mississippi, playing a program of light classics and popular tunes, when their white audience asked if Handy would mind if "a local colored band played a few dances." Handy and company happily took a break while a trio of mandolin, guitar, and "a worn-out bass . . . struck up one of those over-and-over strains that seem to have no very clear beginning and certainly no ending at all."

When it did come to an end, it was met with a hail of coins that Handy says more than equaled what his nine-man band would take home for their entire evening's work. Handy's description of the trio's music makes no mention of the music being blues, and with the crowd's request for dance music from the country trio and Handy's own reference to "over-and-over strains," it seems more than likely that the rural string band played breakdowns and reels, simple country dance tunes that usually consist of two separate sections which repeat as long as the dancers' legs and the musicians' arms hold out. Although usually considered a white musical tradition, that country dance music, like so many of the multicultural sounds that have come from Memphis and the Delta before and since, is the product of a combined Anglo/Celtic/minstrel/slave tradition with no true color.

For Handy, though, it bore a very distinctive hue — the color of money. "My idea of what constitutes music was changed by the sight of that silver money cascading around the splay feet of a Mississippi string band," he later wrote. It was a lesson that Handy would remember well a few years later, when he was leading the hottest band on Beale Street.

2

Birth of the Beale Street Blues

"Nostalgia just ain't what it used to be," goes the old saying, and that certainly seems the case on Beale Street. The one constant that runs through the street's history is that old-timers are always complaining that Beale is just a pale shadow of its former glorious self. W. C. Handy himself may be the Father of the Beale Street Bemoan as well as the Beale Street Blues. In his autobiography, *Father of the Blues* (1941), he writes of his feelings on leaving Memphis in 1917: "There's no denying that Beale Street changed. Even at that moment it was losing something essential to its former character."

Of course, in its long and checkered career, Beale has had more identities than barbecue joints. During the twentieth century alone it's been in a state of constant change, first gaining fame for its turn-of-the-century gambling dens, then evolving into the center of the black vaudeville circuit at the Palace Theatre in the teens and twenties. It survived Prohibition and the depression thanks to Boss Crump–sanctioned speakeasies that provided work for such future blues legends as Peter "Memphis Slim" Chatman. After World War II and through the fifties Beale showcased the new R & B stars and electric blues performers; only with the sixties did pawnshops finally overtake the nightclubs, as the street seemed headed to oblivion, or urban renewal — which of course was the same thing.

No one's even quite sure how the thoroughfare that would become known as "the Main Street of Negro America" first got its
name, though most say it was in honor of a military man named
John Beale, who gained some fame for some now-forgotten hero-
ics in the War of 1812. Until the Civil War, it was primarily the
home of rich white Memphians, who graced it with such imposing structures as the Hunt-Phelan mansion. Constructed in 1841,
this house at 533 Beale served as General Ulysses S. Grant's head-
quarters during the war; it still stands today and was reopened for
tours in 1996. When Grant was in residence, a few blocks toward
the river on the north side of Beale between Hernando and Third
stood one of the city's two public markets, built in 1859 in the European style popularized in New Orleans's French Quarter.

The Civil War left Memphis relatively unharmed, but peace
was hell. In 1862, following the North's victory at the Battle of
Memphis (which despite its grandiose name was a minor naval
skirmish on the Mississippi that lasted just a couple of hours),
Union troops took possession of the city. The presses for the city's
newspaper, the *Memphis Daily Appeal*, were loaded onto a railroad car and taken down to Grenada, Mississippi, where the *Appeal* continued publishing on the run from Union troops. Back at
home, for the remainder of the war, Memphis life and business,
particularly trading in cotton and contraband, went on relatively
undisturbed.

But, like the rest of the South, Memphis took Reconstruction
hard. On April 30, 1866, the city saw the South's first major race
riot. Beale historian George Lee writes in his *Beale Street: Where
the Blues Began* that it was caused by a fight between two young
wagon drivers, one African American, the other Irish American,
which resulted in the latter's death. The fight escalated into a battle between black federal soldiers and local Irish cops bristling
under their new, lower status. However it began, white Memphians rioted for three days, burning, looting, and raping their way
through the black section of town. When it was over, forty-six black
Memphians were dead. No whites were reported killed.

Racial conflict was just beginning. Union loyalists in western Tennessee were frequently attacked, and reports emerged from the city in late 1866 that gangs of unrepentant rebels were confiscating guns from blacks. Things soon got worse for the freedmen and -women, not just in Memphis but in all of Tennessee. In 1866, a secret society was formed in Pulaski, Tennessee, taking its name from *kuklous*, Latin for "circle." The Ku Klux Klan, purportedly modeled after a college fraternity, was organized by a handful of privileged young men, bored with civilian life after their military experiences in the War Between the States. What started as an isolated rash of mean-spirited pranks soon spread throughout the South, degenerating into the violence and terrorism for which the night riders of the Klan are remembered today. As the story goes, in 1867 local heads from the various Klan "dens" met in Nashville to organize under a secret national charter. It was at this meeting that the distinguished Confederate general and prominent Memphis businessman Nathan Bedford Forrest is said to have been installed as the grand wizard of the Invisible Empire of the Ku Klux Klan.

Before the war, Forrest had been Memphis's leading slave trader, the foremost dealer in human flesh in the largest slave market between the eastern seaboard and New Orleans. His market at 87 Adams Street in the north end of downtown which boasted "the best assortment of field hands, house servants and mechanics," earned Forrest a reported one hundred thousand dollars annually. Ever the canny businessman, he showed how healthy and happy his slaves were with daily parades outside his market featuring his slaves singing and playing fiddles. Ironically enough, these performances were some of the first documented public performances by black musicians in Memphis.

Forrest never swayed from his white supremacist convictions. After Emancipation, the ex-general was allowed to legally continue what was for all intents and purposes slavery, running a combination penal farm and cotton plantation for black prisoners on

President's Island just southwest of downtown Memphis. Forrest was considered important enough as a Confederate hero and military strategist that today a statue in his honor stands in the park at Union and Manassas that bears his name. The park and statue continue to arouse protests from the city's African American citizens, but so far with little effect.

Tennessee was particularly ripe for racial strife, and it's no surprise Memphis was the scene of that first post–Civil War race riot. Mountainous East Tennessee, with no plantations requiring a large labor force, had been a Unionist stronghold throughout the Civil War. It was also the birthplace of Andrew Johnson, who succeeded to the presidency following Lincoln's assassination. The Tennessean in the White House gave his home state special attention, putting it through Reconstruction much faster than other Southern states. Cities like Memphis tended to be refuges for freedmen, but the Klan also found safe haven there. Arriving in the city shortly after the Nashville meeting, its first activities were recorded in 1868.

In February 1867, black Tennesseans were given the right to vote, although the best government jobs remained in the hands of carpetbagging whites. When the Klan arrived in Memphis, some newspapers, such as the now-defunct *Avalanche*, supported it. Perhaps its harsh rule of intimidation seemed preferable to the postwar chaos that kept alive Memphis's renown as the wildest city on the Mississippi. In 1867, an estimated three thousand Memphians reportedly were addicted to opium, either smoking it in pipes in the oriental style or taking it orally in socially acceptable laudanum, available at every apothecary. Gambling and prostitution remained popular pursuits, and roving youth gangs made traveling alone at night potentially fatal.

Unlike the night riders who terrorized rural blacks, the Memphis Klan took a less aggressive tack, organizing boycotts of Unionist businesses and showing its strength in parades. There were, however Klan-like organizations of a more sinister nature, such as the Supreme Cyclopean Council. When a clandestine Supreme Cyclopean meeting was broken up on April 6, 1868, at Hernando and Beale, the group's hierarchy was found to include an assassination committee targeting prominent Reconstructionists.

It was a desperate time for proud ex-Confederates, who faced the humiliation of losing the war, their plantations, their slaves, and their rights. Confederate dead totaled 260,000, more than one-fifth of the South's entire white male population. Of the survivors, thousands were maimed. A full 20 percent of Mississippi's total revenues in 1865 went to the purchase of wooden limbs for wounded veterans. White Southerners bitterly watched their former slaves transformed from servile plowshares into electoral swords, wielded against their former owners by radical Republican politicians.

However, that boiling racial cauldron was soon overturned by a tiny mosquito, as yellow-fever-bearing "galley-nippers" forever changed the face of Memphis. The disease had been a problem since the city on the river was founded, and by war's end Memphis had already seen two minor outbreaks. In 1867, a third yellow fever epidemic hit, killing hundreds.

The Mississippi was a lifeline, helping create a bustling economy that had made Memphis the biggest city in Tennessee and brought its commerce, primarily in cotton, up to $51.5 million by 1860. It transported death just as efficiently. The swampy land and frequent flooding made Memphis a breeding ground for mosquitoes and a prime target for mass infection, with a whole world of new and exotic bacteria making its way upriver from the international port of New Orleans. Endemic to West Africa, point of origin for the region's slaves, yellow fever is carried by the *Aedes aegypti* mosquito, which breeds in standing water. The water barrels aboard slave ships provided a perfect breeding ground for the mosquitoes, often making the Middle Passage slaving route from Africa even more dangerous for tropical-disease-susceptible Northern European slavers than yellow-fever-resistant slaves. In Memphis, the city's water cisterns, the fetid Wolf River, and the stagnant Gayoso Bayou proved even more ideal environments for the deadly *Aedes aegypti*, as well as other infectious insects and bacteria in profusion. In the oppressively humid summer heat minor cuts often turned to gangrene, and major infections were almost invariably fatal. In 1873, yellow fever returned, striking five thousand citizens and killing two thousand. An attack of cholera took almost three hundred additional lives.

The worst was yet to come. In 1878 and 1879, twenty thousand Memphians were struck by yellow fever. Almost six thousand died, vomiting the black bile that was the unmistakable sign of the disease. Though the newspapers advertised such "cures" as Tabasco sauce, nothing helped, and a panic seized the city. In September 1878, twenty-five thousand people fled in one two-week period. By the end of the month, there were fewer than twenty thousand left in the city. Of that, fourteen thousand were African Americans. The usual rumors of black men raping white women circulated, customary when white Southerners of the time found themselves in a state of hysteria. The fact that many of the blacks remained in the city to guard the homes and property of their white employers garnered less attention.

The disease forever changed the cultural life of Memphis. Visitors today often wonder why the city has no ethnic enclaves, none of the Little Italys or Greek Towns usually found in cities the size and age of Memphis. The answer is simple: To escape the epidemics, ethnic groups deserted the city en masse, including virtually the entire German population, which took residence upriver in St. Louis. The recently arrived Irish, with no resistance to tropical diseases and without the money to leave, died in the slums of the Pinch district. Wealthy whites left their mansions to their servants' care and fled to the countryside. Most were not so fortunate, as Memphis became a nightmarish plague city. The Shelby County undertaker kept four wagons busy collecting corpses day and night, and in front of the Peabody Hotel "the coffins filled with the dead were stacked up like bales of cotton," according to historian Shields McIlwaine. Hundreds were buried in shallow graves with no markers. Rats from the river made their way up into the town to feed on unburied corpses, spreading further infection.

The city's poor sanitary conditions, which some compared to the original Memphis, in Egypt, were exacerbated by an unusually hot Indian summer. Those escaping the city often carried the disease with them and the epidemic spread as far as Bowling Green, Kentucky. Cities near Memphis, such as Jackson, Tennessee, set up roadblocks, refusing to admit anyone who might have been infected.

Even when the fever subsided, many who had fled refused to return. Of the 7,000 whites who had remained in the city, 6,800 were hit with the fever. Three out of four of them died. Among Memphis's black population of 14,000, the odds for recovery were far greater. Descended from West Africans who were resistant to the disease and who had been hardy enough to survive the incredible ordeal of transportation in festering slave ships, these black Memphians had already withstood generations of exposure to the South's germ pool. Of 10,800 yellow fever cases among the city's African American population, only 800 were fatal.

When the plague was over, the decimated city was no longer even a city; forced to give up its municipal charter, it was reduced to a taxing district. One man's faith in Memphis never wavered, however. As panic swept the city, Robert Church, son of a white riverboat captain and a mulatto woman whose mother, the story goes, was a Malaysian princess, was quietly buying up all the land he could. Church, who had served on his father's boats as chief steward, put to use his skills in buying and selling provisions when he became one of Memphis's first black saloonkeepers after the Civil War. As an enterprising black man, he was a target during the race riots of 1866, but he survived a gunshot wound and went on to become the South's first African American millionaire.

He continued to show his loyalty to the city that had made him rich. While white Memphis was still debating the creation of a segregated park system for itself, Church built a park for black Memphis. Church Park and Auditorium on Beale, east of Fourth Street, opened in 1899, a year before the Memphis city government announced its park system plan.

Church later built the Dixie Park amusement facility, described by W. C. Handy as "a suntanned Coney Island." Dixie Park, with its rides and its bandstand, provided work for brass bands such as Handy's and was a favorite spot for thousands of black Mid-Southerners. One of them was blues singer Alberta Hunter, who grew up in Memphis in the early part of this century. More than seventy years later, writing her autobiography, she recalled with delight how she loved to ride the "Spinning Jenny" carousel at Dixie Park.

It was largely due to Church's efforts that, around this time, Beale Street became the center for African American business and social activities in Memphis. The conversion was in the works even before the war, but a big step came in 1865, just as Reconstruction was taking hold, when Beale became the home of the Beale Street Baptist Church, the street's first black religious institution. At first the church members gathered outdoors in an old-fashioned brush arbor meeting, similar to the camp meetings of thirty years earlier but minus the whiskey. They sang the old shape-note hymns, so called because they were taught in books that used shapes to symbolize the different notes. In 1871, the congregation made the leap of faith and began construction of the historic church that still stands on Beale, just west of Church Park.

The daylight hours saw Beale growing into a thriving center of black commerce, boasting dentist offices, dry goods stores, and, most notably, Church's Solvent Savings Bank and Trust, which opened in 1906. Church lived nearby in an integrated neighborhood at 384 South Lauderdale. His next-door neighbor was Memphis's white postmaster, Robert B. Armour; across the street lived one of the city's leading black music teachers, Mrs. Julia Hooks,

whose two sons went on to run Beale Street's foremost photographic studio, Hooks Brothers. For many years, it was at Hooks
Brothers that any self-respecting entertainer passing through Memphis had promotional portraits taken — including the famous, recently rediscovered photo of Robert Johnson in his razor-sharp
pin-striped suit and fedora.

There were many other thriving businesses on Beale, both
black and white. When door-to-door salesman Jacob Goldsmith
tired of wearing out shoe leather, he opened the first Goldsmith's
dry goods store on Beale. There was Bensiek's Confectionary and
Bakery, famed for its French custard ice cream, and Vacarro's
restaurant, equally renowned for its spaghetti and thick steaks. On
Fourth Street just south of Beale was the Farris Undertaking Company, said to be the first African American mortuary in Memphis.
Farris's fleet of hearses included a custom-built, miniature white
wagon for infants and children.

While a bustling business district energized the area during the
day, that sort of excitement paled compared to the sight of flashily
dressed "high-yaller girls" of easy virtue and murderous gamblers
going about their business to the throbbing rhythms of low-down
blues bands. So it was when the sun went down that the street at-
tained that character Handy held so dear, the one that made Beale
into a musical legend.

As the biggest city in the Delta, the region bounded on the
west by the Mississippi and the east by the Yazoo River, Memphis
was a magnet for thousands of black laborers. Roustabouts would
make their way up Beale from the river after a week of loading and
unloading the huge bales of cotton that provided much of the city's
formidable wealth; lumbermen rode the trains up from Mississippi's heavily forested swamps for a weekend of fun in the big
city. The lumber and turpentine camps in Mississippi often tried
to keep their workers down on the swamp by building small juke
joints on their land. In these "tonks," the men could gamble to the
sounds of itinerant blues musicians, and enjoy the company of

prostitutes imported by the camp's management. The pioneering African American folklorist Zora Neale Hurston wrote of a Saturday night dance at a lumber camp in Florida in her book *Of Mules and Men*, first published in 1935: "Huge bonfires of faulty logs and slabs are lit outside the house in which the dances are held. The only music is guitar music . . . musicians are paid in liquor and the dancing goes on all night."

Like many African Americans from the Delta, George Washington Lee first visited Memphis on a weekend holiday, riding into the city on the Yazoo and Mississippi Valley Railway. Lee, who went on to become one of Memphis's leading black writers and political powers, was impressed by the city, which by then boasted two fifteen-story skyscrapers. When he returned in 1912 to settle in Memphis, the skyline was dominated by the Exchange Building at Second and Madison, nineteen stories tall, while across the street stood the eighteen-story Central Bank and Trust Company.

In 1934, Lee published his important history of the street and the role it played in black life, *Beale Street: Where the Blues Began*. In one of its most famous passages, he described Beale as "owned largely by the Jews, policed by the whites and enjoyed by the Negroes." But he forgot the Italians, who ran many of the street's most popular saloons, and later, its theaters.

The most famous barroom was Pee Wee's, which Handy considered the cornerstone of the Beale scene when he hit town early in the century. Vegello "Pee Wee" Maffei had arrived in Memphis in the 1880s according to Handy, on a freight train from New York, his point of arrival from Italy. Starting with just a dime, legend has it, Maffei was able to win enough shooting craps to open a saloon at Hernando and Beale, later moving to the 317-319 Beale location where Handy found him when the future Father of the Blues arrived from Clarksdale in 1905.

By then, Pee Wee's (or P. Wee's, as the sign outside read, allegedly the result of a sign painter's poor planning) was a well-known musicians' hangout. More than forty years later, Handy, in his autobiography, still remembered the saloon's four-digit phone number, 2893. He had good reason to remember, as Pee Wee and his relatives who helped run the bar were kind enough to allow Handy and other bandleaders and musicians to use the phone to land gigs. So many musicians congregated at Pee Wee's that the instrument storeroom was always full. As Handy recalled, "You couldn't step for the bull fiddles."

It was also a hangout for gamblers, as were most of the other Beale saloons, which stayed open twenty-four hours a day. As Handy described the scene in his autobiography, the clientele "ranged from cooks and waiters to professional gamblers, jockeys and race track men of the period. Glittering young devils in silk toppers and Prince Alberts drifted in and out with insolent self-assurance. Chocolate dandies with red roses embroidered on cream waistcoats loitered at the bar." Occasionally, Handy recalled, rival saloonkeeper Hammitt Ashford, "a striking quadroon," would come in and wager Pee Wee one thousand dollars on a single roll of the dice.

Along with the farm workers and laborers from levee, turpentine, and lumber camps, the riverboats employing black waiters, cooks, porters, roustabouts, and deckhands contributed a constant stream of men who worked hard and demanded hard recreation. Beale's entrepreneurs were only too happy to provide it. Still more customers came from the local railroad yards, which employed a thousand African Americans, more than any other rail yard in the country. And most of the timber cut down in Mississippi by the lumbermen partying on Beale also found its way to Memphis, then the world's largest hardwood market. More than thirty sawmills were kept busy processing the lumber that came in on the river from the lumber camps. In addition, of the city's six hundred factories, forty were dedicated to turning the boards into furniture, providing still more work for a growing black population eager to escape the hardships of plantation life.

Ever since the war, the region's black population had been leaving the plantations. The exodus occurred so rapidly that, in 1867, cotton plantation owners considered various plans to replace their lost labor force, among them importing Chinese workers. That idea had worked successfully for the western railroads, but not on the plantation.

Former slaves continued leaving their plantations in Mississippi and West Tennessee, and Memphis was usually their goal. In 1860, the black population of Memphis was 3,882 strong; a decade later it was 15,471, and continued to grow steadily through the rest of the century. When the 1900 census topped 100,000 Memphians, an event celebrated with fireworks, more than 50,000 were African Americans.

As the new century dawned, Church and the growing black professional class were cementing their holdings, creating their own version of high society based to some degree on the same color-caste system employed by New Orleans's light-skinned Creoles. Church and his friends would hire Handy's well-schooled band for their dances aboard the *Charles Organ* steamboat or at their exclusive Primrose Club and Toxoway Country Club. Meanwhile, the less-privileged rural immigrants were enjoying the considerably earthier pleasures of Beale.

In addition to Pee Wee's and Hammitt Ashford's, there was John Persica's saloon on Hernando. Persica was "the most notorious of the underworld overlords" of the late nineteenth and early twentieth centuries, according to historian William Miller. In addition to his Hernando club, Persica bought the city's old car barn after the electric streetcar lines were consolidated in 1893 and converted it into the Garden Theatre. He also promoted boxing and controlled gambling south of Madison Street.

While most of the saloons in the area were for blacks, the brothels, primarily employing light-skinned black women, were mostly exclusive to white patrons. "Sporting houses," which lined Main Street south of Linden, could also be found along Third, Fourth,

and Mulberry Streets. The biggest and fanciest were on Gayoso
Street between Union and Beale. At 121 Gayoso, Grace Stanley ran
her infamous Stanley Club — that is until a dispute with one of her
"girls" ended with her murder at the point of a knife.

In 1981, John Keck, eighty-four, told the *Commercial Appeal* of
his childhood working at the family livery stable on Second Street
between Beale and Gayoso, where many of the pimps and
madams boarded their horses and parked their carriages. "They
dressed as showy as they could," Keck recalled. Most pimps handled the horses for the madams, but Keck retained a vivid childhood memory of one particularly bold woman, "all painted up
with rouge and a Polly parrot on her shoulder," who drove her
own carriage.

Like the whorehouses in New Orleans and St. Louis, the
Gayoso houses provided employment for Memphis's early ragtime
pianists, including the local legends Willie Bloom, "Bad" Hooks,
"Hatchett," and one Benny Frenchy, the most famous of them all.
In 1938 Jelly Roll Morton told Alan Lomax in a Library of Congress
recorded interview of going head-to-head with Frenchy in a "cutting contest," in which musicians tested their skills. Morton, with
his usual bravado, remembered winning. But the girls loved the
home team, Morton admitted; "the girls would be kickin' and
everybody'd be standing around this guy," he said, recalling how
they'd egg him on: "Oh play it, Mr. Frenchy." The tune Morton recalled Frenchy playing was a typical country ragtime progression
of the sort banjoist/jug-band leader Gus Cannon later recorded in
several sessions, including his "Madison Street Rag." The Gayoso
brothels gave many white Memphians their first dose of syncopation and the blues. Compared to the pallid ballads and sentimental "heart songs" that the Victorian era offered, that "whorehouse
music" would have been exciting in any situation. Given the extra
tang of forbidden fruit, of social and moral taboos being broken all
around, those sexually syncopated sounds proved irresistible.

Though social segregation never wavered, cultural integration was the rule rather than the exception. White Memphis early on embraced the blues and its offshoots, providing regular employment for black musicians on the riverboats and at private parties in the Peabody Avenue mansions.

With the help of government and police corruption, prostitution and other organized crime in Memphis ran fairly smoothly, just as it did in Kansas City, St. Louis, and Chicago. One of the more notorious exceptions around Beale involved saloon keeper "Wild Bill" Latura who, it's said, walked into Hammitt Ashford's saloon in 1908 and, annoyed at the sound of the colliding billiard balls, killed six patrons. Latura was white, his victims black, so naturally Latura was acquitted of the murders. The *Commercial Appeal* protested the verdict, although with regrettable logic: "Those white men who kill Negroes," it reasoned, "usually end up by killing white men." Latura never even went to court when he killed another black Memphian in 1912; but in 1915, angered over a white reporter's reference to him as "Wild Bill," he threatened the newsman and the Memphis policemen who were with him. Finally Wild Bill had gone too far. As he turned to leave, the police fired, killing him with five shots. Pool players on Beale breathed easier.

In the early years of the twentieth century, the fanciest Beale gambling den was the Monarch, the elegantly appointed saloon owned by Memphis underworld figure Jim Kinnane. Built at the then-astronomical cost of twenty thousand dollars, it lived up to its name with a lobby paneled in mirrors and exotic hardwoods, and was also equipped with more practical features such as trapdoors and secret passageways for easy getaways during raids.

Just as the more famous Irish gangs in Chicago battled over the rackets, Kinnane and rival ganglord Ed Ryan fought for dominance of Memphis prostitution and gambling through the turn of the century. By then, however, younger, more reckless men were entering Memphis organized crime, in the same way Chicago's Italian mob would soon be overtaken by Al Capone. Ryan was killed by the young gun Mike Shanley at the Montgomery Park racetrack, a longtime Shanley hangout. A few years later, when the gangster was asked to put out his cigar during a hot-air balloon exhibition, he angrily stormed off. He soon returned with his "boys," taking revenge for the slight by shooting down the balloon.

Kinnane and the Monarch achieved blues immortality in 1935, thanks to Robert Wilkins, a bluesman from Hernando, a town in the Mississippi hill country just south of Memphis. Wilkins, who had moved to the city after serving in World War I, recorded a song called "Old Jim Canan's" [sic] at a Vocalion Records session held in Jackson, Mississippi. In the song, he nostalgically recalls the riotous good times there: "The men and women running hand in hand/going to and fro to Old Jim Kinnane's/Drinking beer and whiskey, sniffing cocaine/and you ask me why I wish I was back in old Jim Kinnane's."

Cocaine also seemed to play a prominent role in another popular Memphis pastime: murder. Whether it was cocaine nerves, a bad hangover, or just a low irritation threshold that incited "Wild Bill's" pool-hall massacre, he wasn't alone in his taste for mayhem. Memphis was setting annual records for homicides early in the century. In 1902, Memphis's ninety-one police officers made 24 arrests on murder charges. By contrast, Atlanta, just a bit smaller than Memphis, had only 6 arrests. By 1910, the court had 105 homicide indictments on its calendar. The numbers continued to rise, with 134 murders recorded in 1916. In 1918, Prudential Insurance statistician Dr. Frederick L. Hoffman crunched some numbers and concluded that Memphis had become the murder capital of the United States — a reputation that plagued the city for years.

In 1900, when the Memphis population topped one hundred thousand, the *Commercial Appeal* estimated that 80 percent of the city's black population, as well as "a considerable number of whites," used cocaine. Even allowing for a touch of hysteria on the paper's part, cocaine use was certainly epidemic. Legally sold in five- and ten-cent boxes in drugstores and groceries (and found, in negligible doses, in that popular new soft drink from Atlanta, Coca-Cola), cocaine played an important role in the city's nightlife, where, as Handy wrote in "Beale Street Blues," "business never closes till somebody gets killed."

Other common sources of cocaine were the patent medicines and tonics sold in the traveling medicine shows that also provided occasional employment to such Memphis blues figures as Gus Cannon, Furry Lewis, and Jim Jackson. Moreover, plantation managers reportedly provided their workers with doses of cocaine to increase productivity. It was a trick first devised in South America by the Spanish conquistadores, who provided their Indian slaves with rations of coca leaves before sending them into the gold and silver mines.

Like the other Beale attractions, cocaine became a popular theme in the blues. The Memphis Jug Band recorded its "Cocaine Habit" in 1930, a song that immortalized one Beale Street purveyor, Lehman's Drug Store: "I Went to Mr. Lehman's in a lope/sign on the window says 'No more dope.' "

As Memphis entered the twentieth century it had survived wars and epidemics and gone from a small river town to a bustling port city. The draining of the Delta in the final twenty years of the nineteenth century created a huge lumbering industry; and when the land was stripped bare, the even bigger business of massive cotton plantations was born. Memphis became a wealthy capital of cotton and hardwood trading. But one thing hadn't changed — the city's untamed frontier spirit. Gambling, drinking, prostitution, drugs; all contributed to the wild times that filled every hour in a Memphis day, and demanded intoxicating, even earthshaking musical accompaniment.

3

▼▼▼▼▼▼▼▼▼▼▼▼▼▼▼▼▼▼▼▼▼▼▼▼▼▼▼▼

Mr. Handy and Beale Street

With the exception of Elvis Presley, no figure in the history of Memphis music has been as revered and reviled as William Christopher Handy.

To the Memphis city fathers, Handy is a musical icon, the Father of the Blues, Exhibit A in Memphis's claim to the title Home of the Blues. As I write this, he remains the only black musician in Memphis to be honored with a statue and a public park in his name — an honor bestowed on him, remarkably, twenty-seven years before his death. The Memphis-based Blues Foundation's national blues honors — the Grammy of the blues industry — are called the W. C. Handy Awards. And as any philatelist could tell you, Handy was a first-class stamp in 1969, decades before Elvis was even a gleam in the postmaster general's income projections.

Nonetheless, although Handy readily admitted that he had not created the blues but merely transcribed and arranged the sounds he first heard in rural Mississippi, he has long been attacked by jazz and blues purists as a thief and a charlatan. When Handy appeared on the *Ripley's Believe It Or Not!* radio program in 1938, New Orleans jazz pioneer Jelly Roll Morton was tuned in. Hearing Handy introduced as "the Father of Jazz" as well as of the blues, the hot-tempered pianist fired off an angry letter to *Downbeat* magazine. "Mr. Handy cannot prove that he has created any music," Morton fumed. "He has possibly taken advantage of some unprotected material that sometimes floats around. I would like to know how a person could be an originator of anything without being able to do at least some of what they created." Of course, Morton's contempt for Handy didn't prevent him from bootlegging sheet music of Handy's "Hesitation Blues" in his early days and later recording several Handy compositions, most notably "Beale Street Blues."

Morton's attack was supported by the pioneering jazz writer Rudi Blesh, among others. In his 1946 book *Shining Trumpets,* Blesh wrote, "Even to claim, or accept, the title of Father of the Blues, as Handy has done, is as absurd as it is presumptuous." He goes on to write that Handy "from the time of his youth [seems] to have been in the un-Negroid tradition . . . a tradition that has always aimed at 'disinfecting' Afro-American music by 'Europeanizing' it." More recently, in his history of American popular music *After the Ball,* music historian Ian Whitcomb belittles Handy as the Stenographer of the Blues, a rip-off artist stealing music from anonymous bluesmen.

Morton's anger is easy to sympathize with — as a bandleader and a composer, his greatest accomplishments were a decade behind him. To see Handy — whose days as a bandleader were more than twenty years behind him and whose most popular songs were a quarter century old — continuing to collect accolades, not to mention huge royalty checks, was more than the poor, embittered Morton could bear. Blesh's argument smacks of an unfortunate brand of jazz racism: Handy, by presuming to incorporate European musical forms and aesthetics into his work, was being "un-Negroid," in other words, diverging from what Blesh had decided a black musician should sound like. It was an opinion frequently expressed by other jazz and blues writers as well, but it's just another way of saying, "Handy just didn't know his place." Whitcomb, writing in the late sixties, reflected the countercultural attitudes of the time. Dignified old Mr. Handy, by leaving Beale

Street, had sold out, becoming a respected music publisher, a member of the establishment, and an exploiter of downtrodden bluesmen.

Ignoring all the revisionist chest-beating, one fact remains: Handy, by writing down the blues and altering it to fit standard musical notation and seeing those compositions enjoy phenomenal commercial success and musical influence, was arguably the single most important figure in twentieth-century American popular music. Handy didn't invent the blues — but then again, no one person did, so far as we know. What Handy did, with such compositions as "The Memphis Blues" and the even more popular "St. Louis Blues," was to add the blues to the vocabulary of popular music, which turned out to be a bit like splitting the atom.

Handy paved the way for the success of the vaudeville blues singers like Ma Rainey and Bessie Smith, the creations of songwriters George and Ira Gershwin, and the musical innovations of Dixieland jazz, big band swing, rhythm and blues, and ultimately rock and roll. Until Elvis Presley transformed himself into the Hillbilly Cat under the watchful eye of Sam Phillips forty years later, no single event of the twentieth century so completely altered the course of America's — and the world's — music. And without the blues, of course, the Hillbilly Cat would have been just another hillbilly.

Handy's journey to mogulhood began with his birth eight years after emancipation in Florence, Alabama, a town that would later be the birthplace of another Memphis music entrepreneur, Sam Phillips, the founder of Sun Records and discoverer of Howlin' Wolf, Elvis, and dozens of other legends. In fact, the town would prove to be something of a Memphis music outpost; Rick Hall's Fame Recording Studio, home of the Muscle Shoals sound, was actually located in Florence, a city that was also the home of soul singer Arthur Alexander.

The son of former slaves, Handy grew up fascinated by the many strains of music that seemed to be everywhere around him. He sang old-time country tunes: "Cornstalk fiddle, shoestring bow, broke in the middle, jumped up Joe." He played fiddlesticks with his uncle Whit Walker, a former slave fiddler, who would play breakdowns such as "Little Lady Goin' to the Country" as the young Handy reached around Walker's shoulder to beat rhythm on the fiddle strings with knitting needles.

Despite his preacher father's disapproval, Handy had caught the music bug early. Perhaps out of guilt at disappointing his dad, he remained rigidly legitimate in his approach and always taught as much music as he played, his dignified, academic air earning him the nickname "Fess," for Professor. Handy remained a bit defensive about his chosen profession throughout his life, long after the wealth and honors had lent his music an air of legitimacy. In his 1941 autobiography, *Father of the Blues*, he wrote, "If anyone owned a dozen cans and piled them on a couple of shelves behind a printed sign, he was a grocer and a businessman . . . but one who contracted for musicians and played for parties over a dozen states was a good-timer and a rounder, if not worse."

Fighting both the general racism of the day and the low esteem in which musicians of all races were generally held, Handy became an overachiever. No rounder he, Handy in his early years led and arranged for bands, played a variety of instruments, and generally showed the business acumen that would later help make him one of the first black music tycoons of the twentieth century.

Handy grew up in the midst of the brass-band craze, so his first instrument was the cornet, on which he took lessons in a Florence barbershop. By nineteen he was teaching music himself; soon thereafter, inspired by itinerant musician Jim Turner, Handy hit the road with Mahara's Minstrels. He performed at the 1893 World's Fair in Chicago, the event generally acknowledged as the birthplace of the ragtime craze. He traveled as far as Cuba with the band, where he recalled first hearing the Afro-Cuban habanera rhythms that would later turn up in the tango section of "St. Louis Blues." By 1902, a married man of nearly thirty, Handy opted to settle down in Clarksdale, Mississippi.

Cotton money had turned the town into one of the wealthiest

in the Delta, and Handy and his band readily found work there, though he later confessed that his orchestra's well-drilled military approach was a little stiff for dancing. Clarksdale and its neighbor across the Mississippi, Helena, Arkansas, would prove as fertile to the blues as it was for cotton. The area later produced McKinley "Muddy Waters" Morganfield, John Lee Hooker, and scores of others on the Mississippi side, and musicians such as Sonny Boy Williamson and George "Harmonica" Smith on the Arkansas side.

It was shortly after arriving in Clarksdale that Handy first heard the blues at a railroad station in nearby Tutwiler. As he waited for a train, Handy recalled in his autobiography, "a lean, loose-jointed negro had commenced plunking a guitar beside me. . . . His clothes were rags, his feet peeped out of his shoes. His face had on it some of the sadness of the ages. As he played, he pressed a knife on the strings of the guitar in a manner popularized by Hawaiian guitarists who used steel bars." It was, Handy wrote, "the weirdest music I had ever heard." But, he confessed, "The tune stayed in my mind."

Not long afterward, when Handy witnessed the popularity of that Mississippi string band southwest of Clarksdale in Cleveland, he began adding the local music to the band's repertoire, arranging such songs as "Make Me a Pallet On Your Floor" for his band. The song would later become a jazz standard played on the riverboats that ran from New Orleans to Memphis to St. Louis. It was also played by guitarist Mississippi John Hurt, who hailed from Avalon, Mississippi, and who began playing around the same time that Handy heard the slide guitar player in the train station. Hurt, who called his version "Ain't No Tellin'," recorded it in 1928 for OKeh Records. On his rediscovery in the 1960s, when Hurt rerecorded the song under its original title, it became a standard of the folk-blues revival.

With his new, "low-down" repertoire, Handy said, "the popularity of our orchestra increased by leaps and bounds." Among the band's new gigs were regular engagements in the section of Clarksdale called the New World, the town's red-light district. It was wide-open by Clarksdale standards, but tepid compared to Beale, as Handy would later learn.

As if music didn't keep him busy enough, Handy was also something of a civil rights worker, distributing the *Chicago Defender* and the other new black-published newspapers from the North. He writes glowingly of the all-black community thirty miles south of Clarksdale called Mound Bayou, and recalls bringing a band there from Memphis at his own expense when the town opened its oil mill, for a celebration that included a speech by Booker T. Washington.

While his sojourn in Mississippi gave Handy a postgraduate course in the blues, he soon outgrew Clarksdale. When the offer came to organize a Knights of Pythias band in Memphis, Handy, still based in Mississippi, began the twice-weekly, seventy-six-mile train commute, in another demonstration of his strong work ethic. His K. of P. band, as he called it, was too formal for dancing and so had to settle for the occasional funeral. Determined to break into the bustling Beale scene, Handy moved his family up to the Greasy Plank section of Memphis into a tiny shotgun house.

Today the phrase "big band" summons images of Benny Goodman, Duke Ellington, or Count Basie leading smoothly swinging ensembles. In the early part of this century, though, bands that were big were anything but streamlined. They came out of the stiffly starched and tightly disciplined military tradition, whose pinnacle was John Philip Sousa's martial march band. Handy confesses that when he came to Memphis it was the Sousa model he had in mind. But as he saw the looser, more syncopated and danceable Beale bands getting all the best gigs, Handy the canny businessman started hiring musicians away from the competition. Adding his old friend Jim Turner, New Orleans trombonist George Williams, and other versatile musicians, he proceed to channel all his considerable energy into becoming Beale's top bandleader.

By the time Handy made his move, Memphis was a thriving

city, fully recovered from the devastating yellow fever epidemics; but the fact that a little more than half the city's hundred thousand residents were black caused a knee-jerk reaction from the city's white power structure. In 1906, the first separate-but-equal "Jim Crow" laws were passed, segregating its streetcars.

Millionaire Robert Church Sr. responded by purchasing one of those newfangled automobiles, but few black Memphians enjoyed his financial privileges. Feisty Alberta Hunter wrote in her autobiography that, when there were no empty seats in the rear of the streetcars, she would merely move the divider separating the black and white sections up a row into the white seats.

There were plenty of other, less ominous, changes in the air as Memphis became swept up in the beginning of a new century. Handy seems first to have envisioned the blues as a spin-off of ragtime, which had itself begun as an attempt to re-create the broken chord patterns of old minstrel show banjo tunes on a piano. When first published, in fact, "The Memphis Blues" was described on sheet music as "a Southern rag." Ragtime instrumentals were on the way out, though, and it was as popular song, with lyrics, that the blues would really catch on.

Handy wasn't the first person to publish a blues song. That honor goes to St. Louis ragtime pianist Artie Matthews, whose "Baby Seal Blues" came out in August 1912. Handy didn't even come in second; Hart A. Wand, a white violinist, published "Dallas Blues" early in September 1912. Handy's "Memphis Blues" hit the streets late that same month, when Handy, frustrated at not finding a publisher willing to invest in a new form of music composed by a black man, published it himself. Legend has it that Handy composed the tune while standing at the cigar stand at Pee Wee's, but his wife later revealed he'd actually written it in a small apartment he used as a studio, writing songs there to escape the chaos of a house full of children.

Music isn't all about getting there first, however; though he came in third, Handy's tune was the hit. A couple of years later, the

ballroom-dancing pioneers Vernon and Irene Castle were introduced to the tune by their bandleader, James Reese Europe. Europe, the Alabama-born African American bandleader who
provided the stylistic link between Sousa-style military band music
and jazz, performed "The Memphis Blues" at a slow tempo during the Castles' breaks and costume changes. Perhaps as a respite
from the more frenetic two-steps of the day, the Castles, prime
movers in the social-dancing revolution that took place in the first
two decades of this century, created a new dance for Handy's tune.

It was the age of the so-called animal dances — the turkey trot,
the grizzly bear, the kangaroo dip, the horse trot, the buzzard lope.
In keeping with that terpsichorean menagerie, the Castles called
their new creation the bunny hug, but soon changed it to the more
polite fox-trot, which became the single most popular and enduring of the ballroom dances.

The Castles gave the credit for those fox-trot rhythms to Europe. But the bandleader, whose career would end in Boston in
1919 when he was stabbed by the drummer in his military band,
the 369th Infantry "Hell Fighters," laid the credit where it belonged. "The Fox Trot was created by a young negro of Memphis,
Tenn., Mr. W. C. Handy," Europe said in a 1914 interview with the
New York Tribune.

That same year, the phenomenal success of Handy's "Memphis
Blues" was overshadowed by the publication of his follow-up, "St.
Louis Blues." His tale of the jilted country girl who lost her man
to the painted charms of that more sophisticated "St. Louis
woman" turned the blues from fad to full-fledged movement. The
song defined the blues, according to music historian Samuel Charters, who wrote, "Until W. C. Handy published his 'St. Louis
Blues' . . . with its opening three-line verse in the classic blues,
there was no way to say exactly what the form of a blues was." Ever
the shrewd song salesman, Handy tossed in a bit of the latest ballroom craze, the tango, a rhythm he remembered driving the
crowds wild back in his days at Dixie Park. Jazz pianist Dave

Brubeck, a pioneer of world-beat rhythms in jazz, credits Handy with beginning that trend with "St. Louis Blues." "A few years ago I looked up 'St. Louis Blues,' " the jazz piano great told me in a 1994 interview. "And the first strain is written as a tango. So, I think all this idea of fusion and everything is all a lot of baloney. What is this tango doing in 'St. Louis Blues,' if there wasn't an influence [in jazz] coming in from Europe or South America right from the beginning?"

Handy's "Europeanization" of the blues inspired what became known as the Golden Age of American popular song, as such blues-crazed composers as George Gershwin wrote "Rhapsody in Blue" (which included a strain from "St. Louis Blues") and the folk opera *Porgy and Bess,* and Hoagy Carmichael composed "Up a Lazy River" and "Stardust."

Equally important were Handy's accomplishments as a pioneering African American businessman. When Handy first published "The Memphis Blues," it was as an instrumental. He had originally written it in 1909 as "Mr. Crump Don't Like It," for mayoral reform candidate E. H. Crump, whose campaign team recognized the benefits of hiring one of those newfangled Beale Street bands to drum up a crowd at campaign stops. Bands were used for everything back then; store openings, funerals, medicine shows, anytime anyone wanted to attract attention. Crump won the election and became "Boss" the same year Henry Ford launched his Model T. Of the two, Crump's machine proved the more durable, and it ran Memphis for the next forty years, largely due to Crump's ability to marshal black support.

If Handy's tune got the job done for Crump, it didn't do much for its composer. Published as "The Memphis Blues," it sold poorly; Handy, desperately in need of cash, agreed to sell his rights to it — a common practice at the time. Handy got fifty dollars and the unsold sheet music; the purchaser added lyrics by George Norton, who was seemingly inspired by Irving Berlin's million-selling 1911 hit "Alexander's Ragtime Band." Berlin had celebrated "the best band in the land" and described how they played "a bugle call like you never heard before" on a "fiddle with notes that screeches like a chicken . . . and the clarinet is a colored pet." Norton extoled the virtues of Handy's Memphis Blues Band, with its "fiddler there that always slickens his hair, an' folks he sure do pull some bow" and "the big bassoon . . . it moans just like a sinner on Revival Day." The lyrics also reveal Handy's appeal to white Memphis, telling how "the whi' folks gently swayed [while] all dem band boys played real harmony."

Handy watched his composition become one of the most successful songs of the young century without earning him a penny. To add insult to injury, Norton's lyrics revealed his ignorance of Handy's band and the new music it played. Germany's Adolph Saxe had invented his saxophone in 1846, but even in the early twentieth century they were still rare enough in America that when Norton tried to describe the instrumentation in Handy's band, he called the sax "the big bassoon." Handy no doubt called Norton a few things himself, but the lyrics certainly played a key role in the song's enduring popularity. Handy reacquired the rights to "The Memphis Blues" in 1940, just as the song was being used in the Bing Crosby film *The Birth of the Blues.* Handy's first royalty check for the tune he'd written thirty-one years earlier was five thousand dollars, a tidy sum in pre–World War II dollars.

Ford's automobile assembly line wasn't the only innovation to create a new industry in 1909. That same year Congress passed the first modern copyright law, guaranteeing copyright owners exclusive rights to their work and giving the publishing firms that filed for the copyrights a 50 percent share. The combination of sheet music, the musical theater that had sprung up from the minstrel shows, and the mechanical royalties from the budding record industry added up to a bonanza for the music publishing business. Not surprisingly, Handy wanted in on the action. In 1914, when he published "St. Louis Blues," he did it with his new partner, Memphis businessman-lyricist Harry Pace. Adding Pace's lyrics, the partners published it themselves — and it became an even bigger success than "The Memphis Blues." A quarter century later,

Handy said the song was still bringing him twenty-five thousand dollars in annual royalties. Handy continued turning out blues, such as "Yellow Dog Blues" (named after the nickname given the Yazoo-Delta railroad) and "Joe Turner's Blues" (in honor of a notoriously dogged lawman who conveyed convicts to the penitentiary in Nashville).

Handy had met his future lyricist, "a handsome young man of striking personality and definite musical leanings," when the latter was a cashier in the Solvent Savings Bank on Beale. Handy, who occupied an office upstairs, soon learned that the younger man, a popular singer at upper-class black functions, was also an aspiring lyricist and publisher who, among other projects, had published W. F. B. Du Bois's short-lived magazine *The Moon.* In 1907 the pair collaborated on a standard nostalgic Southern ditty, "In the Cotton Fields of Dixie." Shortly after the fiasco with "The Memphis Blues," they formed the Pace & Handy Music Company — Publishers. Around 1913, the upwardly mobile Pace left Memphis to become secretary-treasurer of the Atlanta-based Standard Life Insurance Company, though the men continued their musical partnership. Their songs were gaining popularity, but both men cautiously refused to give up the security of their regular jobs — Pace selling insurance, Handy playing for the wealthy black and white Memphians on the riverboats and in such posh Memphis nightspots as the whites-only Alaskan Roof Gardens. Using his Atlanta connections, the racially progressive Pace was able to book Handy's orchestra into a white auditorium in that city, arousing protests from the Atlanta newspapers. Then as now, publicity sold tickets — Handy and company wound up selling out the place for a full week. Buoyed by their success, Handy and Pace soon decided to try their hands in the publishing capital, New York, home of Tin Pan Alley, the songwriting district named for the cacophony of the inexactly tuned pianos ringing from every office.

Before Handy left Memphis, he paid tribute to the street that had been the catalyst for his success. In 1916, Handy and Pace published their "Beale Street Blues," a song that found its way into

the repertoires of everyone from Louis Armstrong to the hillbilly
string band Charlie Poole & His North Carolina Ramblers. "I'd
rather be there than any place I know," they wrote. How right they
were. Beale proved to have been their muse. Handy and Pace
would never write another hit after leaving Memphis.

Though the music came from black traditions and often from
black composers, before 1920 the most popular blues singers were
exclusively white. Former minstrel performer Al Jolson sang on
Broadway in blackface and was one of the biggest stars of the day,
recording dozens of hits. Sophie Tucker was another success story,
a stocky Russian-Jewish immigrant woman whose affinity for the
blues would help make Handy and Pace wealthy men.

Handy never forgot his disastrous business decision with "The
Memphis Blues," and while he would never again sell songs he frequently bought them. In 1918, he paid $125 for "A Good Man Is
Hard to Find." Introduced by former Memphian Alberta Hunter at
Chicago's Dreamland cabaret, the song soon attracted Tucker, who
must have realized its potential as a hit during the eligible-bachelor
drought that was World War I. As Hunter later recalled, the white
blues star "sent over her maid to tell me that she wanted to see me.
I knew she wanted the song and so I didn't go. So you know how
she got it? She sent over her piano player, Ted Shapiro, to listen to
it and learn it, and got somebody to take down the words. But
when she sang it she always gave me credit." Handy and Pace,
nevertheless, got the cash. As one of Tucker's biggest hits, the song
returned its owner-publishers' investment hundreds of times over.

Unfortunately for the Father of the Blues and his partner Pace
(the Stepfather?), the white audience was gaining a deeper appreciation for the new music progeny than they had themselves. In
1921, Pace left the publishing firm to start Black Swan, the first
black-owned record label. Recognizing that (at least in the entertainment business) being black was something of an asset, Black
Swan records called itself "the only true colored record label, all
others are merely passing." Pace had no intention of launching a
blues-only company; he wanted to create a separate-but-equal

record label, one that provided the growing market of black consumers with recordings of everything from the classics to the blues, all performed by black musicians. Black Swan, named for the sobriquet given the African American concert singer Elizabeth Taylor Greenfield of Natchez, Mississippi, held true to the European aspirations of its namesake. When it did release a blues record, Black Swan exclusively featured whiter-sounding classic black blues singers such as Ethel Waters and Trixie Smith. Perhaps the most revealing fact about Black Swan's aesthetic was that the company turned down Bessie Smith when she auditioned for the label.

Pace was the unsung hero in the Handy story; like many who remain in the music business too long, though, Pace eventually lost his edge as an innovator, and his record sales suffered. In 1924, with Bessie reigning supreme in the blues, Black Swan was absorbed by Paramount, the Wisconsin company that was already having success with New Orleans country bluesman Papa Charlie Jackson. The following year, Paramount unexpectedly birthed the new country-blues craze with the recording debut of Texan Blind Lemon Jefferson.

The musical legacy of Black Swan continued through the contributions of a young pianist-arranger Handy and Pace had first hired for their publishing company and who Pace took with him when he started the label. Working for Handy and Pace had been James Fletcher Henderson's first job after arriving in New York from his native Cuthbert, Georgia. In 1923, he formed his Fletcher Henderson Orchestra, the first successful and phenomenally influential black big band in jazz — a band whose ranks would include Louis Armstrong, Coleman Hawkins, and Memphian Buster Bailey (all at the same time) as well as dozens of other jazz greats over the course of its career. Henderson would go on to become the largely uncredited architect of the Swing Era, writing and arranging many of the Benny Goodman Orchestra's biggest hits.

Harry Pace was also the man who got Handy's band on record, arranging a contract for twelve sides with Columbia shortly after the pair's move to New York in 1919. And it was Pace who finally convinced Handy that it was time to give up his bands, concentrate on his songwriting and publishing, and make the move to New York in the first place.

As for Handy, by the time he split with Pace, his biggest successes were also behind him. In 1926, he published *Blues: An Anthology*, a book-length collection of fifty-three songs, including his signature pieces (although he was careful to use his "Mr. Crump" lyrics for "Memphis Blues" rather than George Norton's more famous words) and such oddities as "Jogo Blues," an early draft of "St. Louis Blues." By the 1930s, Handy, then living in an upper-middle-class section of Yonkers, New York, was losing his eyesight, and had turned to composing spirituals. Cynics might suggest that his conversion was inspired by the phenomenal success that Thomas A. Dorsey (the former Georgia Tom, a blues pianist who had accompanied Ma Rainey and written the risqué blues smash "Tight Like That") was enjoying with "Peace in the Valley" and other songs. But Handy certainly seemed sincere; he told reporters, "I hope I live long enough to see a real revival of genuine African spirituals," and composed such songs as "Those Who Sow in Tears Shall Reap in Joy."

Unlike other gospel converts, Handy didn't abandon his secular music. The May 22, 1936, *Press-Scimitar* reported that Handy and his sixteen-piece St. Louis Blues Orchestra were returning to Memphis to begin a week's engagement at the Beale Street Palace Theatre, including, on Wednesday and Thursday nights, two "rambles for white patrons." The Palace's famous Midnight Rambles allowed white Memphians to hear the best black jazz and blues performers who regularly appeared there, though by then the TOBA (the black vaudeville circuit that had gotten its start on Beale) was no longer in operation.

By the thirties Handy had been accepted as a genuine star, even if the Memphis newspapers did so in the absurdly patronizing manner of the day. The April 3, 1936, *Press-Scimitar* called him "an outstanding proponent of jazz and a credit to his race and his nation." An April 22, 1936, article in the *Commercial Appeal* staked a Memphis claim on him, saying he lived in New York for business purposes, but "Memphis has always been his home, the white folks of Memphis always his white folks." The occasion for all this condescending attention was Handy's selection as grand marshal in the first Cotton Makers Fiesta, the "separate-but-equal" version of the city's all-white Cotton Carnival.

Handy wrote patriotic songs for World War II, including "There Is No Fifth Column on Beale Street," celebrating the obvious lack of blond, blue-eyed Nazi spies in black Memphis. In 1947, the W. C. Handy Theater, declaring itself "the only negro theater south of Chicago that is completely air-conditioned," opened on Park Avenue, just east of Airways in Orange Mound, the city's old black community. Jazz trumpeter Cootie Williams came in for the grand opening, and each day's movies began with the playing of "The Memphis Blues" and ended with "St. Louis Blues." The building still stands today, the weathered marquee still bearing some of the glass tubing of the original neon sign in the form of a "WC," a treble clef, and a sixteenth note.

Handy died on March 28, 1958, in New York. He was buried in Woodlawn Cemetery in the Bronx, the burial site of such luminaries as Duke Ellington and Bat Masterson, the western lawman who ended his career as a New York sportswriter. That same year, Handy received the ultimate Hollywood tribute: his own, bizarrely fictionalized film biography. In true Tinseltown tradition, *St. Louis Blues* had a star who looked absolutely nothing like Handy. Nat King Cole even played Handy as clean-shaven, despite the fact that Handy sported a mustache throughout his adult life. Still, with an orchestra arranged by Nelson Riddle and appearances by such musicians as Ella Fitzgerald, Cab Calloway, Mahalia Jackson, Pearl Bailey, Eartha Kitt, Barney Bigard, Lester Young's drumming brother Lee, and a young Billy Preston as the boy Handy, the movie at least featured some worthwhile music.

On Handy's death, the *Commercial Appeal* immediately began raising funds to erect a statue in Handy Park, which the city had named in his honor all the way back in 1931. On May 1, 1960, the statue that stands there today was erected at a cost of fourteen thousand dollars and dedicated at a ceremony in which gospel great Mahalia Jackson sang.

In 1969 the U.S. Post Office honored Handy with a stamp, and the honors continued: New York City paid tribute to the Father of the Blues in 1980, renaming a section of its jazz thoroughfare, Fifty-second Street, "W. C. Handy Place."

His career had begun before the blues were born; by the fall of 1954, as his old patron E. H. "Boss" Crump lay dying and Elvis Presley was just beginning to enjoy some local success with his first Sun singles, W. C. Handy, by then totally blind, was honored as a guest performer with the Dixieland band at Billy Rose's Diamond Horseshoe nightclub in Manhattan. In his lifetime he'd seen the blues go from a folk style in rural Mississippi to the single most important innovation in twentieth-century American popular music. And, unlike virtually every Memphis musician who would come after him, Handy lived long enough to enjoy the wealth and the honors his music had brought him.

4

▼▼▼▼▼▼▼▼▼▼ ▼▼▼▼▼▼▼▼▼ ▼▼▼▼▼▼▼ ▼▼▼

Beale, Black Vaudeville, and the First Blues Boom

The roots of the blues lead back to Senegal in West Africa, but in the form we know it today — "the primary music of the 20th Century," in the words of Dr. William Ferris, director of the Center for the Study of Southern Culture in Oxford, Mississippi — the blues isn't much older than this century.

Gertrude "Ma" Rainey is acknowledged as the first minstrel show performer to bring the blues to the stage. She recalled first hearing the music sometime between 1902 and 1904, when a woman in a small Missouri town sang her an unaccompanied blues. By 1905, Rainey was causing a sensation singing the blues onstage with the Rabbit Foot Minstrels. Like "Father of the Blues" W. C. Handy she admitted she didn't create the music, but by introducing it onstage she earned her own parental title — "the Mother of the Blues."

W. C. Handy first encountered his "lean loose-jointed Negro" playing blues guitar with an improvised slide at around the same time, and soon added "a number of local tunes" to the repertoire of his well-drilled military band. The blues craze, however, was still a decade off. It would take a new idea to find the audience for this new style of music, and that new idea was born, not surprisingly, on Beale Street.

In 1907, F. A. Barrasso, owner of the Palace Theatre on Beale

Street, came up with the notion of organizing his fellow theater owners around the South into a chain specializing in black performers. The idea was based on what northern theaters had done with white vaudeville on the famed Keith, Albee, and Orpheum circuits. Barrasso's chain would feature black minstrel shows like Mahara's, Silas Green's, and the Rabbit Foot Minstrels, as well as bands like Handy's.

The idea finally got off the ground in 1909, when Barrasso's brother Anselmo began the Theater Owners' Booking Association. The TOBA, with its hard working conditions, poor wages, and filthy, overcrowded dressing rooms, was said by some performers on the circuit to stand for Tough On Black Asses. Though the circuit was something of a plantation system for black performers, many TOBA acts were able to step up to the better-paying white vaudeville circuits. And the TOBA theaters at least offered steady work. The white circuits of the time employed a quota system, allowing only one black act per show, severely limiting opportunities for African American performers. For the theater owners the benefits were even greater, giving them a better-organized, more dependable pool of talent.

The timing for the TOBA was perfect. The slavery-to-freedom, rural-to-urban migration that had swelled Memphis's black population had done the same in cities throughout the South. The new city dwellers demanded entertainment, and while the bars and gambling houses on Beale provided recreation for some, others demanded something a bit more respectable and less strenuous. The Beale joints and gambling dens were giving way to larger and more elaborate theaters. In addition, the same year the TOBA was organized, Tennessee established statewide Prohibition — not that that meant very much on Crump-protected Beale. Then as now, the real power in Memphis was wielded by the old cotton interests. All others, whether it be Crump's political machine or the Irish and Italian gangsters running the rackets on Beale and elsewhere, were tolerated only insofar as they served the cotton families' interests. Beale was a useful part of that power structure, providing an outlet for the masses of black workers in and around the city.

Within a decade the Barrassos had built the TOBA into a circuit of more than three dozen theaters, among them the Howard in Washington, D.C., and Charlie Bailey's 81 Theater in Atlanta. It was at the 81 that a teenage Bessie Smith, fresh out of Chattanooga, Tennessee, and years away from her coronation as Empress of the Blues, was hired at ten dollars a week. The Barrassos ran the TOBA until 1921, when it was taken over by Nashville theater owner Milton Starr and Charles Turpin, brother of ragtime composer Tom Turpin ("Harlem Rag"), and one of the few black theater owners in the country. The pair did well, adding new theaters until, by the mid-twenties, the TOBA circuit included fifty venues.

The TOBA played the key role in the evolution of black entertainment from minstrel shows to vaudeville, providing black artists with a showcase that, despite the often difficult working conditions, was a vast improvement over the tent shows traveling through the South. By the early twenties, stars of the circuit included Bessie Smith, Ethel Waters, Memphian Alberta Hunter, comedians Jody "Butterbeans" Edwards and his wife, Susie, and, of course, the first blues star, "Ma" Rainey.

White America's hunger for African American music dates back to the early minstrel shows. But the gentler songs of Stephen Foster ("Old Black Joe"), Dan Emmett ("Dixie"), and James Bland ("Oh! Dem Golden Slippers") degenerated in the late nineteenth century to the genre known as "coon songs." "Coon Coon Coon" and "All Coons Look Alike to Me," the latter written by Ernest Hogan, a black man, are two examples of the grotesque fad. In 1896 Bert Williams and George Walker won fame as Two Real Coons, basically a stripped-down minstrel act. Oddly enough, those songs and those of the minstrel shows helped give white audiences a taste for black music, as opposed to the sentimental ballads that were so popular among white performers and audiences, such as the Civil War hit "Lorena" or Charles K. Harris's smash "After the Ball." Offensive as they were, the coon songs helped open the door for the twentieth century's blues craze.

The craze was further abetted by Thomas Edison, who early in his career had spent some time working at the Memphis telegraph office. There, so the story goes, he could occasionally be found dancing on top of his desk, re-creating the shows he had seen the previous evening in Handy's "grand dance town." But it was in 1877, long after he had moved on and just before Memphis was hit by its yellow fever epidemic, that Edison invented the phonograph. By the 1890s a market had begun to develop for Edison's talking machines. Those Gramophones and Edison's bulky cylinder recordings of opera selections and light classics were then sold in furniture stores; the record store was still a thing of the future. When the more convenient disc replaced the cylinder after the turn of the century, the industry began to boom.

Those new record companies were slow to catch on to the blues, or any black music for that matter. Columbia opened its doors in 1899, but it was almost twenty years before it recorded black artists — and even then its first entry was the very proper Fisk Jubilee Singers, a thoroughly "Europeanized" choir that had been raising funds for Fisk College in Nashville since 1871. Victor was a bit more open-minded. The company had great success with recordings by black comedian Bert Williams, who became a solo act after his partner Walker died of complications from syphilis. (In a grim foreshadowing of the modern AIDS epidemic, the venereal disease devastated the early black musical theater. Along with Walker, syphilis would kill ragtime composers Scott Joplin and Louis Chauvin, and "coon song" writers Ernest Hogan and Bob Cole.) Williams, who had first been turned down by Columbia, recorded his "Elder Eatmore's Sermon" for Victor, selling a then unheard-of five hundred thousand copies. In the wake of that success, Victor went on to cut a half dozen sides with the black Dinwoodie Quartet.

50

For the most part, the success enjoyed by Williams eluded black performers in the first twenty years of this century. Just as Pat Boone would later "cover" songs by Fats Domino and Little Richard in the rock and roll era, white performers sang black material with far greater commercial success than the music's originators, at least at first. Former minstrel performer Al Jolson took his blackface act to Broadway and became one of the biggest stars of the time, recording dozens of hits and going on to make the first full-length talking picture, *The Jazz Singer*. Sophie Tucker's way with a blues song made a fortune for Handy & Pace, publishers of some of her biggest hits.

While Tucker worked the white vaudeville circuits, the TOBA was providing work for the generation of musicians evolving from the military-style brass ensembles of Handy's bandleading days into the full-fledged jazz bands. These men, and occasionally women, played in Memphis in the TOBA's Beale Street pit bands as well as at dances and on the riverboats. While the country blues musicians played in the streets and at the funkier saloons, the theaters belonged to the well-schooled musicians who could play "from the sheets," as the pioneering Memphis clarinetist William C. "Buster" Bailey recalled in the classic collection of jazz oral histories, *Hear Me Talkin' to Ya*.

There was plenty of work for Bailey and other Memphis bandsmen in those days. Just as canny old Mr. Crump attracted the black vote with W. C. Handy's band, every public gathering, political or otherwise, demanded live music to ensure a crowd. In 1916, the eccentric Memphis retailing genius Clarence Saunders founded the world's first self-service grocery, creating the modern supermarket. For the grand opening of Piggly Wiggly No. 1, along with a beauty contest to draw the men and red roses for all the red-haired women, Saunders offered brass band music.

Though not a musician, Saunders symbolized that same Memphis maverick spirit seen in the careers of Handy and Pace and later in Sam Phillips's Sun Records, Jim Stewart and Estelle

Axton's Stax label, Kemmons Wilson's Holiday Inns, Fred Smith's Federal Express, and Isaac Tigrett's Hard Rock Cafes and House of Blues clubs. Virtually singlehandedly, the retailing pioneer created the modern consumer marketplace. In 1923, Saunders lost control of Piggly Wiggly in the mercurial stock market of the day. He continued in the grocery business with the less artfully named (and less successful) "Clarence Saunders Sole Owner of My Name" stores, a grocery chain that folded in 1933. Four years later he was back with his Keedoozle ("Key Does All") stores, a highly complex concept involving a hive of vending machines operated by individualized keys. That Automat approach to groceries didn't work and the chain closed in 1941. His final venture, the Food-electric store — an even more complex variant of the Keedoozle — was within weeks of opening when Saunders died on December 14, 1953. His legacy continues today in Piggly Wigglys all over the South, as well as in his Memphis estate, the Pink Palace — a museum that is the site of the city's only I-MAX giant-screen movie theater, a gadget Saunders surely would have loved.

Just as Saunders's stores and their variety of products proved a strong draw to Memphians, so did the array of sounds emanating from Beale Street. The success of the TOBA brought a multitude of rising black talent to the Palace Theatre. White Memphis had appreciated black music since slavery days. With the Jazz Age in full swing, the Palace instituted its famed Midnight Ramble policy. Special shows for white patrons were held at 11:30 on Thursday evenings.

By then the hunger for blues, jazz, and other African American sounds was being fed by record companies, which had begun realizing that, along with eager white fans, records by black artists were tapping a potential market of 14 million African Americans. Mamie Smith, a pop-inflected black singer from Cincinnati, had scored a hit in 1920 with "Crazy Blues," and the gold rush was on, as record companies searched for black women to record blues songs. Black Swan recorded blues by Ethel Waters and Memphian

Alberta Hunter; when they turned down Bessie Smith, it was because her sound was too coarse, too "low-down" for the label's "dicty" pretensions.

Black Swan wasn't the only label that felt that way: Bessie had also been turned down by OKeh and Edison. In 1923, with the demand continuing to grow and blues singers in short supply, Columbia took a chance, and Bessie's first record for the label was Hunter's composition, "Down Hearted Blues." It had sold modestly for its Memphis-born composer, but when Bessie released her version in June 1923, it became a huge hit, selling 780,000 copies before the end of the year. It was the beginning of the single most important and influential career in the vaudeville-inflected "classic" blues.

A large, imposing woman, Bessie's big voice was custom-made for the primitive early recording technology. There were no electric microphones in the recording studios of the early twenties, and performers had to sing into huge "acoustic horns," the vibrations caused by their voices moving the needles through the wax discs from which the metal masters would later be molded. Other early blues singers such as Alberta Hunter and Mamie Smith projected their voices in the classic light-opera style. Complete with starchy vibrato, it's a sound that hasn't aged well. But Bessie's effortless power allowed her to sing with a direct, natural approach that conveyed real blues feeling. Her title of Empress of the Blues was no mere record company promotion.

Just as Alberta Hunter, composer of Bessie's first hit, came from Memphis, the city and Beale Street would continue playing a major role in Bessie Smith's career. With the success of Handy's blues and the development of the TOBA, Beale had become the first nationally famed black entertainment district, predating New York's Harlem, Chicago's South Side, Los Angeles's Central Avenue, and Dallas's Deep Elum. In 1923, Bessie was the star at the TOBA's flagship theater of one of the Palace's Midnight Rambles. By then the blues craze had grown to the point that she was belting out her hits, "Down Hearted Blues" and "Beale Street Mama," over WMC, which had gone on the air just a few months earlier. That remote broadcast on the *Commercial Appeal*'s new radio station was, in its way, segregated, since it was done from a whites-only Midnight Ramble.

When Bessie's blues were launched into the airwaves from the transmitter atop the roof of the *Commercial Appeal* building at Second and Court Streets, they became part of a twenties craze that would soon surpass the phonograph record. After World War I, radio quickly evolved from being an expensive hobby into a fixture in most American homes. In 1922, $60 million worth of radios were sold. By the end of the decade, sales totaled more than $842 million; it was estimated that more than one-third of American families had radio sets in their parlors.

Though the importance of Bessie Smith's record sales is undisputed, it was those radio broadcasts that gave her a truly national audience, spreading her sound beyond the South in the days when the airwaves were still uncluttered. The pioneering black newspaper the *Chicago Defender* reviewed her first WMC broadcast in 1923, saying the blues singer "gave the air some currents that it will not forget as long as a cloud is left in the sky, and Memphis has its Beale Street. . . . Bessie carried the evening with her blues." Bessie Smith biographer Chris Albertson writes that that WMC broadcast wasn't an isolated incident and that, despite the racism of the region, "It was only in the South that Bessie had a substantial following of whites."

Bessie frequently recorded Memphis-related material. She did several songs by W. C. Handy, including the quintessential version of "St. Louis Blues" (a 1993 inductee into the Grammy Recording Hall of Fame) as well as "Yellow Dog Blues." Her repertoire also included "Beale Street Mama" and "Jazzbo Brown from Memphis Town"; on the latter she's accompanied by former Handy & Pace employee Fletcher Henderson on piano and the Bluff City musician on whom "Jazzbo Brown" ("that Memphis clarinet hound") might well have been based — Buster Bailey.

In 1929 Handy repaid Bessie for recording his music: When the short film script he'd cowritten based on "St. Louis Blues" was set to go into production, the composer suggested the statuesque singer for the lead role. Shot in Long Island, New York, in the days before Hollywood cemented its position as the film capital, the movie portrays the singer being robbed and deserted by her easy-ridin' papa. Thus inspired, she sorrowfully sings the title song, unfortunately accompanied by J. Rosamund Johnson's overbearing forty-two-voice chorus. The seventeen-minute two-reeler had its world premiere on Beale Street at the Daisy Theatre. Bessie, by then struggling through the final days of the blues craze, attended the premiere of the movie, the only film document of the Empress of the Blues. More than sixty-five years later, it was still being shown daily at the same theater, now known as the Old Daisy, when it temporarily housed the Beale Street Blues Museum.

Bessie's career neatly encapsulated the "classic blues era." After learning the music from Ma Rainey, she invested it with her own power. Strong yet vulnerable, she was equally convincing whether demanding sexual satisfaction in "Do Your Duty" or playing the victim in "St. Louis Blues." Her own life offered ample inspiration. She had a habit of choosing the wrong men (and the wrong women, for that matter) and her husbands and lovers usually left her with little of the wealth her singing had earned her. But she could be a tough negotiator when it came to her career. One story has her beating Columbia Records A and R man Frank Walker when she found that she hadn't been receiving her full royalties.

But even her prodigious strength and monumental talent couldn't stand up to changing tastes and times. As the twenties came to an end the blues craze began to fade, as radio and the stock market crash gave a one-two punch to the record business. Without her recording successes to promote her stage shows Bessie's income shriveled, but she stayed on the road.

Bessie Smith's last show also found her back on Beale. By 1937 she was no longer recording, earning her keep performing on the same southern circuit once serviced by the then-defunct TOBA. She supplemented that with tent shows in the smaller, more rural towns, earning a fraction of what she'd made a decade earlier. A comeback might have been in the offing; Columbia Records producer John Hammond had recorded her 1933 session for the label's subsidiary, OKeh, backing her with the cream of the Swing Era's musicians — Benny Goodman, Jack Teagarden, Frankie Newton, Chu Berry, and others who'd learned to play the blues by listening to her old records. Hammond had other sessions planned and was putting together a major black music concert at Carnegie Hall to be called "From Spirituals to Swing," for which Bessie was the leading candidate to represent the classic blues style.

Before she could go back into the recording studio there were still bills to pay, however, so Bessie headed out on a tour of the South with the *Broadway Rastus* show. On September 25, 1937, having finished its Beale Street run, the revue was due to open the following afternoon with a Sunday matinee in Darling, Mississippi. Rather than spend the night in Memphis and race to Darling the next day, Bessie, energized after the evening's performance, had her driver, Richard Morgan, take her to Clarksdale as soon as the curtain fell. Driving down old Highway 61 a few miles north of Clarksdale, the car carrying the blues legend sideswiped a truck stopped at the side of the road. It would have been a fairly minor accident, except that Bessie had been riding with her elbow jutting out the Packard's open window. Her right arm was torn off in the crash. Bessie Smith biographer Chris Albertson's investigation has disputed the commonly told story of how the singer had been rushed by ambulance to a white hospital, where she was refused treatment and bled to death during the delay. According to Albertson, after crashing into the truck, which was reportedly delivering Sunday editions of the *Commercial Appeal* to Clarksdale, the singer was attended by Memphis physician Hugh Smith, who came upon the scene on his way to a fishing holiday. After an ambulance arrived, she was taken directly to the "colored" hospital; after all, this was 1937 in Mississippi; what local ambulance driver would take Bessie Smith to a whites-only hospital? Nonetheless, the story of the great blues singer being turned away to die became one of music's most enduring myths. It was even turned into a play, *The Death of Bessie Smith*, by Pulitzer Prize winner Edward Albee. It was an ironic ending to a groundbreaking career which saw its greatest successes in the South.

If Bessie Smith's life was the classic blues singer's tragic story, Alberta Hunter's followed no such stereotype. Born in Memphis on April Fools' Day, 1895, she ran away to Chicago at age eleven with just fifteen cents in her pocket. She did whatever work she could find, but singing was her first love. She performed at speakeasies such as the Panama, but she found her greatest success at the Dreamland Cabaret. "It was there that I introduced 'Loveless Love,' which W. C. Handy brought to me on a little piece of paper — not even on manuscript," she recalled in *Hear Me Talkin' to Ya*. Her relationship with her old neighbor continued with her introduction of other songs published by Pace & Handy. But black blues singers weren't yet being recorded, and she saw the songs she introduced become huge hits for Sophie Tucker. When the record companies' color line was finally broken in 1921, Hunter enjoyed success on a variety of labels, including Black Swan, Paramount, and Victor. But her precise diction and light-opera vocal style were soon quite passé, as the "blacker" sound of Bessie Smith became the rage. Hunter then tried to break into the pioneering black stage productions of Noble Sissle and Eubie Blake, including *Shuffle Along*. But Sissle preferred lighter women in his shows, and Hunter found herself in the unfortunate position of looking too black for the musical stage and sounding too white for records. Things were looser in Europe and in 1928 she starred in the London Palladium's production of *Showboat* costarring the great black musical theater performer Paul Robeson.

She continued plugging away until 1956, when, just as another

Memphis-bred musical revolution was taking over, Alberta quit show business to become a nurse. She'd occasionally sing, but didn't make her comeback until 1977, when she retired from nursing. Her feisty personality hadn't changed since the days she was playing fast and loose with the segregated streetcars in Memphis, and the eighty-two-year-old singer became an overnight sensation on the TV talk show circuit. She also got her revenge on Sissle, outliving him to team frequently on TV with his old partner Blake. She made new records, starred in the Robert Altman film *Remember My Name*, performed at the Carter White House, and even did a series of TV commercials for Final Net hair spray. Her remarkable comeback included a Memphis homecoming in 1978 in which she received the key to the city, sold out the 2,200-seat Orpheum Theater, and, she recalled with delight in her autobiography, even got a kiss from the mayor. For Alberta Hunter, a life spent in the blues at least had a happy ending.

A half century earlier, it had been a very different story. Then, when the singer was in her prime and the mid-twenties blues craze was in full bloom, record companies wanted no part of her polite style. They were trying to keep up with the public's growing hunger for new blues sounds — a taste that would lead away from the bejeweled women playing the TOBA theaters in southern urban centers and back to the country, to the plantations and rural juke joints.

5

▼▼▼▼▼▼▼▼▼▼▼▼▼▼▼▼▼▼▼▼▼▼▼▼▼▼

Back to the Country

Gnarled black fingers work a broken bottleneck across the strings of a steel-bodied guitar, gleaming in the flickering light of a kerosene lamp. Sweat pours from the furrows in the singer's forehead, as, leaning forward in the rickety straight-back chair, he cradles his instrument, thrashing the strings with his right hand and moaning a deep blues about losing the woman he loves to the undertaker and forfeiting his soul to the devil.

The Delta bluesman is one of the most potent images of twentieth-century music, an inspiration to painters and poets, as well as musicians from W. C. Handy to Eric Clapton to alternative rocker Beck to rapper G. Love. Early in the century, when the blues began emerging from the backcountry labor camps and sharecropper farms of the South, vital regional blues scenes began springing up in Texas, North Carolina, and Georgia. But it was from the Mississippi Delta, with its rich cotton plantations and bustling lumber and levee camps, that the most powerful sounds emerged, forever to reshape the world's music.

They say the Mississippi Delta begins in the lobby of the Peabody Hotel, so it's not surprising that Memphis became the focus for much of that early blues activity. As the most luxurious hotel in the business and cultural center of the Delta, the Peabody was the stopping place for "the best people," from visiting foreign dignitaries to the plantation gentry visiting the city for business or pleasure.

"Memphis was the capital of the land of cotton," says the avuncular folklorist Alan Lomax, whose field recording work with the Library of Congress included seminal sessions with such greats as Son House, Muddy Waters, Leadbelly, and Jelly Roll Morton. "Especially the new land of cotton that was created when the swamps were drained and all that wonderful new alluvial marshland was made available to the plow. And huge fortunes were made and small fortunes were made, and the nearest place to spend your money and have your fun was Memphis. So Memphis became the capital of the blues."

The influence those early blues-singing men and women continue to have on today's music can't be overstated. Their use of the guitar, of bending notes in imitation of the human voice, of spontaneously improvising lyrics and instrumental solos, even their apparent "attitude" — their posture while playing, the way they dressed and held their guitars — has helped shape virtually every facet of popular music to follow.

When W. C. Handy first heard the blues in the central Mississippi Delta town of Tutwiler, it was played on guitar. The blues had its roots in the field work songs and church music of the nineteenth century, but it took Sears Roebuck to provide its signature instrument. When the guitar first became widely and cheaply available around the turn of the century through mail-order catalogs, it made possible the country blues that is now seen as the music's purest form. And, though some musicologists argue that the slide is an African invention, most early bluesmen have traced that innovation to touring Hawaiian guitarists who first popularized their moaning guitar sound in America at the 1893 World's Fair. That Chicago event played a remarkably influential role in American life, introducing new technology and world culture that helped Americans to think more globally. It also served as a potent musical catalyst, helping spread the sounds of ragtime piano, pre-jazz brass bands (including the one featuring the young Handy), Hawaiian guitarists, Swiss yodelers, indeed a whole world of music.

Sears Roebuck and Hawaii are unlikely enough as sources of the blues, but stranger still was the town of Grafton, Wisconsin. Nonetheless, the Dairy State became the home of Delta blues recording in the mid-1920s. The Wisconsin Chair Company was already well established as a manufacturer of phonographs when it decided to launch its Paramount Record label in 1917. In 1921, the company joined the booming blues craze, leasing a couple of songs by vaudeville blues singer Lucille Hegamin. These sold so well that the company started its own series dedicated solely to black performers, the first release of which was Memphian Alberta Hunter's two-sided blues effort, "Daddy Blues"/"Don't Pan Me."

Handy's first blues experience back in 1903 had been with a male singer, but by the early twenties blues were being sung exclusively by women, on record at least. Soon all that would change once again, as the public's seemingly insatiable hunger for blues remained unsatisfied. With the top female blues singers signed to the big-city labels in New York and Chicago, and many recording for several labels under various pseudonyms, smaller record companies began experimenting with more rural sounds, which had been ignored by the bigger labels. In the fall of 1923, OKeh brought Louisville bluesman Sylvester Weaver to its New York studios, where he accompanied vaudeville blues singer Sara Martin on several sides. Although guitar blues certainly predated the jazz-band style favored by Martin, Bessie Smith, and the rest of the "classic" blues singers, it was a new sound on records, and the novelty helped make it a big seller. Another pioneering label was tiny Gennett Records of Richmond, Indiana, remembered for some of the first records by Delta bluesmen, sides by William Harris and "Crying" Sam Collins recorded early in 1927.

But it was Paramount that had the first "hits" by rural, guitar-playing bluesmen. In 1924, Paramount recorded New Orleans bluesman "Papa" Charlie Jackson. Jackson, a former minstrel and medicine show performer, accompanied himself on the banjo-guitar. Rarely seen today (although it's been making something of a comeback as the acoustic blues revival continues to grow), the instrument combines a six-string guitar neck with a banjo body. Fingered like a guitar, it produces a sound somewhere between the two, louder and brighter than a guitar, deeper and more resonant than a banjo. In the days before electric amplification it proved popular in jazz as well as blues; one well-known adherent was Johnny St. Cyr, a member of Louis Armstrong's Hot Five and Hot Seven.

Papa Charlie, beating his raucous guitar-banjo and shouting risqué numbers like "Shake That Thing" and "Salty Dog Blues," was an immediate hit; he recorded for Paramount for the rest of the twenties. The company sold its records by mail order, which gave it a larger exposure among rural audiences who couldn't often get into town to shop for records at the big furniture stores. The company shrewdly included space for suggestions on its order forms, and many customers began requesting more country blues. In 1925, Blind Lemon Jefferson left Dallas and its wide-open Deep Elum district for a Paramount recording session in Chicago that had been set up by pianist Sam Price. Jefferson, with his freely improvisational guitar style and a repertoire of unique blues songs, became the first big star of the country blues. Both black and white guitarists bought his records to copy his licks and learn his songs, but they were far from the only buyers. With Blind Lemon, the country blues craze slipped into overdrive.

Paramount's success with Jefferson and its other guitar star, Georgia ragtime whiz Blind Arthur Blake, didn't go unnoticed by the larger record companies. But a good bluesman was hard to find — literally. While the female singers toured the TOBA theaters, country blues was a much more underground style. To find the next Blind Lemon, record companies organized field trips to the smaller towns of the South in search of talent. Paramount, a relatively small label, lacked the financial resources to send a self-contained, portable recording studio into the hinterlands, and was unable to compete. Instead, the label built its own recording facilities in Grafton in 1929 and supplemented that by sending Jefferson and its other bluesmen to Gennett's studios in Indiana, which at least were closer to the South. It was there that the first great Delta bluesman, Charley Patton, made his first records, on June 14, 1929.

Patton's first record was a coupling of "Pony Blues" and "Banty Rooster Blues," and its A-side became a blues standard, played by just about every Delta blues revivalist. The blond-haired, light-skinned Patton played the deepest blues captured on record in the twenties, a raw, shouted style sung over lurching, ominous guitar accompaniment. Patton, a musical fixture of Will Dockery's plantation in Sunflower County, Mississippi, came to Paramount's attention by way of H. C. Speir, a furniture store owner, record dealer, and self-styled talent scout from Jackson, Mississippi.

By the time Patton walked into Gennett's Indiana studio, the field-recording boom had been going on for two years and had helped revive the moribund blues record business. The large companies had become fairly desperate by 1927, the biggest year for field recording. In 1921 record sales had topped $51 million, representing 100 million of the thick shellac discs, which were still produced using the primitive acoustic recording method. Those numbers plummeted in the next few years, as radio sales boomed and silent pictures drew people out of their parlors and into the local movie palace; by 1925, only 20 million records were being sold annually.

The record industry knew something had to be done to stop the bleeding. Ralph Peer had proven that he could find that something new. Working for OKeh, he'd put together a superb catalog of blues and country ("race" and "old time") records. Victor hired him away, and in early 1927 he led the Victor Records field-recording unit into the South. A stop in Atlanta yielded thirty country music sides but only four songs by a lone bluesman, Julius

Daniels. Undaunted, Peer moved west to Memphis in search of the blues — and hit the mother lode.

With their makeshift recording studio set up in the McCall Building in downtown Memphis, Peer and his Victor team recorded thirty sides in less than a week. The records ranged from hot jazz to fire-and-brimstone Baptist sermons to the raucous sounds of the local jug band. Peer had auditioned Will "Son Brimmer" Shade's Memphis Jug Band on an advance visit and was so impressed he recorded the group first, on the morning of February 24. It was a historic occasion; those Victor sessions by the Memphis Jug Band were the first commercial recordings ever made in the state of Tennessee.

Not quite jazz, not quite country music, the MJB walked a thin line that marked it as one of the precursors of the blues and rockabilly bands that would dominate the Memphis scene less than thirty years later. With its makeshift instrumentation of guitars, mandolins, Shade's harmonica, and, of course, the jug, washtub bass, and washboard, the MJB made music as raw and undiluted as the "white mule" moonshine that regularly fueled their performances. And, just like that moonshine, the band was an important part of social gatherings on both sides of the Memphis color line. The MJB was a mainstay of Beale Street as well as a frequent attraction at parties given by rich white Memphians, among them Boss Crump, the MJB's most prominent and loyal patron.

After the Memphis sessions Peer and company headed to New Orleans for more recordings, but the old record man's hunch about the Memphis Jug Band proved correct. The band's first release, "Sun Brimmer's Blues"/"Stingy Woman's Blues," proved such a hit that in June Peer called them to Chicago to record four more songs. By 1930, the Memphis Jug Band had recorded more than sixty songs for Victor. The group's success made Memphis the jug band capital, spawning such groups as Gus Cannon's Jug Stompers, Jed Davenport's Beale Street Jug Band, Memphis Minnie's Jug Band (basically Minnie with the Davenport group), and even the Memphis Jug Band offshoot group, the Memphis Sheiks, which featured the MJB's Will Shade, Charlie Burse, Jab Jones, and occasional MJB mandolinist Vol Stevens.

Jug bands got their name from the jugs they used as bass instruments. Played by pursing the lips into a brass-instrument-style embouchure and blowing across the mouth of the jug, the jugs made a sound rather like a small, flatulent tuba. To this the bands added a wide selection of other instruments, from guitars, mandolins, harmonicas, and fiddles to washboards, which, scraped with thimbles, became percussion instruments. A one-string bass could be fashioned out of an overturned washtub, with a heavy wire running from the center of the tub to the end of a broomstick. Propping the other end of the stick against the rim of the tub, the wire would be plucked like a bass string, its pitch altered by moving the broomstick, drawing the wire tighter or letting it slack a bit.

Jugs were usually ceramic, but jug players made do with whatever was on hand. Quart beer bottles, gallon wine jugs — any empty vessel with a reasonably small opening worked fine. Perhaps the cleverest jug player was Gus Cannon, who, in order to play jug and banjo at the same time, used a converted coal oil can nestled in a cloth bag and hung around his neck. The effect was much like the feed bags he used to hang around the necks of the mules he plowed with on his rural Tennessee farm.

Jugs were just about all that those jug bands had in common. The Dixieland Jug Blowers were the first commercially successful jug band. Hailing from Louisville, Kentucky, where the first jug bands reportedly began sometime in the teens, the DJB was a fixture of the Kentucky Derby and other high-society soirees. Take away the jug and the DJB, led by violinist Clifford Hayes, was pretty much a "legitimate" little jazz band, no different than the dozens of groups, black and white, that played the region's society dances. The DJB even featured the great jazz pianist Earl "Fatha" Hines on some sessions. The band's guitarist, Cal Smith, remains an undeservedly obscure pioneer of early jazz guitar, whose single-string showpiece, "Blue Guitar Stomp," became a standard among western swing musicians.

In Memphis, the jug band sound was considerably more down-home. The Memphis Jug Band, organized by Will Shade after hearing the Dixieland Jug Blowers' records, flirted with pop and jazz on "Lindbergh Hop" and "Grizzly Bear," but also played blues and country-style dance tunes. Cannon's Jug Stompers, featuring its leader playing minstrel-style banjo in a group that occasionally included bluesman Sleepy John Estes, took a far more rural ap-proach. In fact, if you replaced Noah Lewis's harmonica with a fid-dle player on such Cannon records as "Feather Bed" or "Wolf River Blues," the sound would be fairly identical to the hillbilly string bands of the time, whose records were then so popular among white rural southerners.

Jug band historian Bengt Olsson says Cannon, born in Red Banks, Mississippi, took up the jug at the suggestion of Victor Records, in order to expand on the success of Shade's band. The Memphis Jug Band, with its more up-to-date repertoire, proved the more popular of the two and the group played "stag parties" for white patrons in the segregated Peabody Hotel and the equally ex-clusive Chickasaw Country Club. When Boss Crump would hire a train to take parties of supporters to the wide-open resort town of Hot Springs, Arkansas, for the annual horse races, the Memphis Jug Band provided the entertainment. Memphis musician/pro-ducer Jim Dickinson recalls Shade telling him how the jug band "would turn the washtub bass over for tips and the people would fill it with silver dollars." Known today as the hometown of Bill Clinton, in the twenties and thirties Hot Springs was a wide-open resort town drawing crowds for its widely publicized mineral baths and its less publicized, though just as famed, casinos and brothels. It was a favorite hideout for Al Capone. But if the amusements of Hot Springs were a lot like those of Beale, the racial attitudes weren't. Afraid of running afoul of the notoriously corrupt Hot Springs police, the jug band and its washtub full of silver would stay safely on board the train until it was time to head back to Memphis.

For gigs closer to home, the band worked out of band-leader/booking agent Howard Yancey's office at 316 Beale. Every February, the jug band would head south on Highway 61, playing its way to New Orleans, where the same raucous sounds that kept all shades of Memphis toes tapping would liven up Mardi Gras. The good-time music that attracted the Memphis elite in the twenties endured into the sixties. In 1963, the folk revival group the Rooftop Singers recorded Cannon's "Walk Right In" in a slicked-up arrangement. On the eve of the British Invasion it became one of the year's biggest hits, and Cannon received a portion of the royalties, having sold half the rights to Rooftop Singers Erik Darling and Bill Svanoe. That oldie found new life in 1994 on the soundtrack to *Forrest Gump*. But if "Walk Right In" helped ease Cannon's later years a bit, he wasn't so lucky a couple years later, when his music again topped the charts. When John Sebastian of the Lovin' Spoonful wrote "Younger Girl," a hit for the Critters, he "borrowed" the melody, right down to the hook, from Cannon's minstrel tune "Prison Wall Blues" ("These prison wall blues keep rolling cross my mind").

But Sebastian says he considered the song different enough to be a separate creation, and so gave no credit (or cash) to Cannon. It was an all too common practice of the time. And whether you chalked it up to the freewheeling folk scene or calculated chicanery, the results were the same — the creators of the music rarely, if ever, were compensated for their work. When Jim Dickinson, then a young folkie/rocker, met Cannon in the mid-sixties, the old man was working as a yardman and living in a carriage house, where, Dickinson remembers, he kept a copy of the album he'd made for Stax Records in 1963. "But he had no way to play it; he didn't own a record player," Dickinson recalls.

Cannon certainly didn't worry himself to death over being cheated. He stayed active throughout the sixties, performing at the historic 1969 Memphis Blues Festival as well as at national events such as the Newport Folk Festival, where he could be found in the company of old Beale buddies Furry Lewis, Sleepy John Estes, and Mississippi John Hurt. He died at the age of ninety-six in 1979 and was buried in Walls, Mississippi, beneath a plain stone marker. In 1995, the Beale Street Blues Society began to raise funds for a more fitting memorial to Cannon, one that made mention of his musical contributions. John Sebastian played several benefits for the cause.

The success of the Memphis Jug Band inspired the formation of a number of new groups; some were purely recording units while others played various social functions, both black and white, or worked for tips in Handy Park on Beale. There was Jack Kelly's South Memphis Jug Band, which often included singer/ukulele player Little Laura Dukes, a Memphis jug band mainstay until her death in 1992. Cannon's harmonica player Noah Lewis also regularly performed and recorded with a jug band featuring Sleepy John Estes on guitar, Yank Rachell on mandolin, and Jab Jones on jug. Estes, hailing from Ripley, east of Memphis, also made some powerful blues records with Rachell, from nearby Brownsville, and Jones, who doubled on piano.

The Memphis jug band sound proved such a potent commercial force that some groups adopted the name with no geographical connections. The Beale Street Washboard Band was a Chicago group that featured the New Orleans jazzmen Johnny and Baby Dodds, on clarinet and drums respectively. Not only did they have no Beale connection whatsoever — they didn't even have a washboard. The Bluff City's musical reputation also inspired the Original Memphis Five, an influential band of New York sessionmen that recorded during the twenties, but featured no original Memphians.

Though the jug bands played some of the most enduring Memphis blues, they got little respect on Beale Street. The big theaters hired only "legitimate" musicians, those who could read music and play the popular tunes of the day. Furry Lewis frequently claimed he had played with W. C. Handy's band, but unless Handy was hiring him to entertain during intermissions for his brass band, it seems unlikely. Handy prided himself on an orchestra that employed only the best sight-reading musicians.

When country bluesmen played Beale, it was most likely in the park, playing for tips or in the funkier saloons; sometimes they were booked out of the Beale music contractors' offices to play out in the country for barbecues. Some, like Robert Wilkins, found work in the whorehouses around Beale. His granddaughter Lane Wilkins recalls him telling her about playing in the parlor of one house run by his aunt, a blonde, blue-eyed woman who was passing for white. "He played for her, but he couldn't let anyone know he was her nephew," says the bluesman's granddaughter, recalling his frustration at the racial hypocrisy involved.

Different events called for different music, and while the respectable dance bands were perfect for Saturday night at the country club, when it came to a down-home Sunday afternoon pig roast, a jug band was just the ticket. The jug bands continued performing long after their twenties heyday. Charlie Burse of the Memphis Jug Band recorded with a jazzier combo in 1939 as the Memphis Mudcats, with sax, piano, and string bass in place of the old homemade instruments. Perhaps Burse was just trying to go legit: In a business where respect was hard to come by, the line dividing the musicians on the street and those who played the theaters and honky-tonks was a rigid one. Even in 1993, when seventy-six-year-old blues piano great Booker T. Laury was being photographed for the cover of his first American album, he refused to pose in Handy Park. "I ain't no *street* musician," he angrily told photographer Karen Pulfer-Focht.

Despite class distinctions, the rural sound of those old-time Memphis jug bands was one of the most distinctive elements of the Memphis blues. The city's unique, inseparable mix of black and white culture wasn't the sole property of the rockabilly cats to come. The early blues of the city had an obvious country sound, a legacy of the slave fiddlers and itinerant musicians from the frontier days of the previous century. Both black and white Memphians never lost their rural roots and they came out when inhibitions were down and it was time to party. After all, this is the city that took a lowly hunk of pork barbecue and turned it into the Memphis in May International Festival, an event of global proportions. Memphis's tastes in music were just as unpretentious. And the musicians, far away from the music business centers of New York or Chicago, felt no industry pressures to clean up their acts. If anything it was the opposite. Moneyed Memphians like Crump hired them because they *were* down-home.

That rural sound lived on in the lilting rhythms of Jim Jackson. The Hernando, Mississippi, native became the first solo Memphis blues star with his 1927 Vocalion recording, "Jim Jackson's Kansas City Blues." It can be heard in the banjo-esque, open-tuned guitar of Furry Lewis. And it can most clearly be heard in the music of Frank Stokes and his partner Dan Sane.

The duo personifies the early Memphis blues sound in such songs as "Mr. Crump Don't Like It," "It Won't Be Long," and "Memphis Rounder Blues." They created an immediately identifiable sound as the Beale Street Sheiks. ("Sheiks" were chic in the twenties, thanks to silent-screen idol Rudolph Valentino; the word bore such a sexual mystique that it was even bestowed on a line of condoms.)

Stokes, a blacksmith born in Whitehaven in South Memphis and raised in Tutwiler, Mississippi, had a boisterous baritone voice and played guitar in a fingerpicking style in which his thumb rocked in an anvil-steady rhythm over the bass strings. Sane's own fluid, countrified flat-picking guitar danced around Stokes's like a cloud of flies around a plowhorse. On recordings for Paramount and Victor, their mix of country and blues personified the Memphis "thing," seamlessly blending black and white musical styles.

Walter "Furry" Lewis was one of the most enduring Memphis

bluesmen, enjoying a revived career in the sixties and seventies that lasted until his death in 1981. A natural-born showman, he was equally at home on the TV talk show circuit, in the Burt Reynolds film *W.W. and the Dixie Dance Kings,* or opening the 1975 Rolling Stones tour (at the band's request) at Memphis Memorial Stadium, now known as the Liberty Bowl. With his gift of salty gab ("I don't need no wife," Lewis would respond when asked if he was married; "not as long as the man next door has one"), Lewis is remembered as one of the most colorful, beloved figures in the Memphis blues. But photographer/artist manager Dick Waterman, a key figure in the revival of the careers of many of the old country bluesmen, says Lewis was not exactly the happy old man he appeared. "He could be very bitter," Waterman told me, recalling the bluesman's anger at receiving no money from Joni Mitchell's "When Furry Sings the Blues," although she would visit him in a limousine when she was in Memphis.

Whatever bitterness he may have harbored never came out in his music. Born deep in the Delta in Greenwood on the Yazoo River, Lewis sang with wry good humor, backed by the gentle, countrified rhythms of his guitar. There was always a gracefulness to his playing, as well as a bit of the old jug band sound in his sliding bass lines. Whether in his delivery of the murder ballad "Stack O Lee" (named after the ne'er-do-well son of a Memphis riverboat captain) or his romance-with-finance proposition, "I Will Turn Your Money Green," or his version of the Tennessee railroad ballad "Casey Jones," Furry's sound was unmistakable.

The Reverend Robert Wilkins was another enduring Memphis bluesman. From Hernando, Mississippi, just south of Memphis, Wilkins played masterful, highly personalized guitar accompaniments to such wide-ranging compositions as his tribute to "Old Jim Canan's," or "That's No Way to Get Along." In the sixties, as he was a Church of God in Christ preacher, Wilkins saw no reason to abandon those great guitar arrangements, and wrote new gospel lyrics to his old blues tunes. Converting "That's No Way to Get

Along" to tell the story of the "Prodigal Son," Wilkins saw his song sell millions of copies on the Rolling Stones' *Beggars Banquet* album. Memphis blues historian David Evans has written that Wilkins earned no money from the song, but Wilkins's granddaughter disagrees. Lane Wilkins says that the Stones had learned it from an uncredited tape and believed it was in the public domain. When Wilkins's publishing company, Wynwood, contacted the Stones, she remembers, "There was no argument, they were very cooperative." She's not sure what the settlement was, "but our financial picture did change," she says, adding that they were able to move to a larger house set on a full acre of land. Wilkins, who died in 1987, remained a fixture of the Memphis blues revival into the seventies, playing his gospel music at such events as the 1969 Memphis Blues Festival. Lane has written and performed a one-woman play in memory of her grandfather, *Last Train Song*, and written several books about her grandfather's life and times.

Memphis Minnie quite literally made a name for herself in Memphis as one of the city's best guitarists. She was born Elizabeth Douglas in 1897 in Louisiana, as she sang in "Nothing in Rambling," and "Raised in Algiers" a town just across the Mississippi from the French Quarter. She picked up guitar early on, receiving one for Christmas in 1905. By then the family had moved to Walls, Mississippi, close enough to Memphis for the youngster to run away there with regularity. Strong and independent, she soon earned a reputation for toughness, both as a person and a musician. In so doing, she, like her spiritual sister Lil Hardin Armstrong, crossed a social barrier every bit as established as the one dividing the races.

Minnie occasionally played in jug bands on Beale, most notably Jed Davenport's, with whom she later recorded. She even toured for a while with a Ringling Brothers circus troupe. But her preferred performance setting was the guitar duet. In fact, despite the popularity of the Memphis Jug Band and the romantic image of the solo bluesman, the duo was probably the most common

Memphis blues style. Most of the Delta bluesmen, from Charley Patton to Tommy Johnson to Son House, all preferred working with a second guitarist, a combination more cost-effective than a band but more versatile than a solo act. Performing with her husband of the moment, Minnie became the most successful country blues singer to come out of Memphis, scoring several major blues hits, the best known of which is "Bumble Bee."

The importance of a hit song is often overlooked in blues history, though virtually every successful blues singer had a signature song. That oversight may be due to the fact that much of the modern interest in early blues originated among sixties folk revivalists fascinated by the guitar virtuosity of a Blind Lemon Jefferson or a Blind Blake. While the success of the most popular blues records may have been helped by performers' instrumental skills, the hardworking people who laid down their seventy-five cents for those records weren't musicians and couldn't have cared less about open tunings or double thumbpicking. It wasn't instrumental technique, but the emotion in the voice and the lyrics, the danceable beat, the ironic humor or stark imagery in a well-turned phrase: "Wonder if a matchbox hold my clothes." "I got me a bumblebee, don't sting nobody but me." "Now she's gone, but I don't worry. I'm sitting on top of the world." "The blue light was my blues and the red light was my mind."

The troubador image was yet another contribution of the country blues singers. Today, singer-songwriters are the norm in popular music; most contemporary pop, rock, and R & B singers are assumed to have written the songs they sing, but that's only been the case since the sixties and the era of Bob Dylan and the Beatles. In the twenties, popular singers got their material from the vast song publishing industry that had been booming since the turn of the century. Sophie Tucker, Al Jolson, and Bing Crosby weren't expected to write the words they sang.

In the blues it was a different story. The lyrics may often have been borrowed, but they were at least strung together by the person singing and playing the guitar or the piano. Some bluesmen proved remarkably evocative and original folk poets. Robert Johnson, who hailed from Robinsonville, another Mississippi Memphis suburb, is the best known, through such songs as "Love in Vain," "If I Had Possession over Judgment Day," and "Hellhound on My Trail." But though less celebrated in legend, there was Skip James of Bentonia, Mississippi, whose "Must Have Been the Devil" provided the model for Johnson's "Hellhound." James's music is at least as powerful as Johnson's, from James's eerie vocal timbre to his haunting, minor-keyed guitar parts that seem to float in the air. Tommy Johnson, of Jackson, Mississippi, was another masterful, all too frequently overlooked, Delta bluesman. His "Big Road Blues," recorded in Memphis on one of Ralph Peer's Victor field trips, was one of the most influential blues records ever made, his lyrics and "dropped-D" guitar arrangement (in which the low E string is tuned down a whole step) being copied by hundreds of other blues players for decades to come. When Bonnie Raitt recorded her first album in 1971, the first blues on the record was "Big Road Blues." But Tommy Johnson was no one-hit-wonder, his repertoire including emotionally evocative blues like "Maggie Campbell" and his doom-laden ode to drinking Sterno, "Canned Heat Blues," the song that provided the name for one of the sixties' most popular blues revivalist bands.

Charley Patton is generally considered the originator of the Delta blues style, his thrashing guitar and hoarse, shouted vocals seemingly dredged up from some primeval Delta swamp. Before he died in 1934, Patton inspired hundreds of players, including such key figures of Memphis music as Chester "Howlin' Wolf" Burnett and Roebuck "Pop" Staples of the Staple Singers. "Me and Charley Patton lived on the same plantation, Will Dockery's," Staples recalled more than a half century later. "He used to play at the country stores, sit out there on the grocery store and play and entertain all of the people, maybe on a Saturday. Everybody'd go up to the big store when he'd play." Another Patton follower was

Son House, who played in a slightly more refined manner. Some film of House performing in the sixties survives, revealing him to be a riveting performer, seemingly possessed by his music.

The list goes on; the sheer numbers of blues musicians from Memphis and its nearby Delta towns are staggering, far greater than the concentration in any other region. But there was no single Delta style, with various towns each bringing their own flavor to the blues, all of them tempered by the bluesmen's frequent visits to Beale. Memphis was the big time, the Hollywood, Paris, and Manhattan of the blues all rolled into one, a place to record, get photographs taken, book gigs, and get drunk, stoned, and laid.

In 1928, Mississippi John Hurt made the trip to Memphis from Avalon, just north of Greenwood. He came to record for OKeh, on the suggestion of his friends Shell Smith and Willie Narmour. Narmour & Smith, a white fiddle-and-guitar duo, had known Hurt since 1923, when Narmour, the fiddler, first hired Hurt to play rhythm guitar for a dance when Smith couldn't make it, yet another case of music's blurring of racial lines. Narmour & Smith were very successful in their own right, and the duo's "Carroll County Blues" remains a fiddle standard.

Of course, Mississippi John isn't remembered for his backup guitar skills. His records didn't sell very well at the time. But when he was rediscovered some thirty-five years later, his warm voice and gentle, easygoing guitar style made him one of the most frequently copied performers among sixties folk-blues revivalists.

As the twenties drew to a close, time was running out for what is now seen as the golden age of country blues recording. The record business was one of the industries hardest hit by the crash of the economy. Then as now, entertainment was one of the first things to go when household budgets were cut. In 1927, bolstered by the field recording trips, $100 million worth of records were sold. By 1933, that figure had plummeted to $6 million. As record companies slashed their budgets, the field trips that brought Memphis music to national attention were among the first items to go.

Memphis Minnie was one of the last country blues stars to enjoy success as the depression was taking hold. The novelty of a guitar-wielding woman able to beat the mighty Big Bill Broonzy in a guitar contest might have been a factor. But it was her songs, "Bumble Bee Blues," "Me and My Chauffeur," and dozens more, sung in that tough, no-nonsense voice, that sold those records.

Even in the depths of the depression, the Memphis blues thrived on Beale. Peter "Memphis Slim" Chatman recalled in an interview in Arnold Shaw's excellent book about the early independent R & B labels, *Honkers and Shouters*, that the Midway Cafe at Fourth and Beale was the most jumping club on the street when he began playing there in 1931. "The Midway sold whiskey. They had gambling and they paid the police off — it was during Prohibition. Beale Street was full of such clubs, though I think the Midway was the most lively. Sometimes I'd be playing there in the middle of the day, it was that busy. We didn't know what time it was, night or day."

By the time Slim was playing those joints, Minnie, buoyed by her record sales, was gone, following the migration out of the South to Chicago. She'd made the move in 1930 with husband/partner Kansas Joe McCoy, part of the prominent Jackson, Mississippi, blues family that included guitar/mandolin virtuoso Charlie McCoy, a frequent recording partner of Tommy Johnson and other bluesmen. Memphis Minnie remained an exciting and adventuresome musician through the forties and fifties, "going electric" and continuing to expand her repertoire far beyond country blues. Biographers Paul and Beth Garon report that she was a member of the Chicago musicians' union, unusual for a blues player, and that she augmented her blues repertoire with such swing standards as "Jersey Bounce" and "How High the Moon."

One of her earlier recordings shows just how advanced a musician she was. "Soo Cow," recorded in 1931, soon after the couple left Memphis, is thumping, primordial rock and roll. Joe McCoy's guitar plays a walking boogie-woogie bass line while Minnie rocks the house, albeit on acoustic (the introduction of Gibson's ground-breaking "Charlie Christian" ES-150 electric guitar was still five years away). On the record, Minnie slides up the neck to play a solo that would have sounded right at home twenty-five years later on a reverb-soaked Sun Record.

She continued performing, becoming a key figure in the early days of electric Chicago blues. But after a major stroke in the early sixties, she returned to Memphis a broken woman. She lived out her days in a local nursing home, unable to take part in the blues revival of the sixties that made stars of many lesser musicians. Still, there were consolations: She lived until 1973, long enough to see her old records reissued and such Memphis Minnie songs as "Me and My Chauffeur" revived by singers like Maria Muldaur.

Minnie wasn't the only Memphis blues musician to provide a foretaste of the rock revolution to come. Robert Brown, better known as Washboard Sam, was born in Lawrence County, Arkansas, northwest of Memphis. The illegitimate son of Frank Broonzy and half brother of Big Bill Broonzy, Washboard Sam came up the hard way in the levee and lumber camps of the Delta. He augmented that hard-earned income as a street musician on Beale, singing in a booming voice and scratching out rhythms on his washboard. He played the percussion instrument popularized by the jug bands with sewing thimbles over his fingertips and a phonograph turntable for a cymbal. After moving to Chicago in 1932, he hooked up with such Beale homeboys as his half brother Bill, Sleepy John Estes, and Yank Rachell. Washboard Sam recorded in 1941 and 1942 for the RCA Bluebird label with Broonzy on guitar and Memphis Slim on piano. Prime examples of the Bluebird beat, the regularized rhythm that steadily led the way to postwar rhythm and blues, those sides are driven by Sam's washboard and a shouted vocal style that would become popular through such pioneering rockers as Big Joe Turner and Wynonie Harris.

The Bluebird sessions included his "Rockin' My Blues Away," "Diggin' My Potatoes," and "Soap and Water," songs that displayed his proto–rock and roll style. "Rockin' My Blues Away" speaks for itself. (Of course, Frank Stokes was singing about rocking more than ten years earlier, in lines like "Every time I feel like rockin' I feel like rockin' downtown.") "Soap and Water" found new life more than fifteen years later when Sun Records rocker Warren Smith took Brown's classic put-downs ("You must have been your mama's only child. You should have been a gorilla, man you sure is wild") and made them do the bop under the title of "Miss Froggie." Washboard Sam himself remade "Diggin' My Potatoes" for Chess Records in 1953 as full-tilt rockabilly, featuring his sly vocals against Big Bill's distorted, frenetic electric lead guitar and Chess sessionman Ernest "Big" Crawford's jumping, double-slapped bass. It rocked like crazy, and predated Elvis's first Sun sides by a year. But being ahead of your time isn't usually a very good career move; Washboard Sam's hits would remain a decade behind him.

Washboard Sam's Bluebird labelmates included the duo of John Lee "Sonny Boy" Williamson, who hailed from just east of Memphis in Jackson, Tennessee, and Mississippi Big Joe Williams, inventor of the nine-string guitar, whose driving style helped pave the way for the electric blues to come. The two recorded together but issued the records under their individual names; Williamson wrote "Good Morning Little Schoolgirl," one of the most frequently performed songs of prewar blues, while Williams recorded his classic "Baby Please Don't Go" just five days after Pearl Harbor.

By the time those recordings were made, the Delta scene was in major transition. Robert Johnson, though often hailed as a founder of the Delta blues, was in many ways the last of the prewar Delta bluesmen, and his contemporaries would go on to become the first generation of electric bluesmen. Johnny Shines, born in the Memphis suburb of Frayser, was one of Johnson's running buddies. Robert Junior Lockwood, who would become one of Chess Records' top sidemen in Chicago and a longtime associate of "Sonny Boy Williamson II," Aleck "Rice" Miller, was Johnson's common-law stepson. Both men would adapt to the electric sounds to come. Relatively few of Johnson's associates, among them Dave "Honeyboy" Edwards (who claims to have been with Johnson when he was poisoned by a jealous husband), have kept the old-time Delta sounds alive.

Johnson's life, almost all of it spent within fifty miles of Memphis, has remained shrouded by legend. His mystique was enhanced for many years by the fact that no photos of him were known to exist. Two were discovered several years ago, one a photo-machine snapshot, the other a formal studio portrait taken at Beale's Hooks Brothers studio on one of his stays in Memphis. The most widely repeated part of the myth tells of Johnson as a struggling, but inept, musician ridiculed by older men like Son House, until one dark midnight when the young man made the trip to the famed Delta crossroads where Highway 61 meets Highway 49. There, he allegedly met a shadowy figure who took his guitar, tuned it, and handed it back to him at the stroke of midnight. Instantly, Johnson was transformed into a virtuoso guitarist and singer, but at the cost of his soul. The myth was aided by Johnson's tortured compositions, agonized vocals and violent, untimely death on August 16, 1938; in a gruesome coincidence, thirty-nine years later Elvis Presley would leave this world on the very same day.

It's a great story and, along with inspiring the awful movie *Crossroads*, it was endlessly repeated in 1990 when Columbia rereleased Johnson's complete recordings in a boxed set that "went gold" and made the *Billboard* charts more than fifty years after the bluesman's death. But it does a great injustice to Johnson, a versatile performer who did indeed compose some of the darkest, most harrowingly poetic blues to come out of the Delta, but who also was equally at home with the hokum ragtime of "They're Red Hot" or the Bo Carter–like double entendres of "Terraplane Blues."

What Johnson did better than any of his contemporaries, both vocally and instrumentally, was to take advantage of the new subtleties made possible by the improved recording techniques of the late 1930s. He didn't have to thrash his guitar like Patton or House and he didn't have to contort his voice to be heard. Patton recorded as if the studio was just another rowdy juke joint, and he needed to be the loudest thing in the room. Johnson sang and played to the microphone as if it were a woman to be seduced — a situation with which he was no doubt familiar. Frank Sinatra similarly revolutionized pop singing a few years later, taking advantage of better microphones to bring new intimacy to the form. Indeed, what others saw as Johnson's shyness may have actually been a demonstration of the musician's sonic sophistication. Don Law, the engineer who recorded Johnson in 1936 and 1937, recalled that Johnson was so shy that, when he recorded, he could only do it facing the wall, not looking at the engineers and other waiting musicians. But it could well have been that Johnson played and sang close to the wall's hard surface to amplify his voice and guitar, letting the sound bounce back at him, using a technique later called "corner loading" to create a richer, fuller recording.

Whatever it was, it worked. It's almost sixty years and a world away from the days Johnson made those records. His stomping grounds thirty miles south of Memphis in Robinsonville have been transformed into a thriving casino capital, while Highway 61 has become a gridlock of commuting gamblers. But the unearthly power of Johnson's music remains as potent today as it was in 1938, and it's Johnson, not Satan, who deserves the credit. Though he was born black, dirt-poor, and illegitimate in the heart of the Delta, he managed to create a body of work that continues to move and inspire millions all over the world. In 1994, he was honored with a first-class postage stamp in a special commemorative blues and jazz series. Johnson's life had been hard-lived and short, but for the purposes of the U.S. Postal Service his act was cleaned up posthumously: Based on the penny-arcade machine snapshot, its painting of Johnson captures the somber cast of his eyes, but eliminates the cigarette that dangled from his mouth in the original photo.

One of Johnson's stampmates was McKinley "Muddy Waters" Morganfield, a fellow Delta bluesman who got his start in Johnson's style. Muddy Waters learned music on Stovall's Plantation near Clarksdale, playing in string bands, where he backed up fiddler Son Sims and mandolinist Louis Ford, as well as playing in the solo styles of his neighbors Johnson and Son House. He recorded in both settings in 1941 for folklorist Alan Lomax, setting down his music on the disc-cutting machine Lomax carted around the South for the Library of Congress, despite hostile white sheriffs who harassed the folklorist, suspecting him to be a Communist labor organizer. Those early sides have recently been reissued in their entirety on CD, showcasing Waters's acoustic slide guitar work and budding style. But it would take the combination of a guitar amplifier and the urban environment of Chicago — or North Mississippi, as it was called by the huge numbers of Delta expatriates living there — to bring out Waters's particular brand of musical genius. For other men, including Howlin' Wolf in West Memphis and Sonny Boy Williamson in Helena, Arkansas, the raw electric style that would later become known as Chicago blues was not only born in the Delta but was perfected there as well.

The South's black population continued its move northward, a move footloose musicians readily joined. Some great Memphis bluesmen were yet to emerge, however. Booker T. Washington "Bukka" White was a slide guitarist whose guttural vocals and intense, driving slide guitar were first recorded in 1930 in a Memphis session that produced "The Panama Limited," a song that showcased White's trademark slide-guitar train imitation. The depression and the end of Memphis field recordings delayed his next record until 1937, when his "Shake 'Em On Down" became a sizable hit, but a shooting landed him in Mississippi's notorious Parchman prison farm. By 1940 he was free, and recorded a dozen sides for Vocalion Records that, along with being some of the last recorded prewar Delta blues, are true classics of the style.

Bukka White's frequent accompanist was former Memphian Washboard Sam. By then, though, the rural sounds of the acoustic Memphis blues were passé, as more sophisticated musicians like T-Bone Walker were becoming the stars of the day. World War II would forever change the face of the blues, as Charley Patton's generation gave way to Robert Johnson's, and the future electric blues stars like Waters, Wolf, Sonny Boy Williamson No. 2, and dozens more brought the Delta blues with them to Chicago.

The world of music obeys its own rules, however, and in the early sixties, the old-time acoustic Delta blues would again be king. Young white middle-class folkies became hooked on ancient 78 RPM records and headed South in search of their heroes. In Memphis, Furry Lewis, Gus Cannon, Bukka White, and members of the Memphis Jug Band remained part of the city's musical life, and young white Memphians like Jim Dickinson, Sid Selvidge, and Lee Baker all learned music from the older black men. Mississippi musicians like Skip James, John Hurt, and Eddie "Son" House were largely retired until young white fans from the North set out to find them. Young Californians John Fahey and Bill Barth found Nehemiah "Skip" James sick in a Tunica hospital, recalls Dick Waterman, who the very same day found Eddie "Son" House living in Rochester, New York. "It was Sunday, June 21," Waterman recalls of that 1964 day, adding that it was the same day civil rights workers Goodman, Schwerner, and Chaney were murdered. Waterman and some friends had driven down from New York to look for House, starting out from Memphis and traveling through the Delta with Robert Wilkins as their guide. When they learned House was living in Rochester they backtracked, dropping Wilkins back in Memphis and driving straight to upstate New York. With so many bluesmen emerging from obscurity, the world of folk-blues was turned upside down, Waterman recalls. "Delta blues or traditional blues went from where you would listen to Josh White or Brownie [Mcghee] & Sonny [Terry], and then suddenly all of these legends who had just been names on discs, they were back, they were right in front of you playing. [For] the gathering at Newport in 1964, which was MC-ed by Sam Charters, Son House was sick, but there was John Hurt and Skip James and Bukka [White] and Fred [McDowell] and Sleepy John Estes, Hammie Nixon, Robert Pete Williams, Gus Cannon."

The men became stars of the folk circuit, traveling the world playing clubs and festivals modeled on the Newport event and making new records which, though they seldom matched the music they'd made in their primes, nonetheless sent thousands of young urban kids to sit glued to their stereos, trying to decipher their fingerings and tunings. The result was a Delta blues revival that continues on today's pop charts, as one of those kids grew up to be Eric Clapton, whose 7-million-selling *Unplugged* album featured a healthy dose of old-time acoustic blues and whose 1994 all-blues *From the Cradle* set featured several more acoustic numbers.

That modern revival has again inspired controversy over whether white boys like Clapton can play the blues, or should even try. A recent wrinkle on the old debate of authenticity is the growing number of young black musicians who are taking up acoustic country blues, players like Keb' Mo', Corey Harris, and Alvin "Youngblood" Hart, all of whom grew up much further removed from the tradition than the Mississippi-born, Memphis-bred harmonica master Charlie Musselwhite. Should a person's color be considered the ultimate proof of authenticity, or is that idea just another example of musical racism? Many, myself included, believe the latter. The old argument that white players are merely copyists won't really wash either, as true musical innovators of any color are few and far between. There are as many African American copyists in the blues as European Americans.

There are at least as many opinions about the blues as there are blues performers. And it's not a new situation. Back when the blues was still in its golden age of the twenties and thirties, the plantation owners of the time — like Nathan Bedford Forrest a century earlier — viewed their musician/sharecroppers as proof they had "happy niggers" down on the farm; left-wing labor organizers saw the blues as the voice of protest of the black proletariat; recording company executives, for their part, thought the blues was their own key to the bank. For the men and women who created the blues, the music was a way to make a few bucks, forget the cares of the day, maybe attract some members of the opposite (and in some cases the same) sex, and just to generally have a good time, a rare commodity for poor black men and women in Memphis and the Delta.

Whatever it was, the blues genie had busted out of the bottle, coming out of Memphis and the Delta to seep into every crevice of American popular music and go on to shape the music of the world. Produced by a people that had survived incredible hardship, the music inherited its creators' resilience. It continues to change and mutate as we approach the turn of the millennium. The purists try their best to put the stopper back in that bottle, but it's too late. The blues has caught that Greyhound bus and gone.

6

▼▼▼▼▼▼▼▼▼▼▼▼▼▼▼▼▼▼▼▼▼▼▼▼▼▼▼

Jazz on Ol' Man River

One of the treasured myths of American music tells how jazz was born in the saloons and whorehouses of New Orleans's Storyville district and then traveled up the Mississippi to Chicago. Like most myths it contains some truth, but jazz as we know it today was more a creation of the river itself than of any single city. The population of musicians plying the bustling Mississippi riverboat trade freely shared ideas, tunes, hot licks, and instrumental innovations, creating such unlikely jazz pockets as the river town of Davenport, Iowa, revered by vintage jazz fans as the birthplace of Bix Beiderbecke. Not surprisingly, Memphis, as the first major riverboat port upriver of New Orleans, played a vital role in the development of jazz.

Jazz had its roots in the brass band tradition that flourished across the country after the Civil War. In every city, town, and hamlet, no self-respecting civic and social club went without sponsoring a brass band, and no event was complete without a local band playing marches, quadrilles, light classics, and other popular tunes of the day. In New Orleans, the city's ubiquitous French influence made itself felt, as musicians there incorporated European sounds; when ragtime became a national craze after the Chicago World's Fair of 1893, those new syncopations were digested by the brass ensembles. But what separated the brass bands of New Orleans from their brethren upriver was an emphasis on improvisation.

"We were playing in Memphis at the same time they were playing in Storyville in New Orleans," Memphis jazz pioneer William C. "Buster" Bailey recalled in *Hear Me Talkin' to Ya*, the important collection of oral histories by early jazzmen. "The difference was that the New Orleans bands did more improvising. Ours [in Memphis] were more the note variety. We played from the sheets."

Right from the first stirrings of jazz, New Orleans musicians frequently found themselves in Memphis. Most passed through on the riverboats; some, like innovative New Orleans trombonist George Williams, came for the opportunities offered by the city's biggest and busiest bandleader, W. C. Handy. Bailey, who played with Handy as a teenager, recalled that the most respected musicians on the scene in those days were the ones who played in the circus bands. The split-second shifts of key, tempo, and dynamics demanded of musicians accompanying fast-moving circus acts required a technical facility far beyond that of most bandsmen. "During the off-season, a lot of them would play in the local bands led by Handy, George Bynum, Stewart, et cetera," Bailey said.

Bailey, born in Memphis in 1902, took up clarinet at thirteen, around the time he heard Handy's band play at the Clay Street School behind his house. Like many young musicians, Bailey learned the new popular tunes by buying magazines such as *Etude*, which provided arrangements of waltzes, mazurkas, ragtime songs, and light classics. "Every month they'd publish two new numbers and we'd learn them — but with a beat."

The Memphis musicians had that danceable beat and were familiar with the blues, through Handy's compositions at the very least, if not from the itinerant rural bluesmen along Beale. But one ingredient was still missing from the jazz recipe: improvisation. It was the success of a white group, the Original Dixieland Jazz Band, whose recordings became huge hits in 1917, that started Bailey and the rest improvising in earnest.

In addition to the influence of the ODJB records, Bailey recalled, "Some of the boys had drifted up from New Orleans. There
was George Williams, around 1912, 1913, a great trombone player
and a very good musician, composer and arranger who also improvised. He played with Handy's reading band."

And if Williams helped Memphis musicians learn to improvise,
Memphis, through Williams, gave something very important back
to New Orleans, according to veteran Crescent City bassman
George "Pops" Foster. "The first slide trombone I ever saw was
brought down to New Orleans by a cousin of mine, George
Williams," Pops recalled in his late-sixties autobiography, *Pops Foster: New Orleans Jazzman.* "George had gone up to Memphis and
gotten a job with W. C. Handy's band. He got the slide trombone
there and brought it back with him on a visit. Up until then there
was nothing but valve trombones." Try to imagine Dixieland jazz
without the signature sound of the "tailgate" slide trombone.

Bailey became fascinated with the new sound coming from
New Orleans, and in late 1917 the young clarinet virtuoso traveled
down to the Crescent City on a vacation that changed his life.
"We only stayed a week. I was in high school at the time. I heard
Johnny Dodds at Tom Anderson's. And I heard [Armand] Piron,
Mutt Carey, Clarence Williams," Bailey said, reciting some of the
city's foremost jazzmen. "After that trip, I came home and started
jazzing it up in Memphis."

Back then, most people wouldn't have known what Bailey
meant by "jazzing it up." "Jazz" was a brand-new musical term.
When Bailey began playing outside the melody, he said, "I
wouldn't have known what they meant by 'improvisation.' But 'embellishment' was a phrase I understood. And that's what they were
doing in New Orleans — embellishment. In my day in Memphis,
if a guy played with a good swinging beat, he was a good ballroom
man. Before 1917 [when the Original Dixieland Jazz Band burst on
the scene], the word 'jazz' didn't exist — not around my city
anyway."

"Jazz" (also called "jass" in its early days), like "rock and roll" a couple of generations later, had its origins as a slang term for sex. The ODJB's success made it part of the national musical language (and standardized the spelling). Of course, the word's risqué roots no doubt boosted its popularity in that age-old search by hormonal, rebellious young people looking for edgy, exciting new ways to express themselves and, if at all possible, worry their parents as well.

The all-white ODJB got its start in Chicago, but it was in New York that vaudeville star Al Jolson got the band its groundbreaking gig at Reisenweber's Restaurant. They were an instant hit, the lively music providing needed relief on the home front from the shortages and news of casualties of World War I.

Of course, the ODJB was to jazz what Pat Boone would later be to rock and roll, "covering" the real thing, presenting it in a more acceptable manner (and complexion). But just as Sophie Tucker paved the way for Bessie Smith, the ODJB created an appetite for Sidney Bechet, Joe "King" Oliver, and other early black jazz greats. And the inspiration provided by the ODJB's success shouldn't be discounted; young musicians like Bailey saw that you could get rich and famous playing that new music, and the Jazz Age had begun.

Bailey remains the unsung hero of Memphis jazz. In many ways his career, which survived changing tastes and styles and lasted until his death in 1967, exemplified the life of a Memphis jazz musician. A well-schooled musician with superb technique and superior reading skills, Bailey could also play the blues, improvise with the best of them, and swing like crazy. In his later years, living in New York, he made a musical trip back to the Home of the Blues with the 1958 album *All About Memphis*, which included Handy's "Memphis Blues" and "Beale Street Blues" as well as such locally flavored originals as "Chickasaw Bluff" and a tribute to the city's red-light district, "Hatton Avenue and Gayoso Street."

But in 1919, just seventeen years old and hungry to make his name in the brave new world of jazz, Bailey moved to Chicago just two weeks shy of his high school graduation. "All my friends were going. There was better money there, I thought, and there was a little girl who had gone there that I wanted to follow. At that time, everybody from New Orleans and many people east of the Mississippi and as far west as Arkansas were migrating North. The word was there was lots of money in Chicago."

Thousands of black southerners were giving up on dear old Dixie. Seeing no end to the Jim Crow laws and eager for the opportunities they were told were waiting, they headed north. The *Chicago Defender*, the leading African American newspaper, encouraged the exodus, announcing that the "Northern drive" would officially begin on May 15, 1917. Henry Ford had done his part early on, integrating his automobile assembly lines in Detroit, and there was plenty of work in the slaughterhouses and oil refineries around Chicago.

The migration intensified during World War I, as northern industries advertised in the *Defender* and other black newspapers, actively recruiting southern black labor for the jobs left vacant by drafted workers and the closing of European immigration. Between 1910 and 1920 more than 450,000 southerners, the vast majority of them black, moved north, more often than not with Chicago the goal.

The loss of its black laboring class was not going unnoticed in Memphis, which struck back with an advertising campaign of its own. "Stay in the South," shouted a full-page advertisement in the *Commercial Appeal* in 1923, over a cartoon portraying a giant image of Booker T. Washington halting a northbound train carrying a saucer-eyed black man. "When a negro justifies help, sympathy and 'backing,' he can get a quicker response from a Southern white man than from anybody else in the world," promised the ad, sponsored in part by the newspaper and such vested interests as the Gayoso Lumber Company and the Southern Cotton Oil Company, two firms feeling the pinch as its workforce headed north.

Too little, too late. The targets of that ad were all too familiar with the reality of what that "quicker response" would be. The Ku Klux Klan, which had steadily declined in power and influence with the end of Reconstruction, had been revived in full force, inspired by D. W. Griffith's epic *Birth of a Nation*. During the 1920s, the Klan boasted 4 million members, most of them in the South, though the Midwest remained a racist hotbed. In Richmond, Indiana, the Gennett record label kept itself afloat in the twenties alternating recordings by some of the day's best black jazz and blues musicians with sessions by local Klansmen.

The northern migration continued unabated. In fact, just a few months after that *Commercial Appeal* ad, another one ran admitting defeat. "The negro exodus to the North has been reckoned with and accepted. He has turned his back on the most fertile land in the world. . . . No further organized effort will be made to induce him to remain." Between 1920 and 1930, almost three-quarters of a million more southerners migrated north.

For Bailey, the move north proved a smart one. He quickly found work with the popular Erskine Tate Orchestra at the Vendome Theater and began enjoying the greater freedom and respect granted him. "The Tate band in Chicago was composed of all legitimate musicians and I was regarded as a legitimate musician too. In Chicago, I started studying with Franz Schoepp, first clarinetist of the Chicago Symphony. Benny Goodman started studying with him two or three years later."

The Memphis teenager's reputation soon began to spread. He recalled proudly that the New Orleans émigrés to the Windy City, a group that included Joe "King" Oliver, Freddie Keppard, Sidney Bechet, Jimmie Noone, and Manuel Perez, "all used to come in [to the Vendome Theater] to hear 'the young kid, a hell of a clarinet player, playing all the overtures.' At night, I'd sit in at places like the Panama Cafe, Royal Gardens, Dreamland, Elite Cafe No. 1 and Elite Cafe No. 2."

That combination of classical technique that saw Bailey

through his day gigs and the improvisational skills that kept him busy at night in the speakeasies and private clubs would continue to mark generations of Memphis musicians down to Phineas Newborn Jr. and James Williams. It served Bailey well in a career that saw the young man move on from Erskine Tate to the groundbreaking Fletcher Henderson Orchestra, where he shared a bandstand with a host of jazz revolutionaries and legends-to-be, including Louis Armstrong and Coleman Hawkins. With its leader's arranging skills and that formidable lineup of soloists, the Henderson band set the model for all swinging big bands to follow. Bailey also played the down-home blues as a session man with Ma Rainey, Alberta Hunter, and Bessie Smith. He featured prominently on the latter's recordings, including one about "that clarinet hound," "Jazzbo Brown from Memphis Town." Bailey's skills took him from the Roaring Twenties to the more streamlined swing of the thirties, when he played in Lucky Millinder's band. He remained a popular session musician in the Swing Era, recording with Billie Holiday, Mildred Bailey, Lionel Hampton, and Teddy Wilson.

In Millinder's group, Bailey met tuba/bass player John Kirby and later joined him in what became *the* groundbreaking "chamber jazz group," the John Kirby Sextet. The lineup was Kirby on bass, Bailey on clarinet, Russell Procope on alto sax, Charlie Shavers on trumpet, Billy Kyle on piano, and O'Neil Spencer on drums. The group caused a sensation playing flawless swing in a smooth, restrained style and syncopating the classics in such pieces as "Mr. Haydn Gets Hip." As jazz critic Nat Hentoff said of the group, "This was cool jazz before Miles Davis. . . . This was tightly linear interplay before the Gerry Mulligan Quartet. This was a prototype of how disciplined jazz could be before the Modern Jazz Quartet."

After Bailey's death in 1967 at the age of sixty-four, his bandmate Procope gave much of the credit for the Kirby band's sound to the versatile musician, calling him "the most underrated clarinet player who ever lived. Buster Bailey was a genius. . . . Buster could play anywhere, whether it be the Philharmonic, a pit band, a radio program, or a blues session."

Bailey did all that and more, playing in the Broadway pit band for *Porgy and Bess* in 1953–54 and occasionally performing with classically trained musicians. But Bailey grew up in a time of strict segregation, and he had no illusions over the social limitations forced on him. "When I started you couldn't even think, if you were a negro, of making symphony orchestras," he said. "The only regret I have is that I didn't have a chance to make it in symphony music."

If Bailey, as the first prominent Memphis jazz musician, found the odds against him, the second faced an even more stacked deck. Lil Hardin wasn't merely black, she was female at a time when a woman's place, if not limited to the kitchen and the bedroom, was at best in a ceremonial position at the front of the stage, singing in a pretty gown.

But Hardin was a piano player, Memphis born and bred. A neighbor of Bailey's (and quite possibly that "little girl" he mentions as one of the reasons he moved to Chicago), she began studying in the first grade under the prominent Memphis piano teacher Miss Violet White. Lil moved to Chicago with her parents in 1918 at the age of fifteen (although Louis Armstrong biographer James Lincoln Collier suggests she might have shaved a few years off her age). While exploring her new city, which she called "heaven," she stopped at Jennie Jones's music store at 3409 State Street for new sheet music. She couldn't remember the title of the song she wanted, so she played it, and played it better than the salesman could. She wound up with a three-dollar-a-week job demonstrating sheet music. But even the most difficult music must have seemed easy compared with convincing her middle-class mother to let her work there.

"As soon as I got to the music store, I got busy playing all the music on the counter and by 2 P.M., the place was packed with people listening to 'the Jazz Wonder Child,' " she later recalled in *Hear Me Talkin' to Ya*. The music store doubled as a booking agency, so young Lil got to meet and play with all the New Orleans transplants who had wound up in Chicago after the closing of New Orleans's notorious Storyville red-light district. "Almost every day there was a jam session and I took charge of every piano player that dared to come in," she recalled with matter-of-fact pride. The only one who gave her some trouble was Jelly Roll Morton. Playing for an audience of musicians at the store, Morton pulled out all the stops, banging out his "whorehouse music" with every flourish he could think of. After his flamboyant performance, Hardin said she was "thrilled, amazed and scared. . . . But do you think the people were satisfied? No, they wanted Jelly Roll to hear me play."

Hardin was as clever as she was talented. "Suddenly remembering that he had played nothing classical, I sat down to the piano very confidently, played some Bach, Chopin and 'The Witches Dance,' which they especially liked. The session ended with me still the winner."

With her mix of skill and showmanship, Hardin soon found a spot in the New Orleans Creole Jazz Band. This was the last thing Lil's parents wanted. Like other upwardly mobile blacks of the time, they wanted their daughter to at least have a career in "legitimate" music or teaching, something as far removed as possible from the sounds of Beale Street, New Orleans, and the Chicago speakeasies. Moving to the North, they had hoped to leave that low-down southern music behind them. In a rare interview quoted in *Louis Armstrong: Portrait of an American Genius*, her mother, Dempsey Hardin, echoed what other middle-class Memphis blacks thought of the blues, calling it "worthless immoral music, played by worthless immoral loafers expressing their vulgar minds with vulgar music."

Faced with a parental attitude like that, could any self-respecting teenager resist? Her bourgeois parents' dreams of sending their daughter to Nashville's Fisk University went unfulfilled. Instead of making the dean's list, Lil made history.

She soon earned a name for herself as one of Chicago's best
jazz pianists, but her place in the jazz hierarchy was cemented
when she joined Joe "King" Oliver's band in 1921. A couple of
years later, Oliver introduced her to his new second cornet player,
a chubby twenty-two-year-old just arrived from New Orleans, "Little" Louis Armstrong. Lil, recently married to a dashing singer
named Jimmy Johnson, making good money on her own in the
clubs, and enjoying her status at the top of the Windy City's budding jazz scene, wasn't much impressed with the shy, awkward
country boy. But sharing a bandstand with him soon gave her second thoughts, and the two became an item, divorcing their re-
spective spouses and marrying on February 5, 1924. Perceiving the
talent in her new husband, Lil convinced Louis to leave Oliver, his
idol and father figure. It was the first step in turning Armstrong into
the single most important jazz musician of the twentieth century.

"I thought the main thing to do was to get him away from Joe
[Oliver]. I encouraged him to develop himself, which was all he
needed. He's a fellow that didn't have much confidence in himself
to begin with," Hardin recalled.

"If it wasn't for Lil, Louis would not be where he is today," New
Orleans trombonist Preston Jackson stated flatly in the fifties, long
after Armstrong's place in the jazz pantheon was ensured. "She inspired him to do bigger and better things." Bassist Pops Foster
agreed, recalling that it was Lil who helped Louis learn to read
music. Together they composed the jazz standard "Struttin' with
Some Barbecue," and Hardin played piano on the classic Hot Five
and Hot Seven recordings, regarded by critics as cornerstones of
early jazz. Collier calls those sides "the most important set of
recordings of 20th Century improvised music."

"Most of the tunes Louis composed, Lil wrote the music to.
Louis would play the melody and Lil would write it down just as
fast as Louis played," said Preston Jackson. "When playing some of
Louis Armstrong's records recorded by the Hot Five, notice the
foundation. It will speak for itself."

The couple divorced in 1932, because, Foster said, "she just got tired of Louis smoking that stuff. He smoked pot just like you smoke regular cigarettes." But the pair remained close friends throughout Armstrong's life. Lil stayed active in music, but never remarried and died onstage in 1971, while performing in a memorial concert for her late ex-husband. Sharply dressed in a beautiful gown, she died at the piano, in the middle of playing "St. Louis Blues," a favorite of Louis's, and, fittingly, the biggest hit written by her hometown hero W. C. Handy.

On her own, Lil never achieved the prominence of a Mary Lou Williams, who walked through the door Lil had opened and became one of the Swing Era's best pianist-composer-arrangers. Lil had learned her parents' lessons all too well, and her playing usually displayed her classical training more than the "vulgarisms" of Beale. Of course, it certainly didn't help that her replacement in Armstrong's recording band was Earl "Fatha" Hines, one of the great innovators of jazz piano. But if she failed to please the critics, the musicians loved her. Among Lil's fans was Alberta Hunter, whom Hardin frequently accompanied at Chicago's Dreamland. "I know I don't want no musicians who know all about music playin' for me," Hunter asserted, but for one exception. "Then there was Lil Armstrong — she played a mighty blues." "Louis should give more credit to Lil than to anyone for teaching him how to play," said Pops Foster. "She was a great piano player and a great musician."

As Memphis jazz pioneers, Bailey and Hardin laid the groundwork for what would become a very well traveled path. Another Memphian who became a respected name in jazz was drummer Jimmy Crawford, who would go on to fame in the thirties with Jimmie Lunceford and would continue recording and performing into the fifties and sixties with such artists as Dinah Washington. Early in his career, producer Quincy Jones *(Thriller, Bad)* produced Washington's classic *Swingin' Miss D* LP. One of the highlights, he recalled, was working with Crawford. "He can give me spirit, time, enthusiasm, sympathy with the musical situation, a professional attitude and musical discipline."

For Crawford, it all started on Beale. Luckily for him, his family, unlike the Hardins, bore no prejudice against Beale and the blues. "When I was a kid in Memphis, Tennessee, my aunt used to carry me to the old Palace Theatre," Crawford recalled years later. "It would be around 1924, I guess, and there I saw Ma Rainey, Bessie Smith, Ida Cox, Baby Cox and Butterbeans and Susie. That was the time of the T.O.B.A. circuit and there was a pit band led by Charlie Williams," Crawford said in Stanley Dance's 1974 book *The World of Swing.* "My interest in drumming began right there."

Crawford was fourteen when he made that first visit to Beale. A couple of years later he was a student at Manassas High School in North Memphis. His gym teacher was a musically inclined young man named Jimmie Lunceford, who was forming a student band. With Crawford on drums, Lunceford's group of teens would evolve into one of the hottest bands of the Swing Era.

Around the time of Crawford's Beale indoctrination, white Memphis was getting a look at the Beale Street talent during the popular Midnight Rambles, the whites-only shows held at 11:30 P.M. Thursday nights. Rambles were frequently broadcast on Memphis's flagship radio station, WMC, which had gone on the air early in 1923. The Beale evenings provided some relief from the station's staple diet of "snappy" (in the slang of the time) white pop music. Provided by so-called jazz bands, all of them lily-white in personnel and musical style, the music was often a mix of incompatible styles ranging from light classics to attempts at the blues. Among the bands were the Washington Syncopators, the Burks Band, Gasper Pappalardo & his Hotel Gayoso Orchestra (who, according to listings in the *Commercial Appeal*'s "News and Notes of the Radio World," claimed to play both jazz and grand opera — now *that's* fusion) and the Jolly Jazz Boys. The last was a typical hot-cha group of the day whose WMC broadcast, according to one *Commercial Appeal* review, included "Ten-Ten-Tennessee" and "a host of other snappy numbers."

No matter how feeble the attempts, it seemed everybody wanted to be part of the Jazz Age. In the early twenties, syncopa-

tion ruled the nation, and even the Salvation Army Band got
caught up in the epidemic, jazzing up its repertoire of hymns. In
the July 10, 1923, *Commercial Appeal*, Salvation Army commis-
sioner William Peart defended his band's syncopated rhythms.
"We prefer melodies with zest and swing in them." He was certainly not alone. "We didn't call it jazz back then," recalls Rufus
Thomas. "We called it 'syncopation.' "

Not everyone jumped on the jazzwagon. A 1925 *Commercial
Appeal* editorial called the Charleston "one of the latest offerings
of musical degenerates" and said a local bandleader who "jazzed"
a classical piece "ought to have bowed his head in shame that
[such] beautiful music is butchered and debauched."

The newspaper had won a Pulitzer Prize in 1923 for its campaign against the Ku Klux Klan, but when it took on jazz, the
Commercial Appeal was fighting a losing battle. Jazz was here to
stay. And when the "hot" sounds of the twenties gave way to the
smoother swing style of the thirties, Lunceford and his Manassas
kids were in the forefront. Born in Fulton, Missouri, near the center of the state, Lunceford studied under jazz pioneer Wilbur
Sweatman and majored in music at Fisk University in Nashville.
After failing to make a name for himself with bands up north, he
migrated to Memphis for the steady paycheck of a Manassas High
School teacher and leader of the school orchestra. "He formed
the school band and out of that we got a little dance group," Crawford would recall. In 1927 Lunceford's Chickasaw Syncopators
went professional, and within a few years, with Crawford on drums
and Memphian Moses Allen on bass, the Lunceford big band was
earning a reputation as the most danceable black swing band.
Memphis remained Lunceford's adopted home, and when he died
in 1947 he was buried there.

Leonard Feather's *Encyclopedia of Jazz* calls the Lunceford
band "the best-disciplined and most showmanly Negro jazz orchestra. . . . The Lunceford band ranked with those of Ellington,
Basie and Goodman among the few lastingly important big jazz orchestras of the 1930s."

Lunceford definitely had the "Memphis thing," that combination of versatility and showmanship that he shared with Handy, Buster Bailey, Elvis, B. B. King, Otis Redding, and the other Memphis music stars. "One of the real problems in trying to analyze the so-called Lunceford style is that there isn't a single style but several," wrote jazz historian Gunther Schuller in his book *The Swing Era*. "There may have been, especially in later years, a Lunceford beat or a Lunceford tempo, but the band's very versatility would almost by definition preclude a single stylistic approach."

Like Bailey and Hardin before him, Lunceford combined discipline, a finely honed jazz sense, and a keen commercial instinct. His influence continued not only in jazz, but in rock and roll as well. Dave Bartholomew, the brilliant New Orleans producer-bandleader who helped create the Crescent City R & B sound and was a key figure in the career of Fats Domino and dozens more, was a former Lunceford bandsman. An even more vital link to the rock era was the protorock act the Treniers. Twin brothers Claude and Cliff Trenier cut their first records in 1946 as members of the Lunceford aggregation. But it was the following year, after they had stripped down to the smaller sort of band coming into vogue at the dawn of the rhythm and blues age, that they began making history. Music historian James Marshall calls the Treniers "arguably America's favorite rock 'n' roll act in the days before rock 'n' roll had a name."

Even Lunceford's advance man, Dave Clark, was ahead of his time. Clark, a West Tennessean who first joined Lunceford in the reed section, soon found the business end of the band more to his liking. As the band's advance man, Clark's job was to visit cities ahead of the band and create a buzz. In 1938, Clark convinced Martin Block, host of New York City's groundbreaking *Make Believe Ballroom*, the program that revolutionized radio by using recorded rather than live music, to play Lunceford's "St. Paul's Walking Through Heaven with You." To accomplish that feat, Clark had to pose as the station manager's chauffeur, as WNEW's studios weren't open to blacks in the late thirties. Clark's mas-

querade earned him the distinction of being, some say, the record
industry's first radio promotion man.

Lunceford's influence in rock and roll found its way into the
MTV era, with British pop groups Fun Boy Three and Bana-
narama having a 1982 hit with Lunceford's swing classic "It Ain't
What You Do (It's the Way That You Do It)" reaching No. 4 on the
British charts. The Lunceford legacy also continued in Memphis,
as Manassas High remained the city's jazz high school, turning out
such great players as Booker Little, Harold Mabern, Frank
Strozier, and even the versatile Isaac Hayes.

Versatility continued to be a prerequisite for Memphis jazz
players. They were expected to be excellent reading musicians,
great improvisers; and, of course, they had better be able to play the
blues. The Beale theaters continued to provide a training ground
for musicians. Leaders like Bill Harvey provided work and training
for such players as saxophonist Fred Ford, who even as this is written remains a key player on the Memphis scene with his partner,
organist Honeymoon Garner.

Today's generation of Memphis jazzmen still say that, to survive
in the city's scene, you better be able to do it all. "You had to deal
with all the functions that went on in the community," says jazz pianist Mulgrew Miller. Born in Greenwood, Mississippi, (also the
hometown of bluesman Furry Lewis), Miller received his jazz
training at Memphis State and on the local club circuit. An important part of his training was his position as keyboardist at Eastern Star Baptist Church in the Crosstown section of Memphis. It
was pianist James Williams's family church, and, as he was about
to head for New York, he wanted to leave the congregation in good
hands. For a few months, worshipers were treated to the world-class
double bill of both Williams and Miller playing for services. Miller
says that his gospel experiences still shape his playing today, in yet
another example of the communal nature of the Memphis music
scene. "You didn't grow up just learning jazz. You grew up learning classical music, you grew up playing in church. On Saturday

night you played for the high school dance or in the R&B band, whatever kind of function that was needed."

Miller is one of many disciples of the man many consider to be the greatest Memphis jazzman of them all: pianist Phineas Newborn Jr. Phineas grew up in just the sort of eclectic musical environment Miller spoke of. In the forties, his father, Phineas senior, was one of the most in-demand drummers on Beale, playing in most of the top bands, including the one led by Al Jackson Sr., father of the future MGs drummer. Phineas senior also had a long association with Beale bassist and bandleader Richard "Tuff" Green. After catching a Green performance at Nashville's Plantation Club in 1940, *Downbeat* called his group "the South's biggest little band." Green's group was home to many of Memphis's finest musicians, including at various times, along with Phineas senior, vibraphonist-arranger Onze Horne and tenor saxophonist Ben Branch. In 1949, Green, Newborn, and Branch were injured in a band bus crash outside Memphis that killed three members of the band. Green quit touring after that, while Phineas senior, with his two sons quickly coming of age, decided to form a family band. Calvin played guitar, and the brilliant but tragically unstable Phineas junior played piano.

A few years earlier, in keeping with the Memphis tradition, the younger Newborns had made their debut on Beale at the street's legendary amateur contest. "My brother and I played at the Palace Theatre. I guess I was about 10 and he was about 11," Calvin recalled. "We won the amateur show at the Palace. [Master of ceremonies] Rufus Thomas awarded us a $5 bill." The pair played a piano duet on "Hey Ba Ba Re-Bop," said Newborn. "I sang and did a little act on the bottom of the piano and my brother played his behind off on the top."

Phineas junior continued playing his behind off. It was, in fact, that portion of his anatomy that caused him to alter the pronunciation of his first name. Phineas senior preferred the rather unorthodox "Fine-us," even spelling it phonetically on the family band's equipment. But Calvin recalls that in high school groups of girls would follow his elder brother down the halls, commenting on his rear view, "Look at that fine ass." Not surprisingly, the painfully shy and introverted young musician soon began using the classical pronunciation of "Phineas." Still, his closest friends and knowledgeable jazz fans continue to refer to him as "Fine-us." These include bassist Ray Brown, who performed with the pianist frequently in the fifties and who in 1993 recorded the tribute "Phineas Can Be."

In the early fifties, the Newborn family band was one of the hottest acts on the Memphis club scene, boasting Phineas's blues-to-ballads-to-bebop-to-boogie piano stylings, Calvin's wild guitar playing and even wilder showmanship, and Phineas senior's rock-solid rhythm. Calvin says the Newborn family band had a particularly strong influence on a young white musician who often came by to see the group at such local nightspots as the Flamingo Room at Hernando and Beale or the Plantation Inn in West Memphis. "He got rhythm from my dad, he got boogie-woogie from my brother and he got his poise from me," asserts Calvin. Of course, there are dozens of musicians around Memphis who'll tell you just how much Elvis got from them, but Calvin has a point. Back then, the youngest Newborn was a wild man, famed for a stage act that included leaping into the air in midsolo, a routine that earned him the nickname "Legs." "I had more hang time than Michael Jordan, and I'd be playing the guitar all the while," he says proudly.

Along with their regular gigs on Beale and in West Memphis, the Newborn family band helped B. B. King make his first recordings in the studios of WDIA. As he became a blues star, King filled his big band with a whole host of Memphis jazzmen.

"B.B.'s first bands had Phineas and they had Calvin, too," says jazz pianist and Phineas historian James Williams. "Jamil Nasser, then [known as] George Joyner, was his bass player. He [King] bought George Coleman his first tenor."

Most of the R & B bands around Memphis in the fifties were

made up of jazzmen. Howlin' Wolf's "Oh Red," recorded at Sam
Phillips's Memphis Recording Service, includes a tenor sax solo
that quotes the opening phrase of Charlie Parker's "Ornithology."
On Beale, Clubs like Sunbeam Mitchell's Club Handy drew touring blues and R & B singers and their jazzy bands. Charles Neville,
of New Orleans's famed Neville Brothers, was part of that mid-
fifties scene, courtesy of Uncle Sam. "When I was in the Navy I
was stationed at Millington [the naval base north of Memphis],
and I used to play this joint on the corner of Beale and Hernando,
it was called Mitchell's Hotel and the club was called the Club
Handy, right across from Handy Park," Neville recalls. "I used to
play at Sunbeam's place and that's where I met Phineas [New-
born], old man Phineas and Phineas [junior], George Coleman,
Bill Fort, Barry Harris, Fred Ford. . . . Little Willie John's band
would come to town, Roscoe Gordon's band, all those cats were
jazz musicians and the same scene that would happen at Sunbeam's place was happening at the Dewdrop on LaSalle Street in
New Orleans."

But Phineas junior didn't want to just to play blues for a living
and jazz after hours. A couple of years after those early B. B. King
sessions, the pianist, like so many Memphis jazzmen, left for the
jazz capital of New York. Blessed with dazzling technique, an un-
erring sense of swing, and deep blues feeling, Newborn formed his
own trio in 1955. He earned rave reviews for a 1956 appearance at
New York's Club Basin Street. In 1958, he teamed with bassist-
composer Charles Mingus to provide the music for jazz-loving
filmmaker John Cassavetes' *Shadows*. A year later the pianist traveled to Europe with the Jazz from Carnegie Hall tour.

"It just stunned the entire jazz world when he came on the
scene," said James Williams. "I wasn't around when he made his
greatest impact initially. But from his recordings and talking to
Oscar Peterson, or Andre Watts, or Andre Previn, or George Shear-
ing, you just mention his name and you stop them dead in their
tracks." A video of a 1962 TV appearance by Newborn shows why.

The short-lived *Jazz Scene USA* presented a half hour of Newborn in a trio setting, playing such dazzling piano showpieces as his "Blues Theme for Left Hand Only."

As always in the music business, talent alone wasn't enough to guarantee commercial success, and Newborn's genius proved too fragile. Problems with drugs and alcohol exacerbated his already delicate emotional makeup, and the pianist was occasionally committed to mental hospitals during the sixties and seventies. In the late eighties he could be found scuffling around Memphis, unable to find work. Producer-musician Jim Dickinson remembers Newborn often sitting down uninvited at the Peabody Hotel piano to play incredible, impromptu jazz concerts until the management finally barred the unshaven and unwashed genius from the premises. In 1989, Newborn, weakened by drug and alcohol abuse, died of heart problems at fifty-seven.

His old B. B. King bandmate George Coleman has been far more fortunate. At King's suggestion, he switched from alto to tenor, the horn he used on some of King's early classics. But he's best known for working with a bandleader whose personality is the ultracool yin to B. B.'s charming, ebullient yang: Miles Davis.

Coleman had joined the Davis band in 1963 at the recommendation of tenor giant John Coltrane, a reference that must have been hard to question. After he joined, Miles went through one of his periodic band changes and he sought his new tenor player's counsel.

"I asked him who he liked to play with and he recommended Frank Strozier on alto and Harold Mabern on piano. . . . that's where I got all those Memphis musicians," Davis later wrote in his autobiography. Even Davis, who personified "cool," both musically and personally, got pretty excited about the bumper crop of jazz talent emerging from Manassas High School in Memphis. "They had gone to school with the great young trumpet player Booker Little, who soon after died of leukemia, and the pianist Phineas Newborn. I wonder what they were doing down there when all them guys came through that one school?"

Mabern and Strozier only lasted a few months in the group, but Coleman remained one of Davis's favorite players. His tenor plays a leading role on the classic live recordings Davis made at Lincoln Center in 1964. Now available as a two-CD set, they feature one of Davis's best bands — the leader on trumpet of course, with Coleman, pianist Herbie Hancock, bassist Ron Carter, and drummer Tony Williams.

Today, Coleman is universally respected in jazz and has tutored such younger musicians as David Sanborn. His recent recordings, including *My Horns of Plenty* and *James Williams Meets the Saxophone Masters*, in which Coleman can be found playing with Joe Henderson and Billy Pierce, reveal that Coleman's playing has only improved with age.

Yet, unlike the cliché of the jazzman who looks down his nose at anything except pure jazz, Coleman still loves to play the blues, especially with such old Beale buddies as Roscoe Gordon and Bobby "Blue" Bland. In a 1992 performance at Manhattan's Sweetwater's nightclub, Bland looked into the audience to see Coleman sitting there and invited him onstage. "We had a nice little impromptu session," Coleman told me a few months after the reunion. "Bobby said, 'Can you still play the blues, George?' I said, 'Well, I, you know, *might* be able to get through a chorus or two.'"

The sounds of Beale are still in his soul, but Coleman, who makes his home in New York, speaks for many expatriate Memphis jazzmen when he says of his former hometown, "The tradition and the heritage is there, but as a rule, we don't get the recognition we deserve . . . from our hometown crowd. We tend to fade into the background, and they adhere to Kenny G or somebody like that, not realizing that we are world-renowned jazz musicians from Memphis."

And nowhere is that more true than in the short, tragic life of Phineas Newborn Jr. "They just took him for granted," Coleman says of his old friend. "One of the great geniuses of the piano, beyond a shadow of a doubt. He should have a statue or something erected out on Beale Street. He should have a street named after him."

Today James Williams champions Phineas Newborn's memory in particular and Memphis jazz in general, in much the same way Wynton Marsalis does for New Orleans. Williams's two 1993 albums, *The Memphis Convention* and *The Memphis Piano Convention*, combine the talents of such internationally known players as Coleman, Mabern, and Calvin Newborn with lesser-known Beale Street regulars like Herman Green and such up-and-coming Memphians as Tony Reedus. In 1994, Williams formed a unique multipiano group featuring himself, fellow Memphians Mulgrew Miller, Harold Mabern, and Donald Brown, and the young pianist Geoff Keezer. The group recorded and toured to rave reviews as the Contemporary Piano Ensemble, playing four pianos simultaneously in a tribute to Newborn and Memphis jazz.

"New Orleans, contrary to popular belief, was no more of a jazz town than Memphis," Williams asserts. "But they've hyped all that, because they've had higher profile names, whether we're talking about the great Louis Armstrong or Wynton and Branford [Marsalis] or whatever. But there was a lot of years in between that, you know. You're taking about sixty years in between the time that one was born and the other one was born."

Even discounting hometown pride, Williams has a point. New Orleans may well have been the birthplace of jazz, and Louis Armstrong's importance can't be overstated. But Memphis produced outstanding jazz players and bandleaders with far greater consistency. From first-generation players like Buster Bailey and Lil Hardin through the big band of Jimmie Lunceford and on to the great individual players of the forties and fifties, Memphis has quietly been a major influence in the course of jazz. But the city's Home of the Blues title often obscures its jazz heritage.

Along with Hardin, Bailey, Lunceford, Newborn, and the rest of the better-known players, Williams cites such lesser-knowns as "pianist Jimmy Jones, who for years accompanied people like

Sarah Vaughn and Billie Holiday; and when Duke [Ellington] was ill or he needed somebody to do some arrangements and Billy Strayhorn was too busy, Jimmy Jones would come in there and not only write the arrangements but would fill in for the Duke [on piano]. We've got *too* much of a legacy. It's too important to let it slide by."

But it is sliding by. Although most of the bands in the Beale theaters and clubs were more jazz than blues oriented, that fact is now rarely acknowledged. There are no jazz clubs on Beale today. Sadly, there seems to be little audience for the music as well. In recent years, when promoter-fan Irwin Sheft's World Class Jazz organization has promoted concerts by such internationally renowned players as James Moody and Clark Terry, the shows usually sell only a hundred tickets or so. Without an audience, jazz in Memphis seems in danger of extinction — even as Williams, Coleman, and the rest of the Memphis jazz mafia perform to sold-out houses all over the world.

▼▼▼▼▼▼▼▼▼▼▼▼▼▼▼▼▼▼▼▼▼▼▼▼▼▼▼▼

7

Country-and-Western Tennessee:
The Beale-Opry Connection

George Dewey Hay couldn't carry a tune, couldn't play guitar, never wrote a song, and never had a hit record. So why is he arguably the single most important figure in the history of country music? The answer: Hay was the man who started a little radio barn dance called the Grand Ole Opry. The Opry turned Nashville into the country music capital of the world and created a major segment of the popular music industry — but the roots of the Opry, known as the "Mother Church of Country Music," lead straight to Beale Street.

The Opry began inauspiciously enough, on November 28, 1925, when Hay — who less than a month earlier had been hired away from Chicago's WLS to help start up Nashville's new WSM station — presented a program featuring a seventy-seven-year-old fiddler from Laguardo, Tennessee. Uncle Jimmy Thompson, with his down-home wisecracks and backwoods reels and breakdowns, impressed Hay so much and drew such an enthusiastic audience response that within a month, on the day after Christmas, Hay announced that the station "has arranged to have an hour or two every Saturday night" dedicated to what he called the "old familiar tunes," and country music's Ground Zero was born.

Years later, after the Opry had grown into a certified, dyed-in-the-gingham American institution, Hay would recall that the initial inspiration for his Nashville barn dance had come to him in his early days as a reporter for the *Memphis Commercial Appeal.* Hay was sent to Mammoth Spring, Arkansas, to cover the funeral of a World War I veteran. While there, he was invited by "a truck farmer [who lived] in an old railroad car . . . to attend a 'hoe-down' the neighbors were going to put on that night until the 'crack o' dawn.' " There, the farmer fiddled the evening away with two other musicians as twenty people danced.

So the story went, and as creation myths go it's a pretty good one: one that casts Hay's Opry in the ideal image of a homespun show put on by simple country folks for simple country folks. But in order to accept that story, one has to ignore the rest of Hay's Memphis days and nights. A closer examination of Hay's background points to a far more likely source of inspiration to the east of his primitive Ozark paradise: the Beale Street Palace Theater and the black vaudeville shows that packed the house there.

Hay, a WWI vet himself, came to Memphis and the *Commercial Appeal* in 1919. Then twenty-four, he had grown up in the small town of Attica, Indiana, in the northern part of the state. To the inexperienced Hay, Memphis must have seemed as wild and exciting as it did to the poor black sharecroppers and lumbermen who regularly spent their week's wages on a Beale Street Saturday night. As a reporter Hay also witnessed the bloody aftermath of many of those wild nights; he learned about America's reigning murder capital from the underbelly up, working the paper's police beat from 5 P.M. to 3 A.M. There was plenty to cover, including 137 homicides in a single year, he recalled in a 1952 interview with the *Nashville Tennessean.*

But Hay was headed for bigger things. He soon combined his experience covering the city's criminal element with his newcomer's fondness for southern culture in a humor column called "Howdy, Judge." The column, purportedly taken verbatim from municipal court cases, featured black defendants almost exclusively and was written in broadly humorous, minstrel-style dialect.

It was a huge hit, which was no big surprise: Minstrel humor, though offensive today, was quite popular in venues like the *Commercial Appeal* at the time. The front page had a daily cartoon feature called "Hambone's Meditations," by J. P. Alley, in which Hambone, an elderly black man, held forth in molasses-thick dialect. "Dey jes' ain' no sech thing ez me en a brass ban' workin' at de same time!!!" one caption read; "Ef dey's a chicken dinnuh cookin' in de neighborhood, de pahson's nose kin jes nachly lead he mouf right up to it," went another.

That type of "humor" may make it seem as though the *Commercial Appeal* was stuck in a Civil War mindset, and indeed such cartoons would have been right at home in the paper a hundred years before. But it's worth noting that Memphis didn't hold the patent on latter-day minstrel comedy. A few years later, one of the biggest *national* radio hits would be *Amos & Andy*, in which two white minstrel-style comedians continued to propagate the blackface tradition; it was a holdover that would persist into the television age.

With "Howdy, Judge," Hay became one of the city's most popular columnists, but he had bigger ambitions. On January 20, 1923, when the *Commercial Appeal* put radio station WMC on the air, Hay found his true calling, combining a natural affinity for the new medium with the promotional skills of a born public relations man. Hay became radio editor for the *Commercial Appeal*, putting together the "News and Notes of the Radio World" page, which in its first few months consisted largely of self-congratulatory stories about WMC and telegrams from listeners picking the station up as far away as Canada and Minnesota. Hay wrote small features about the performers on the station, praising them in the same flowery prose in which he would later write of the Opry stars; in those early WMC days, though, it was largely the white popular music of the day, a mix of semiclassical groups and collegiate jazz bands, that Hay promoted. Describing a performance by the Jolly Jazz Boys, for example, Hay's radio page commented enigmatically that "a host of . . . snappy numbers were shot to the winds."

Similar words were used in another venue in the fall of 1923, when Bessie Smith performed on WMC, in a broadcast of one of the Beale Street Palace's Midnight Rambles. "Bessie Smith, known from coast to coast as a singer of blues that are really blue, gave the air some currents that it will not forget . . ."

That review appeared not in the *Commercial Appeal*, but in the pioneering African American newspaper the *Chicago Defender*, purportedly contributed by its "Atlanta correspondent." Yet, Bessie Smith biographer Chris Albertson credits the comment to "a white reporter working for the *Commercial Appeal*." Considering that Hay was the newspaper's radio reporter and that he was always looking for ways to promote the station outside the city, that "white reporter" was almost certainly Hay.

Hay, by then working on WMC as an announcer, around this time began calling himself the "Solemn Old Judge," exploiting the popularity of his humor column. He punctuated his on-air commentary by blowing a steamboat whistle in tribute to the Mississippi flowing just a couple of blocks west of the station. Both his nickname and that whistle would become trademarks of Hay's Grand Ole Opry. And Hay was just as aggressive a reporter as he was a promoter: When President Warren G. Harding died in office in August 1923, less than three years after winning the first presidential election in which women voted, Hay broadcast the news of Harding's death as it came into the newspaper office via the Associated Press wires. Few radio stations at the time had newswires; Hay had scored a national scoop. He was fast outgrowing the river town that had been his inspiration. His future lay in radio.

In 1924, shortly after Bessie Smith made her second, even more successful appearance on WMC, Hay left his dual job as newspaperman and radio announcer to become a full-time announcer on Chicago's WLS. When the station had approached him, Hay, not really interested in leaving Memphis, had demanded the princely sum of seventy-five dollars a week; to his surprise, the station agreed. At WLS, owned by Sears Roebuck (the call letters stood for "World's Largest Store"), Hay used both his Solemn Old Judge persona and his steamboat whistle as host of the fledgling *National Barn Dance*.

The folks up north ate it up; Hay soon proved he was worth that seventy-five dollars a week, winning *Radio Digest's* golden loving cup as the most popular radio announcer in the country. By 1925, he'd decided he'd had enough of the North and returned to his beloved Tennessee, this time to get Nashville's new radio station WSM up and running.

And did he ever. Hay did with the Opry just what Sam Phillips would do a few decades later: He created a way to sell black-style entertainment to a larger white audience. The Grand Ole Opry was less a barn dance than a down-home mix of vaudeville with plenty of minstrel-show touches. Replace the Opry's fiddle bands with blues and jazz combos and you had the makings of a typical TOBA show at the Beale Palace.

Even the inspiration for the Grand Ole Opry's name was provided by a black musician. DeFord Bailey, "the Harmonica Wizard," opened Hay's barn dance one evening with "The Pan American Blues," a train-imitation song. Hay, following a network classical music program, introduced Bailey, who played his train-imitation blues. "For the past hour we have been listening to music largely from grand opera," Hay told his listeners. "But from now on, we will present the Grand Ole Opry." Bailey's importance to the Opry was central, but the racial lines held firm, and he received little recognition and no respect. Hay referred to Bailey in Opry publicity as "our mascot" and paid him far less than the other Opry performers. By 1941, when a new generation of Opry stars that included Roy Acuff, Ernest Tubb, Minnie Pearl, and Bill Monroe had risen into place, Bailey was fired. The excuse Hay gave was that he had refused to learn new music. "Like some members of his race and other races, DeFord was lazy," Hay wrote patronizingly in his 1946 book, *A Story of the Grand Ole Opry.* Bailey would tirelessly refute the claim until his death in 1982.

Even the minstrel humor Hay had held so dear and found so profitable at the *Commercial Appeal* (in 1926, after moving to Nashville, he published a popular book of old "Howdy, Judge" columns) was a prominent feature of early Opry broadcasts. Indeed, a broad nostalgia craze was sweeping the country in reaction to the modernism of the Jazz Age, a movement apparent in a number of projects launched by automobile magnate Henry Ford during the period. Seeking to preserve the simpler good old days his assembly lines and automobiles were obliterating, Ford poured money into the small-town ideal of Greenfield Village. More to the point, Ford stoked the nation's fondness for old-time music, producing a number of fiddle contests during these years. Ford and Hay were playing to the same audience; the Opry was founded on a steady diet of hoary comic stereotypes and sturdy old-time music.

But the Opry's first real star didn't play fiddle. Uncle Dave Macon was a banjo wizard whose repertoire consisted largely of minstrel songs. These included "Jordan Am a Hard Road to Travel," which Macon learned from minstrel show performers at his parents' boarding house in Nashville. Macon performed on the show from its beginnings until his death at eighty-two in 1952, just two years before Elvis auditioned for the Opry. Presley's mix of jump blues and country was right in keeping with the tradition of Uncle Dave, whose music was set so firmly in the old minstrel style that many black listeners in the Delta believed he was one of their own. Adding to that illusion was Macon's accompanist Sam McGee, a white guitarist who was a master of blues and ragtime. DeFord Bailey's harmonica blues were also an Opry staple in those early days, as was the blackface minstrel comedy of Lasses White and Honey Wilds.

Of course, many of the fiddle tunes the Opry groups played had their origins in African American traditions. The bluesy inflections and syncopations that so readily distinguish American fiddlers from their more stately Irish and English counterparts can be traced to the slave fiddlers who figured so prominently in the music of the eighteenth and nineteenth centuries. Around thirty years after his Ozark hoedown initiation, Hay recalled the tunes that his Arkansas trio of fiddle, banjo, and guitar performed: "Old Dan Tucker" (which had its origins in nineteenth-century minstrelsy), "Casey Jones" (which folklorist Alan Lomax calls one of "the great black railroad ballads"), and "Turkey in the Straw" (which bluesman Big Bill Broonzy also fiddled, and which was itself a descendant of the minstrel tune "Zip Coon").

Even the show's trademark burlesque of the hillbilly lifestyle may have come about as a way to obscure the show's black origins. Roy Acuff told me in 1991, less than a year before his death, that the early Opry bands, "The Gully Jumpers, the Fruit Jar Drinkers — George D. Hay, the Solemn Old Judge, gave them all these names. They wasn't calling themselves that when they come here." Hay also insisted that the groups, most of which were made up of respectable professional men such as physician Dr. Humphrey Bate (whose band Hay christened the Possum Hunters), trade their business suits for outlandish hillbilly garb. Take away the overalls and straw hats and Hay's show might have been mistaken for one of the Beale Street Midnight Rambles that Hay attended and broadcast for the *Commercial Appeal*'s WMC. In its early days, the Grand Ole Opry was essentially a Beale Street show passing for white.

• • •

The lines between black and white music, then, were already well blurred by the time the Grand Ole Opry appeared in 1925, but no one obliterated them more completely than the first star of country music; Meridian, Mississippi's Jimmie Rodgers.

Though he was known as "the Singing Brakeman," Rodgers never actually had a full-time railroad job, according to his biographer, Nolan Porterfield. The performing bug had bitten Rodgers early. At age twelve, he won a talent contest in his hometown; three years later, he ran away to join a medicine show — a kind of rural, entry-level vaudeville and minstrel show of the sort that gave black and white performers from bluesmen like Furry Lewis and jug band king Gus Cannon to country star Roy Acuff their start. Rodgers probably learned much of his blues repertoire from black railroad workers working the routes between Memphis and New Orleans, but his own experience was largely limited to part-time railroad work that supplemented his musical engagements. By the time of the blues craze of the early 1920s, Rodgers was already singing the blues and accompanying himself on guitar.

Rodgers's dreams of the big time came true in the summer of 1927, in the Tennessee-Virginia border town of Bristol, when he auditioned for Ralph Peer at a Victor Records field recording session in an old warehouse. Peer was in many ways the father of field recordings, having led the 1923 OKeh field trip to Atlanta that produced the first recordings by Fiddling John Carson, the records that set off a country-music boom similar to the blues craze begun a few years earlier by Mamie Smith's "Crazy Blues." Peer's earliest experience in Tennessee had occurred at the other end of the state, in Memphis, where the Victor executive held the state's first recording session the preceding February. Peer's time in Bristol from late July through the first week of August proved even more lucrative. The seventy-six recordings he made there included the debuts of both Rodgers and the Carter Family, arguably the two most important acts of early country music.

The story goes that Rodgers and his band, which he called the Jimmie Rodgers Entertainers, quit their job playing a mountain resort ninety miles away and headed to Bristol with dreams of becoming recording stars. Just before their audition, however, the band fired Rodgers, dubbed themselves the Tenneva Ramblers in honor of Bristol's state-straddling status; and recorded three nondescript string band records. Undaunted, Rodgers auditioned as a solo, cutting a pair of old-fashioned "heart songs," "Sleep Baby

Sleep" and "The Soldier's Sweetheart." Peer liked him enough to record him, but apparently didn't think much of his discovery. When Rodgers's wife, Carrie, suggested Jimmie record his composition "T for Texas," Peer claimed he never recorded more than two songs in a first session (though he'd done three for the Ramblers). Years later he would recall his first impression of Rodgers as "a bus boy in a roadside cafe, singing nigger blues."

It was those blues that made the Mississippian a star and made Peer, who published his songs, a very wealthy man. In November 1927, Rodgers finally got to record his first "Blue Yodel (T for Texas)," and saw it sell close to 1 million copies. It would be the biggest hit of a phenomenal career cut short in 1933 when Rodgers died of tuberculosis.

Today Rodgers is known as the father of modern country music, but at its heart his music revealed the deep commonality between white and black musicians in Tennessee and Mississippi. And Peer's other major country music discovery also owed a debt to black musical traditions. The singing Carter Family from Maces Springs, Virginia — Maybelle, her sister Sara, and Sara's husband, A. P. — had an uncredited partner who gathered and arranged the folk songs they recorded: a black musician named Lesley Riddle who was quite literally instrumental to the group's success.

Lesley Riddle, an East Tennessee native who played mandolin and guitar — the latter in a country-blues style reminiscent of his contemporary Furry Lewis — frequently traveled into the mountains with A. P. Carter to collect songs. As A. P. wrote down the words, Riddle would learn the melody and develop the guitar parts, later teaching them to Maybelle. In fact, many of Maybelle's best-known arrangements, in a bass-picking format known universally as "Carter style," seem to have come directly from Riddle, including the guitar showpiece "Cannonball Blues."

The watershed success of Peer's two Bristol discoveries, Rodgers and the Carters, reveals just how ingrained the mix of black and white musical traditions was in country music, in sharp contrast to its usual reputation as an exclusively white tradition. Peer would return to Tennessee on other field trips, though he never came close to repeating his success with Rodgers and the Carters; yet the die had been cast. Country music would take its place as a paradoxical American music. Seemingly the pure expression of white mountain folk, it is in fact a rich hybrid of black and white musical strains. And while on the surface it came to seem even more definitively linked with Nashville than jazz with New Orleans, country's very home base was a minstrel-style radio broadcast that had Memphis, Tennessee written all over it.

Nevertheless, from the 1930s on — with Nashville only 210 miles away and the Opry fast turning that city into the country music capital — most ambitious Memphians of a country bent reversed Horace Greeley's maxim and headed east.

There were some exceptions. Memphis even had its own western swing band, though the music hadn't even earned the name yet. The Swift Jewel Cowboys got their start in 1933 in Houston, Texas, but when the band's organizer, Frank Collins, manager of Swift & Company's Houston factory, was transferred to the oil and shortening concern's Memphis plant, he brought the band with him. On November 4, 1934, the Cowboys first broadcast on WMC; a couple of years later they could be found on the city's other major outlet, WREC. But even the Swift Jewel Cowboys seem to have caught that versatile "Memphis thing." Despite their cowboy garb, the band soon had as much swing as western in their sound, with the addition of jazzman Farris "Lefty" Ingram on clarinet, sax, and fiddle, and David "Pee Wee" Wamble on cornet. Before too long the group was augmenting mesquite melodies like "My Untrue Cowgirl" with hot renditions of "Rose Room," "The Memphis Blues," and the Cab Calloway–inspired "You Got to Ho-De-Ho (To Get Along with Me)."

Wamble, who was part of the band by 1938, had played in regional dance and jazz bands, working such nightspots as the Wishbone Club in Memphis. There, he would later tell country music historian Tony Russell, he played six-night engagements for only nine dollars plus tips. The steady paycheck and regular promotional work for the Swift company, playing supermarkets and company functions, was a dream come true for Wamble. And while the band's Texas roots and trick-riding stunts helped draw crowds, when it came to the Cowboys' radio shows and records, the folks in Memphis and elsewhere seemed to prefer the band's modern repertoire. "Mr. Collins thought that it was leading away from the old cowboy style," Wamble recalled. "But [he] did have to admit that it drew new and more listeners to our program."

The band proved important to two well-known Memphis-bred musicians — harmonica player Jimmy Riddle, who played on the Cowboy's final recording date in 1939 and later gained fame performing on the Grand Ole Opry with Roy Acuff and on TV's *Hee Haw*; and saxophone player Bill Justis, who was the group's mascot. "The only reason I figured that he got in there," Wamble said, "was that his dad and Mr. Collins were real good friends." Justis would later become one of Memphis's more successful homegrown musicians as an A and R man with Sun Records and also made a huge hit under his own name with the instrumental "Raunchy." In 1958, Justis left Memphis for Nashville, where he had a successful career recording and scouting talent for Monument Records.

Though the Swift Jewel Cowboys continued their careers until 1942, those 1939 sides were to be the last commercial country recordings made in Memphis until Sam Phillips opened his Memphis Recording Service in 1950. Chicago, New York, Los Angeles, Cincinnati (with Syd Nathan's independent King label), and Nashville were establishing themselves as recording centers, but World War II shut down the recording industry; raw materials like petroleum and shellac, needed to make the thick 78s were commandeered by the military.

A few years after the Swift Jewel Cowboys rode into the sunset, the Delmore Brothers, Alton and Rabon, could be heard broadcasting on WMC, aided by local harmonica players Wayne Rainey and Lonnie Glosson. Alabama musicians who had been fired from the Grand Ole Opry for excessive drinking, the Delmores alternated sweet, close-harmony ballads with a primordial brand of rock and roll, a driving country boogie that found an audience in the Home of the Blues, just as young rockers-to-be like Johnny and Dorsey Burnette were coming of age. But to make records, the Delmores traveled up to the King studios in Cincinnati, where Syd Nathan was becoming a major challenger to Nashville's budding country recording industry.

Another brother act, Charlie and Ira Louvin, the heirs to the Delmores' smooth vocal style, arrived in Memphis in 1947. They came from Knoxville, where they had worked for that city's famed grocer and country music entrepreneur, Cas Walker. Country singer/promoter/disc jockey Eddie Hill convinced Ira and Charlie to make the Memphis move, and the duo honed their plaintive vocal harmonies working three radio shows a day in the city, and booking appearances throughout the region, usually with Hill's group. But Charlie Louvin has recalled that in the city of Memphis, where black entertainment reigned, even for much of the white audience, country music was a tough sell. The Louvins wound up working in the Memphis Post Office, but the postmaster gave the brothers such a hard time about missing work to play music that in 1954 the Louvins moved on, first to Birmingham, then to Nashville a year later.

After the Nashville move they wound up on a 1955 tour that included the young Elvis Presley on the bottom of the bill. It was shortly after he signed with Colonel Tom Parker, who was trying to promote his boy as a country act. It wasn't quite working, Louvin said. "Country people didn't exactly know what he was doing."

Neither did Ira, Louvin recalled. "Ira thought his music was a little too close to black and he told him so." Given his love of blues and R & B, that might have been something of a compliment to Elvis. But the remark was couched in typically Ira Louvinesque terms, Charlie told me ruefully. "Ira called him 'a white nigger.' I would imagine that that statement probably cost the Louvin Brothers' music catalog a couple million dollars, 'cause Elvis was on record saying the Louvin Brothers were his favorite country singers. He got that from his mother." Gladys Presley had been a fan of the Louvins since their Memphis days, but Ira's remark kept Elvis from recording any of the brothers' songs. "It was a bad thing, but there was no way I could control [Ira]," Charlie said. "Jack Daniel's controlled him." The Louvins did have a much more direct influence on two other rock and rollers, Don and Phil Everly, the Kentucky duo who took country music's close-harmony brother-act tradition into the rock era, and themselves went on to provide the model for the vocal harmonies of John Lennon and Paul McCartney.

It was tough to make a living in country music in the Memphis of the late forties and early fifties, as singer-guitarist Malcolm Yelvington can testify. Yelvington recalls the days when the area's top acts had radio shows to promote personal appearances. That's how the Delmores, Slim Rhodes and his family, blind bandleader Bob McKnight, and others survived, he says. "They'd play regional, Mississippi, Missouri, Arkansas, where they could go and get back in one night, 'cause they had live radio shows the next day." In the forties, the more family-oriented acts might play school auditoriums for twenty-five cents a head. But as country music changed in the fifties, and small honky-tonk country bands such as Yelvington's own came into vogue, they worked the roadhouse circuit. Yelvington, who at seventy-eight was finishing an album for Sun Studio's 706 label when I spoke with him early in 1997, remembers how dangerous those joints could quickly become, even if you minded your own business.

"We played this place between Ripley and the Mississippi built on stilts about twelve-foot high. The people would come in with overalls and hip boots and what-all. One guy came in there the last Saturday night we played there, pulled an old gun out, and started shooting through the ceiling. Everybody got out of there fast, including me and my band."

Yelvington's band and others like it took as their models the popular groups led by Hank Williams, Red Foley, Hank Snow, and Ernest Tubb, which blended western swing innovations — twin fiddles or lead guitars playing in harmony, as well as boogie-woogie beats — with traditional, hard-country songwriting to come up with the style known as honky-tonk.

Musically, Charley Pride was a country traditionalist, but being black, he was innovative without even trying. Modern country music's first African American star was born in Sledge, Mississippi, just to the west of Como, the hometown of bluesman Fred McDowell. Pride grew up listening to the Grand Ole Opry on his family's old Philco radio. The first country singer he saw in person was the Louvins' mentor, Eddie Hill, the Memphian who often played in front of the Sledge town grocery on Saturday afternoons. "No one ever told me that whites were supposed to sing one kind of music and blacks another," Pride wrote in his autobiography, *Pride.* In Mississippi and Memphis, many people, of all shades, sang both.

Pride's other love, baseball, brought him to Memphis as a young man, where he pitched for the Memphis Red Sox at Martin Stadium in the final days of the Negro Leagues. He recalls auditioning for Sam Phillips in the early sixties, after Phillips's Memphis Recording Service had given way to the more spacious Phillips Studio on Madison. Sam was still looking for something new, but Pride — a black man who could sing with a white feel, in a reversal of Phillips's famous maxim about Elvis — apparently wasn't it. Ironically enough, RCA, the label that a decade earlier had bought Presley's contract from Phillips, thought otherwise. The label signed Pride in 1965, on the strength of a session he recorded with former Sun producer Jack Clement. The date of that session — August 16 — proved luckier for Charley Pride than for Robert Johnson and Elvis. In just a couple of hours on that summer day, he recorded two of his biggest hits, "Snakes Crawl at Night" and "Just Between You and Me." His color remained a problem in the racial climate of Nashville in the sixties, and Pride had to be careful in choosing his material. For example, he couldn't sing "Green Green Grass of Home" in concert because of the line describing his love's "hair of gold." "A black man singing about his blond girlfriend was potential trouble," he recalls. Green grass or no, Pride managed to walk the color line, emerging as one of the decade's biggest country stars.

The Memphis-Nashville connection continues today, with young singers such as Mark Collie, Kim Hill, Jesse Hunter, Philip Claypool, and Andy Childs all boasting a connection with the city on the Mississippi. But the modern country singer who most strongly identifies with her Memphis roots is Deborah Allen, whose two most recent albums, *Delta Dreamland* and *All That I Am*, both take lyrical and musical inspiration from the Home of the Blues and the Cradle of Rock and Roll. She even wrote and recorded a Christmas song with a hometown flavor, "Walk All the Way to Memphis."

Allen's song came on the heels of one of the biggest recent trends in Nashville: Memphis song titles. Pam Tillis had a hit with "Maybe It Was Memphis"; Trisha Yearwood topped the charts with "Wrong Side of Memphis"; Confederate Railroad sang about the charms of the "Queen of Memphis"; Rodney Crowell recorded "Rose of Memphis." Memphis also turned up in the Grammy-winning *Rhythm, Country & Blues* album project, which combined Memphis soul and Nashville country. Produced by Don Was and featuring a core band including two prominent Memphis country musicians, guitarist Reggie Young and steel guitarist Robby Turner, the album served as a reminder of just how close those two strains of music have always been — much closer than even the 210 miles that separate the two music capitals.

8

▼▼▼▼▼▼▼▼▼▼▼▼▼▼▼▼▼▼▼▼▼▼▼▼▼▼▼

Memphis Rocks

Inspired by Beale Street, George Dewey Hay fathered the Grand Ole Opry. A little more than twenty years later, another Memphis radio man named Dewey went to the Beale well and came up with a different vision, one that had even more far-reaching influence. Dewey Mills Phillips didn't invent rock and roll, he's just the guy who brought it home.

Beginning in the fall of 1949 as the pioneering host of WHBQ's *Red Hot & Blue* program, Phillips was an advance scout for what would become the rock revolution in Memphis. He broke the segregated city's musical color line, playing black rhythm and blues records for an audience largely comprised of white teenagers.

In July 1954, he became the first disc jockey in the world to play Elvis Presley's debut record, "That's All Right"/"Blue Moon of Kentucky," spinning the test-pressing acetate brought to him by his friend Sam Phillips over and over again. After setting the precedent, he did the same for the first records by Carl Perkins, Jerry Lee Lewis, Johnny Cash, Roy Orbison, Billy Lee Riley, and the rest of the Sun Records pantheon of first-generation rockers. Those rockabillies (a word Perkins says Dewey coined) forever changed the world's music — and Daddy-O-Dewey, with his nonstop barrage of lightning-fast hillbilly hipster jive and signature catch phrases, pulled the trigger on that musical and social upheaval. Quite simply, Dewey Phillips owned the Memphis airwaves throughout the fifties and into the sixties, from the first stirrings of rock and roll to the beginning of Stax Records and the southern soul movement.

Beyond hard-core Elvis fans and rockabilly devotees, Phillips remains largely forgotten outside Memphis. Cleveland's claim to house the Rock and Roll Hall of Fame was largely based on disc jockey Alan Freed's use of the phrase "rock and roll" to describe the R & B records he played on his *Moondog Matinee* show on that city's WJW radio station. Phillips, who was spinning B. B. King, Big Joe Turner, and Howlin' Wolf records while Freed was still hosting a light classical program in Cleveland, is still not, as of this writing, a member of that hall of fame. The twenty-fifth anniversary of Phillips's death on September 28, 1993, went unnoticed by the anniversary-loving national media — even by the syndicated newspaper feature "This Day in Music," which chose instead to report that, on that date in 1987, Smokey Robinson and Gladys Knight appeared on *The $100,000 Pyramid.*

But the faithful who gathered at their tiny transistor radios will never forget the rock and roll gospel according to Daddy-O-Dewey. "You don't come any closer to what rock 'n' roll was all about than him on the radio," says Wayne Jackson of the Memphis Horns. As a West Memphis teen, Jackson kept his ear glued to *Red Hot & Blue,* and he can still recite his favorite Phillips routines almost forty years later. He's not alone. "Get you a wheelbarrow full of whatever, roll it up through the front door, and dump it out and tell 'em Phillips sentcha," laughs Rufus Thomas, recalling Daddy-O-Dewey's most famous shtick.

Like Elvis a few years later, Dewey Phillips was exactly the right man at precisely the right moment. When Phillips began his radio reign, Rufus Thomas was already famous locally as the multitalented performer and master of ceremonies at the Beale Street Palace amateur nights, and was just about to join WDIA as an announcer, a relationship that continues to this day with his Saturday morning blues program. WDIA made broadcasting history on

October 25, 1948, when its financially strapped owners, figuring
they had little to lose, made the groundbreaking decision to hire
Memphis's first black radio announcer: teacher/author/black community leader Nat D. Williams.

Williams became the Jackie Robinson of Memphis radio. But
breaking the broadcasting color line didn't mean that radio became integrated. Instead, as had happened with the successful
local black newspaper the *Tristate Defender*, Williams's success
inspired WDIA's white owners to turn it into the nation's first all-
black-staffed radio station. With a license that limited broadcasting
to daylight hours — a common restriction for smaller stations —
WDIA played blues, swing, gospel, the pop sounds of Billy Eckstine and Nat King Cole, and the latest in rhythm and blues. The
latter phrase was created in 1949 to describe the new, high-energy
music coming from the small bands that spread like kudzu in the
years following World War II. It was coined by a young Jerry
Wexler, when the future Atlantic Records mogul was just a rookie
reporter at *Billboard*.

World War II had effectively knocked the Swing Era flat, breaking up the big touring bands with the one-two punch of draft no-
tices that decimated their ranks and gas rationing that sidelined
their band buses. But after the troops came home in 1945, all the
postwar partying required a jumping sound track. Some big bands
tried to reorganize after the war, but with improved amplification
small groups and jump-blues combos proved they could be just as
loud. It didn't take long for nightclub owners and dance promoters to realize they could fill their places with music and customers
for much less than the cost of a big band.

Louis Jordan of Brinkley, Arkansas, about forty miles west of
Memphis, is generally considered the father of modern R & B, his
arrangement of "Let the Good Times Roll" remaining the traditional opener for every B. B. King show. Jordan, a brown-eyed
handsome man with a sharp sense of humor and red-hot band,
found his most faithful disciple in Chuck Berry. The first great

rock and roll songwriter, Berry took the jiving hipster attitude of such Jordan classics as "Saturday Night Fish Fry" and "Choo Choo Ch' Boogie" and shifted them to a teenage perspective in such rockers as "No Particular Place to Go" and "Maybellene." And Jordan was far from alone amid the icons of jump blues: Big Joe Turner led a movement of blues shouters that included Wynonie Harris (whose huge hit "Good Rocking Tonight" inspired the young Elvis) and Roy Brown (who wrote "Good Rocking Tonight").

The late forties were a wide-open time in the recording industry, recalls Atlantic producer-engineer Tom Dowd. Jukebox operators and record buyers were demanding new music in the postwar boom, causing a rush by record companies to record everything they could before a threatened musician union recording ban took effect. It was a period when the union periodically declared recording bans that amounted to labor strikes, as musicians called for increased royalties or protested the use of recorded music instead of live entertainment.

A few years earlier, during the Second World War, Dowd had helped develop the atomic bomb as a teenage physics prodigy with the Manhattan Project. Surveying the devastating effect the bomb had had on the people of Hiroshima and Nagasaki, a crushed and disillusioned Dowd gave up physics and turned his engineering genius to recording. In New York, the young freelance engineer worked to beat the ban, recording everything from beboppers to banjo bands. Every studio was working overtime, he recalled, and just as the situation gave beginning engineers like Dowd some welcome opportunities, it did the same for young black musicians experimenting with new forms of the blues. Those records found homes in jukeboxes throughout the South — and on the airwaves at stations like WDIA and Nashville's WLAC.

WDIA's experiment proved wildly successful, as sponsors lined up for the privilege of paying premium advertising rates to reach the huge, previously ignored black audience. WDIA historian Louis

Cantor states that the 1950 census put the black Memphis population at 147,141, or 37.3 percent of the total population. Adding the outlying rural counties within WDIA's listening area, where the population ratio was even higher for blacks, Cantor estimates WDIA's black audience as nearly half a million strong. That audience quickly became loyal listeners to disc jockeys like Thomas, Williams, Gatemouth Moore, Maurice "Hot Rod" Hulbert and A. C. "Moohah" Williams. They regularly tuned in for such programs as *Delta Melodies* and *Sepia Swing Club*, both of which Hulbert hosted with Jekyll and Hyde flair, turning properly reverential for the former's gospel and manically hip for the latter's R & B.

It was a different world after the war, and WDIA tapped into the growing affluence of the Memphis black community amid the postwar boom in construction and manufacturing. Integration was still a couple of decades away, but some of the old Jim Crow laws had begun loosening in Memphis and elsewhere. In 1947, Jackie Robinson became the first black man to enter baseball's major leagues. In 1948, Ernest C. Withers broke the Memphis police force's color line, becoming one of the city's first nine black policemen and part of the first black Memphis patrol car team. It was no revolution: Black police officers still weren't allowed to arrest white lawbreakers; they could only detain them until a white officer arrived. But it was a start, and it was very good news for Memphis blacks. With black officers patrolling Beale, there was less potential for police harassment. Today, Withers recalls with a chuckle how he used to let black farmers sleep it off in the wagon yard just south of Beale if they'd done too much celebrating after bringing in their crops. White cops were rarely so understanding.

In his off-hours, Officer Withers was a photographer, a hobby he'd picked up in high school when he took some snapshots of a visiting Mrs. Joe Louis. He took his hobby with him into the army and to the South Pacific, where he made a tidy side income photographing his fellow GIs for them to send the folks back home. Business was so good, he says, that his superior officers accused him of running a whorehouse. Nothing else, they reasoned, could draw such big crowds of GIs.

To this day, Withers is rarely seen without a camera; for the past fifty years he has documented black Memphis, from the Negro Baseball League's Memphis Red Sox to church functions, lodges, and social organizations. And his photographic documentation of the Beale Street scene in the second half of this century is among our richest testaments to its vitality.

At the same time that that new invention, television, was causing such excitement up North, the success of WDIA was the biggest broadcasting news in Memphis and the Mid-South. The popularity of the station drew the interest of one ex-Mississippian then breaking into the tough blues scene of wide-open West Memphis, Arkansas. B. B. King, who'd gotten some of his early guitar lessons from his cousin Bukka White, recalls arriving at the bus station in downtown Memphis and walking in the rain out to 2074 Union. Tapping on the control-room window that faced the street, he managed to talk his way in to audition with "Nat Dee" Williams, who, a few years after becoming the station's first black air personality, remained its most popular. Williams called in station manager Bert Ferguson, who saw potential in the twenty-three-year-old cotton picker turned guitar picker, and gave King a fifteen-minute spot. It was unpaid, of course, but it did allow King to promote his personal appearances. Since King had been a frequent performer at the Palace's Amateur Night shows (where the dollar bill every entrant received was reason enough for King to ride across the Mississippi in the back of a bus), it seems likely Williams and Ferguson were already familiar with him.

Whatever the reason, King got his break. Dubbed "the Beale Street Blues Boy," he became one of the top stars at the station. He soon parlayed that status into a performing and recording career that took him from the southern chitlin' circuit of juke joints and small-town theaters to concert halls the world over.

When he got his start, King's program was a throwback to the old medicine shows: Along with singing the blues and promoting his club dates, King peddled the patent medicine Peptikon. It sold like hotcakes, King recalls, but it wasn't until years later that he found out its biggest attraction was the fact that it was 12 percent alcohol. "Those church folks weren't drinking it for their rheumatism," he says with a laugh.

King was the station's biggest success story, but WDIA spawned many more. If the white folks at the other Memphis radio outlets looked down their noses at the music and personalities heard on "The Mother Station of the Negroes," as it called itself, they couldn't argue with the profit margin. Yet its success was limited, since WDIA's license in those early years prohibited broadcasting past sunset. Some Memphis radio outlets that had evening licenses figured they could fill that profitable gap. Hoping to capture the WDIA audience, they launched evening R & B shows of their own hosted, however, by white announcers who knew little about black music.

One of those stations was WHBQ, whose program director, Gordon Lawhead, began a fifteen-minute segment in the middle of 1949 that he called *Red Hot & Blue*, taking the name from a patriotic musical film of that year starring Victor Mature, not exactly a king of the blues himself.

"We watched WDIA . . . just making money hand over fist and they had to sign off at sundown," Lawhead says of his show's inspiration. "But I wasn't really hip about the things that should be played for this audience," he confesses. "Dewey was."

Born in Crump, Tennessee, Dewey Phillips moved to Memphis in 1942 from the West Tennessee town of Adamsville. The teenager developed a taste for the blues the way most Memphians did, with clandestine visits to the clubs and barbecue joints of forbidden Beale. By early 1949 Phillips was working at W. T. Grant's five-and-dime near the Gayoso Hotel at Gayoso and Main, where WHBQ was then located. His job description was counter clerk, but Phillips as usual defied description.

"Dewey was hawking records at Grant's just like those guys down on Beale Street were hawking people to come into the pawnshops," recalls veteran disc jockey George Klein. "You'd walk in Grant's and he'd say, 'Hey, Mother'—he called everybody Mother—'Come here, I got a hot one for ya, let me lay this one on ya, ol' buddy.' And you'd walk over and he'd play you a really good record."

Those were still the days when radio announcers spoke perfect grammar in well-modulated tones, but WDIA had proven the old rules no longer applied. After putting up for a while with "that idiot" (Lawhead's words) crossing the street to pester them into giving him some airtime, WHBQ gave Dewey a shot—though not much of one: Phillips got a fifteen-minute slot, for which Lawhead confesses, "We paid him absolutely zero."

He did give Phillips a few pointers, showing him how to run the radio control board, a skill Lawhead says Dewey never quite mastered. Phillips was later given his own studio so that on occasions when he broke the equipment the station wouldn't be totally incapacitated. Lawhead also gave Phillips some tips in reading advertising copy, and claims to have given him what would later become his catch phrase. "I suggested that when he was reading a spot, to say, 'Go in and buy this and tell 'em Phillips sent you.'"

To Lawhead's amazement, the response was immediate and overwhelming. "The day after, we got seven postcards asking for specific rhythm and blues music. And the next day we got seventy; and the next day we got seven hundred. It was a monsoon of mail." *Red Hot & Blue* was soon expanded to three hours, from nine to midnight, and Phillips also began an afternoon show at 2 P.M. that mixed country records in with the rockabilly and R & B. Dewey's salary rose from nothing to $125 and then to $250, a sizable sum in fifties radio. And of course those were the glory days of payola, a time when independent label owners like Syd Nathan of King Records paid so much money to disc jockeys to guarantee that his records got played that he actually listed the bribes on King's ledger

Twin pillars of early-century Memphis music history: (*above*) W. C. Handy (*center, with trumpet*), author of "Mr. Crump Don't Like It," and E. H. "Boss" Crump, Mayor of Memphis, who looks as though he does.

Beale Street, Main Street of the Blues: (*above*) A friendly frisk during its heyday, and a daytime stroll in the early 1960s, when the music spots were being replaced by pawnshops.

Giants of the 1920s, rediscovered: (*above*) Gus Cannon (b. 1885) of Cannon's Jug Stompers, whose music was selling millions in the 1960s, and Alberta Hunter (*left*) (b. 1895), whose greatest fame came in the 1970s.

Jimmie Rodgers (*right*), the Singing Brakeman, cruised through town during the 1920s; the Louvin Brothers (*below*) (Ira, *left*, and Charlie), who showed up twenty years later, ended up working in the Memphis Post Office.

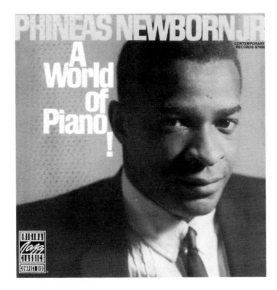

Musicians who
found an early
berth in Sam
Phillips's Memphis
Recording Service:
primal bluesman
Howlin' Wolf (*above
left*), sophisticated
stylist B. B. King
(*above right*), and
jazz pianist Phineas
Newborn Jr. (*left*).

In Elvis Presley, Sam Phillips found everything he was looking for: a white singer who sang R&B like a Beale vet, shopped at Lansky's, and could put his arm around Jane Russell without getting locked up.

Above: Sam Phillips (*right*) and deejay Dewey Phillips (*left*) with Johnny Cash, the first Sun discovery after Elvis to break into the national country charts — and Carl Perkins (*left*), whose "Blue Suede Shoes" gave the King a run for his money in early 1956.

One label, two pianos, two very different men and their wives: Sun's Jerry Lee Lewis (*above*), being shod in 1958 by fifteen-year-old Myra, and Charlie Rich (*below*), the Silver Fox, with his wife Margaret Ann in the 1970s.

books as business expenses. Some Memphis music insiders esti-
mate Dewey pulled in as much as $100,000 annually from record
companies.

Record companies, then as now, weren't known to throw
money away, and Dewey gave them their payola's worth. Although
his influence would be felt most strongly among the teenage rock
generation, everyone in Memphis listened to Daddy-O-Dewey.
"He was just as popular with the black audience as he was with
whites," acknowledges Rufus Thomas. "Dewey was the most popular disc jockey that ever hit the city of Memphis," Sam Phillips
says. "He appealed to the white collar, the blue collar and the no
collar. You could not cover the spectrum [of listeners] he had,
from policemen to city officials to all kinds of politicians and even
some of the preachers, whom I know personally hated what our
music was, [but] they loved Dewey Phillips. He was just one of
these totally natural, totally unexplained personalities that made
contact in the first degree. Dewey Phillips played as important a
part as anybody in the history of the record and music industry toward the acceptance of black music crossing the barrier of the
races."

It's the old Memphis story of social segregation versus cultural
integration. Despite the social segregation enforced by the Jim
Crow laws and strict codes against race mixing, the sheer numbers
of black citizens in Memphis, many of them employed in white
households as maids and cooks, ensured a high degree of cultural
integration.

And in Memphis, music has always been a bridge between the
races. Early in the twentieth century, W. C. Handy frequently
played for white audiences and the Beale Street Palace packed the
house for its whites-only Midnight Rambles performances. Pro-
gramming black music to a white audience in Memphis is a tradition as old as radio itself. Remember that in 1923, the *Commercial
Appeal*'s radio station WMC was broadcasting Bessie Smith live
from the Beale Palace Midnight Ramble. Nonetheless, when

Phillips hit the airwaves, Thomas says flatly, "He was playing rhythm and blues when whites playing rhythm and blues wasn't cool."

Phillips kept people laughing so hard no one seemed to notice the cultural revolution spinning on his turntables. A few treasured tapes of his broadcasts survive, and in 1995 the Memphis Archives label released a full-length CD of *Red Hot & Blue* broadcasts. Daddy-O-Dewey is heard in full rave, sputtering rapid-fire impressions, scrambling the English language with references to the mezzanine floor of the Hotel Chisca [WHBQ's new location] as the "magazine" (and then, after Chuck Berry's hit, as the "Maybellene") — in short, complete, irresistible chaos, all in the space of a few seconds.

He did beer commercials, suggesting listeners who didn't want to drink the stuff could "freeze it and eat it, open up a rib and pour it in." George Klein, then working for Dewey as a gofer or, as Dewey put it, "my little cohort buddy" recalls helping Phillips set up four turntables with copies of Conway Twitty's "It's Only Make Believe" and playing them all simultaneously for a bizarre out-of-phase echo effect. Record producer/musician Jim Dickinson listened to Dewey while growing up in East Memphis and credits Phillips, along with a chance meeting with the Memphis Jug Band, with changing his life and setting the direction he follows to this day. He remembers Dewey's skill with a microphone, changing the direction from which he spoke into it in order to create varied effects and different tones. Word spread fast about *Red Hot & Blue*, with its combination of funky R & B by the likes of Little Richard and Dewey's manic presentation. Klein had first heard of Dewey through the grapevine at Humes High School. "Everybody was saying, 'Hey man, this guy at night is playing some great music. You ought to listen to this really crazy wild guy at night.' "

Rock and roll may be the first music to be defined, not by its sound, but by who listened — and danced — to it. With its steel guitars and fiddles, country music, for example, is defined by sound. A Hank Williams record or a George Strait record is always country music, whether it's being heard by a crowd at the Grand Ole Opry or a Japanese audience in Tokyo. But depending on who was playing it and who was listening to it, the same record, the same sound, could be either rock and roll or rhythm and blues.

In terms of music or performance style, the R & B and jump blues of men like Wynonie Harris, Big Joe Turner, and Louis Jordan was virtually indistinguishable from what later would be called rock and roll. The difference was that those men's audiences were primarily adult blacks. Dewey played those same records for white teenagers who, then as now, were always in the market for something new to dance to, especially if that something also annoyed their parents (many of whom had probably shocked their own parents twenty years earlier by doing that "dirty dance," the Charleston). All that was needed to complete the budding musical revolution was a charismatic young white singer.

And there was one man who recognized that fact: Sam Phillips. Sam, who hailed from W. C. Handy's hometown of Florence, Alabama, was by then well established in Memphis as an engineer at WREC. His duties included running remote broadcasts for big bands at the Peabody Skyway, at the time the ne plus ultra of sophisticated Memphis nightspots. But the energy had long since gone out of the Big Band Era, and Phillips figured there had to be something better than the Miller-less Glenn Miller Orchestra and the other "sweet" bands he beamed nightly to middle-aged white Memphis. Sam was nothing if not restless and energetic, his hotel work for WREC being just one of the many jobs he held to support his wife Becky, his young sons Knox and Jerry, his mother, and a deaf-mute aunt. He also helped maintain the Peabody's public-address system and worked a daily shift at the radio station.

Phillips had been listening to Dewey for a few months when, in January of 1950, he sunk around a thousand dollars into renovating a small auto repair shop at 706 Union Avenue and converting it into the Memphis Recording Service, a storefront recording studio. He managed to pay the seventy-five dollar monthly rent by doing custom recordings of weddings, funerals, conventions, and the like, in those dark ages before the camcorder. But his real love was the sideline he developed recording local blues artists for big-city labels like Chicago's Chess or L.A.'s R.P.M. and Modern.

The time was ripe for such a venture. There had been no regular commercial recording in Memphis since the big labels like Victor and Vocalion had ended their field recording trips during the depression years of the thirties. But the music never stopped; by the end of World War II, a new generation of bluesmen had come of age, performers who sprang from the deep roots of Delta blues but added the raw, distorted power of modern electric guitars and amplified harmonicas.

One of them was Izear Turner, a preacher's son from Clarksdale, Mississippi, who had taken up piano after hearing Pinetop Perkins on Sonny Boy Williamson's radio show. Within a few years years he was playing in the local big band the Top Hatters. But in the late forties small bands were in vogue, and Ike, as he called himself, organized a leaner, meaner group of his own. In 1951, B. B. King heard them and suggested they try their luck at the Memphis Recording Service. The first session yielded "Rocket 88," called by many the first rock and roll record. Sung by baritone saxophonist Jackie Brenston, the song features Turner's hammering piano and Willie Kizart's distorted guitar, reportedly the result of his amplifier falling off the roof of Ike's car.

Released on Chess (under the name "Jackie Brenston and his Delta Cats") the song went to No. 1 in 1951, and Ike was soon working for Sam as both session bandleader and informal talent scout (working with Delta's black club circuit, Ike often sent musicians to Sun and personally brought in young James Cotton from West Memphis joint scene, Sam Phillips recalls). With his position as the only regular studio in town willing to record blues musicians and with the aid of the Ike and his own tireless forays across Memphis's color line, Phillips soon had his hands full recording

B. B. King, Howlin' Wolf, Walter Horton, Little Milton, Junior Parker, Joe Hill Louis, James Cotton, Doctor Ross, and dozens of other bluesmen of the Memphis region.

The blues had changed since the days of Charley Patton and Furry Lewis. The Gibson guitar company, whose acoustic models were the favored instruments of prewar blues musicians, introduced an electric guitar in 1936 that was to become the first commercially successful amplified Spanish (as opposed to Hawaiian-style) guitar. The instrument was first popularized by Texas-born jazzman Charlie Christian in his groundbreaking recordings with Benny Goodman, but it soon spread to hot-rhythm western bands and into the blues. Blues players who had been playing those steel-bodied Nationals mainly because they were louder than wooden guitars (as well as being handy six-string bludgeons when a juke joint gig turned ugly) were quick to adopt the electrics.

All too often in electrifying the blues, something of the old raw emotion was lost. Many singer-guitarists saw an opportunity to ride the electric uptown, smoothing out the rough edges of the blues and competing with crooners like Nat King Cole. T-Bone Walker was the most successful of these, playing Charlie Christian–influenced guitar and singing in a mellow baritone. Transplanted from Texas to California, where he founded that state's thriving jump-blues style, he was hugely influential broadening the public's appreciation of the blues, taking the music to posh supper clubs far removed from the music's juke-joint roots. Even Muddy Waters's first recordings after arriving in Chicago reflected some of Walker's influence. Walker was the first of the urbane urban electric bluesmen, although Lonnie Johnson had pioneered a sophisticated jazz-blues style in the late twenties, recording with Duke Ellington and others. Walker's music seemed to point to the future of the blues, but that most adaptable and resilient musical style was to take many different roads to many different futures.

Waters was still driving a tractor on Stovall's Plantation outside Clarksdale, around eighty miles south of Memphis on Highway 61, when he was first recorded in 1941 by folklorist Alan Lomax. Cut on a huge three-hundred-pound disc machine Lomax toted throughout the South in a special rig designed for his car, those records remain among the most important blues documents ever made. Rereleased on CD in their entirety in 1993, they provide a powerful portrait of the blues on the brink, as Waters performs in a style that was a natural extension of Robert Johnson's. In five years he would record a few sides for Columbia in Chicago in the style known as the "Bluebird beat," a standardized, piano-led band sound that was the signature style of Bluebird Records blues releases. That modern approach was a favorite of Waters's mentor, Big Bill Broonzy, though for Muddy it would prove a dead end.

A year later Waters made his first sides for Aristocrat, the tiny independent label owned by Phil and Leonard Chess that was soon renamed Chess Records. His first records, anchored by Sunnyland Slim's piano, were undistinguished Bluebird-style efforts. Then Waters returned to his Delta roots with "I Can't Be Satisfied," sung in an urgent wail over a duet between his own jagged slide guitar and the percussive, slapped bass of Ernest "Big" Crawford. Waters's Mississippi mud turned to paydirt: With its raw Delta flavor, the record caught the ear of an audience homesick for the South and weary of the blues crooners' uptown sounds, and the "Chicago" blues was born.

But it was Waters's chief Chess rival who truly kept the Delta sound alive. Chester "Howlin' Wolf" Burnett was born in 1910 and raised around West Point, Mississippi, near Dockery's plantation — and Charley Patton. Like other plantation kids, he grew up learning to farm, chop cotton, and plow with mules. His strong build promised a good future in sharecropping and earned him the early nicknames of "Big Foot Chester" and "Bull Cow," but his keen mind and natural leadership ability told him there was more to life than spending your days memorizing mules' behinds. He found it, as did his neighbor Pop Staples, on the porch of the plantation store, where as a boy he came under the spell of Patton. "I liked his sound," Wolf recalled in 1968. "So I got him to show me a few chords, you know. So every night that I'd get off work I'd go to his house and he'd learn me how to pick the guitar." Those lessons took hold, and the ferocious, elemental power of Patton's music continued to burn at the heart of Howlin' Wolf's sound until his death in 1976.

For a budding bluesman, the Delta in the thirties was a great place to find teachers. Wolf took up harmonica, he said, after Sonny Boy Williamson No. 2 (Rice Miller) married his half sister Mary. But unlike the itinerant bluesmen who traveled through the South playing at the plantation stores, country barbecues, and lumber camps, Wolf was of a more serious disposition. At first his music was more of a sideline; he took care of his growing family by farming, working on the plantation by day and playing gigs at night, occasionally performing with his half brother-in-law Sonny Boy, Sonny Boy's frequent accompanist Robert Junior Lockwood, and his stepfather, Robert Johnson.

Wolf was drafted into the army during World War II. After the war, like many of his fellow ex-GIs, he couldn't bring himself to return to the life he had left behind. He decided to try his hand at music for a living. He made his way north to the rough joints of West Memphis, Arkansas, which had never lost its century-old reputation as Memphis's tougher, more rural little sister. Arkansas had legalized liquor after Prohibition in 1935, four years before whiskey started pouring legally in Memphis. West Memphis, with its gambling joints and saloons, soon earned the nickname "Little Las Vegas." In 1941 the *Commercial Appeal* took notice, complaining about the town's Eighth Street district, fast developing into a rougher version of Beale. The ambitious Wolf, a stern bandleader who allowed no drinking in his ranks, soon expanded his performing beyond those bars, broadcasting over KWEM radio. With his booming voice and riveting stage presence, it wasn't long before he became the most popular blues performer in the area. "He was very, very unique," recalls Rufus Thomas, who remembers Wolf from such Eighth Street joints as the Little Brown Jug. "His voice of all things was different. At one time he drew more people at the Paradise Club than Ray Charles. People were hanging out of every little hole, every crack. They were there to see Howlin' Wolf."

And though he recorded up-tempo boogie tunes and other modern sounds, it was his electrified and electrifying versions of the old Delta blues he first heard at Dockery's that would remain his most powerful performances. Like those of his mentor Patton, his songs often drove along over just one chord, and Wolf delivered them in a booming, distorted voice that resembled the older man's sound. But there was something else going on, as against that droning chord and signature guitar line (the best example of which is his "Smokestack Lightning"), Wolf's raspy voice created a trance-like effect — the most primal, otherworldly sound in the electric blues.

Some historians, including the Smithsonian Institution's Berniece Reagon, cite Wolf's early Memphis recordings as the first example of the modern blues band. While that may be debatable, there was no questioning Wolf's raw, undiluted power. This was party music, but it was some of the scariest party music ever made.

"Wolf was, and still is, probably *the* most exciting person to record in the studio of any person I ever recorded, black or white," recalls Sam Phillips, who first recorded Wolf for Jules and Lester Bihari's West Coast–based Modern label. "It was just his soul coming out his mouth."

But it was Wolf's half brother-in-law Sonny Boy Williamson who was arguably the South's most influential blues bandleader. Sonny Boy, based in Helena, Arkansas, had built a huge following and sold a mountain of flour for KFFA's *King Biscuit Time* program. While his namesake, John Lee "Sonny Boy" Williamson No. 1, had led the way to the modern blues band in such prewar recordings as "Good Morning Little Schoolgirl," Sonny Boy No. 2 helped realize that sound. In a series of classic records for the short-lived Trumpet label of Jackson, Mississippi, he pioneered the electric blues; they remain a model for countless bands today, as a growing number of revivalists including Fabulous Thunder-birds leader Kim Wilson (notably on his *Tigerman* solo album), Pat Boyack & the Prowlers, and Rusty Zinn have been forsaking the slicker Chicago style for Williamson's rougher, more individual-ized Delta approach. Williamson, a stunningly original songwriter as well, kept this sound alive when he later recorded for Chicago's Chess label.

The blues wasn't the only music that saw a movement from sleeker sounds to rougher, edgier ones. As these bluesmen seemed to turn the clock back from the more urbane sounds of the R & B balladeers, a parallel phenomenon was occurring in Nashville. Just when it looked as if the pop crooners like Jimmy Wakely or Bob Wills's singer Tommy Duncan were taking over country music, along came a rawboned young man from Montgomery, Al-abama, named Hank Williams. Williams, who received early mu-sical tutoring from a black street singer known only as Tee Tot, had a bluesy country style, a plaintive voice, and elementally simple, direct lyrics that grabbed the Nashville establishment by the throat and wouldn't let go.

By the end of the 1940s, it seemed as if the entire music world was ready for something different, something that felt less studied and more authentic. For Dewey Phillips and Sam Phillips, that something new could be found on Beale Street and the jukes of West Memphis. "I just did not feel that the gutbucket Southern blues that was here was being displayed as something that we should not only not be ashamed of, but was the real-life essence," Sam Phillips says in explaining why he opened his Memphis Recording Service. "I wasn't out to change the world or anything like that; I was out for these people to be heard."

Phillips instinctively recognized the power of the music, its function as the emotional release for a people who, through the historical force of oppression and the legal force of Jim Crow laws, was not allowed many other outlets of self-expression. "I knew what they were going through; they were people laboring under very difficult personal circumstances physically, but most especially emotionally. And not because they were beaten as slaves every day or anything like that; but that they, over all the years, were having to live their lives within themselves to such a degree. I felt that these people must have something to say."

Phillips was quickly surprised at just how much they had to say, and just how many people wanted to hear them say it. His records were soon in demand from the bigger independent labels that, through Phillips, found a treasure trove of southern blues.

And soon there was even more recording going on in Memphis. WDIA began cutting records in the early fifties, freelancing B. B. King's first sides in the WDIA studios for Nashville's Bullet label. The station started a short-lived Tan Town label for local talent, but it wasn't until program director David James Mattis began his Duke Records in 1952 that the young R & B singers in the area had an outlet. James even designed the label logo, a stylized Cadillac grille. With WDIA off the air after dark and the studios empty, Mattis had the perfect facility to record such young Memphis talent as the Beale Streeters, a recording band that featured Roscoe Gordon, Earl Forrest, Bobby "Blue" Bland, and Johnny Alexander. After changing his name to Johnny Ace, Alexander became Duke's biggest star with the hit single "The Clock," written by Mattis — and accidentally became an even bigger star on Christmas Eve, 1954, when, showing off for a girlfriend, he lost a game of Russian roulette. Dead at twenty-five, almost exactly a year after the death of Hank Williams, Johnny Ace was one of the first rock and roll martyrs, becoming the center of a death cult of fans who turned his posthumous "Pledging My Love" into a million-selling hit. (Twenty-two years later, "Pledging My Love" would be the last song Elvis Presley would record, with a studio band, in Graceland's Jungle Room.)

Singer-pianist Roscoe Gordon is remembered as one of the most influential Beale bluesmen of the fifties. Rufus Thomas remembers him performing without a bass player and not needing one. "He carried his bass [lines] with his left hand," Rufus says, still sounding impressed almost forty-five years later. "The piano was the dominant instrument at that time anyway. And he carried the bass and when he finished playing a gig at night they had to have the piano tuned all up for the next week. He'd tear a piano up. He had good big hands, heavy hands." And that big heavy left hand played that Memphis bass line, the behind-the-beat sound that became the signature of local R & B.

Even with all that hometown talent, Mattis, like many small label owners, needed capital to get his label off the ground. So he took in Don Robey, owner of the Peacock Records gospel label, as a partner. A bad move. Robey, a black Houston businessman who had once controlled that city's cab business, applied his same strong-arm gangster's style to the music business. In short order, Robey took over Duke, moved it to Houston, and within a few years had turned Bland into the label's most consistent hit maker. His Peacock label, meanwhile, continued recording gospel; Louis Cantor's fine book on WDIA, *Wheelin' on Beale*, quotes gospel historian Kip Lornell as saying that of ninety gospel groups active in Memphis during the fifties, Robey's Peacock recorded fifty-three. With its smoother R & B approach standing in contrast to Phillips's rougher-edged cotton-patch blues, Duke paved the way for Stax and the golden age of Memphis soul.

It was a heady time in Memphis. WDIA, Dewey's *Red Hot & Blue*, and Sam's Memphis Recording Service were all tapping into a new energy and their enthusiasm was spreading across the barriers of race and age. WDIA's middle-aged black listeners were tuning into Daddy-O-Dewey at night and Memphis teens were checking out the blues and gospel sounds on WDIA, attending the Midnight Rambles at the Beale Palace and the W. C. Handy Theater in Orange Mound.

It all came together in 1952, after Sam Phillips, tired of making hits for other people, decided to set up his own label to record many of the same bluesmen he had been for other labels. But there was a sound he heard in his mind that combined all the various strains of Memphis music: the gospel, the Delta blues, the R & B, and the country music. One night he brought Dewey the first record by a teenage kid from the Lauderdale Courts housing project that Phillips thought might be able to put it all together. It was July 7, 1954, that Dewey first set his turntable needle down on that 78 rpm acetate of "That's All Right"/"Blue Moon of Kentucky."

"He played that mother over and over and over," says Sam. "And he would not have done that except for the response. No hype was done, absolutely. Elvis, really, had very few friends. It was just more or less an experimental thing when Dewey played Elvis. We weren't prepared for the release of it." The following night, as every Elvis fan knows, Dewey became the first man to publicly interview Elvis, talking to him casually with the microphone open. After their chat, the story goes, the nervous young Elvis asked Phillips when he was going to interview him. "I already have," came the reply.

Daddy-O-Dewey's fame grew apace with Elvis's, and all the record men came to pay homage, from Leonard Chess of Chess Records to Atlantic's Jerry Wexler. "Dewey was one of those black-voiced Caucasoid poets," Wexler wrote in his autobiography, *The Rhythm and the Blues.* "A dazzling technician at the turntable, directing comments into the mike for public consumption and, a nanosecond later, off-mike for the delectation of the hangers-on in the control room. 'Spinning this out for all the Little Richard fans,' he announced, before covering the mike and adding 'and raunchy motherfuckers' while reaching for the ringing phone."

Phillips and Elvis had a falling-out in 1956, according to Jim Dickinson, when on a visit to Graceland Dewey picked up the test acetate of "Hound Dog," which RCA Records, Elvis's label, hadn't yet released. Phillips proceeded to feature the unreleased song on his radio show and on his new TV show, which Dickinson described as "way beyond Ernie Kovacs" in terms of cutting-edge TV comedy. It would be years before Elvis forgave Dewey for stealing the record.

The music Dewey played was still rocketing in popularity as the fifties drew to a close — and teens were as much fans of Dewey's antics as they were of rock and roll, watching his afternoon TV show *Pop Shop* as well as listening to his radio program. The writing was on the wall, though, and it was in the form of a playlist. Just as big labels and big business gradually converted rock and roll into an industry that, in the name of efficiency and consistency, began to cut much of the heart and soul out of the music, the same thing was happening in radio. The new Top 40 radio format came into vogue in the late fifties, favoring heavy airplay for a carefully chosen roster of 45s over colorful deejay patter; jocks were expected to stick to prescribed playlists like gospel.

The music business has never been very kind to its pioneers, and Daddy-O-Dewey's radio days were numbered. Even in the twilight years of *Red Hot & Blue,* Phillips remained influential: The man who had set the rock revolution spinning also helped usher in the golden age of Memphis soul, according to Memphis Horn Wayne Jackson, who credits Phillips with making his group The Mar-Key's "Last Night" a hit in 1961 for the newest record label in town, Satellite. "Dewey jumped on that record and he would play it three or four times in a row on the air and he would do it two or three times daily," he remembers. Jackson says "Last Night" sold three thousand copies in Memphis alone, attracting the attention of Atlantic Records, which had earlier distributed Carla Thomas's Satellite hit, "Gee Whiz." "Last Night" went on to sell more than a million records for Satellite, which was forced to change its name to Stax in the middle of the record's run after a Satellite Records in California threatened a lawsuit.

The record's success, Jackson believes, was directly responsible for Atlantic altering its initial agreement with the newly renamed label. Instead of releasing the Memphis artists under the Atlantic name, as the label had done with Carla, the rest of the Stax stable began appearing on Stax nationwide. The label went on to become the most successful and longest-running Memphis record operation. "That was directly attributable to Dewey Phillips," Wayne Jackson states flatly.

It couldn't stop the inevitable, however. Within a couple of years, Dewey, unable to adapt to Top 40, was off the air. "Dewey just didn't fit the mold," said George Klein. A broken man, Phillips shuttled around to smaller stations in Little Rock, Millington, and other towns in the region, where his old reputation as the king of Memphis radio still provided him with work.

Several car wrecks in the fifties left Dewey saddled with a leg brace and suffering constant pain. Already a heavy drinker (although never on the air, insists his friend Sam Phillips), he became addicted to painkillers. After he and his wife separated Phillips became virtually homeless, staying with family members and old friends. Most veterans of the Memphis music industry have a collection of Dewey-in-decline stories, of bailing him out of jail or picking him up in various hospitals, where he'd often go in futile attempts to obtain drugs. Sam Phillips and Elvis occasionally provided money for Dewey and his family, but the comeback that the former radio star frequently spoke of never materialized. On September 28, 1968, Dewey Phillips was staying with his mother when his heart gave out and Daddy-O-Dewey died in his sleep at the age of forty-two.

"He was top dog," recalls Rufus Thomas. "There was none before him and there was none after. Dewey was the only [white disc jockey] doing black music. I believe he was doing it before [Alan] Freed." Klein agrees, adding that Dewey was the man who took rock and roll into its second phase. "Alan Freed came up with the name, but he was still playing Big Joe Turner and Little Richard and Fats [Domino]," Klein said. "Dewey started using it in white rock 'n' roll music. Dewey was the first guy I know that started playing those white rock 'n' roll guys like Bill Haley and Carl Perkins and Eddie Cochran and Buddy Holly."

"He had the best ear for putting things together," Sam Phillips told me. "That type of thing had no format and that was the beauty of it. You never knew what to expect from Dewey. I am real careful about saying anything is unique. But Dewey was as close a thing to being unique in this profession as anybody.

"Somebody like that guy Dewey Phillips comes along that is absolutely not supposed to make it in quote-unquote communications. . . . He doesn't talk right; he doesn't do this right; he doesn't do that right; he's not conventional," Sam continued, his voice rhythmically rising and falling like a preacher getting ready to drop the hammer. "[But] he makes it! And he makes it bigger than anybody who's ever been a DJ in this city. It's a damn *fact*!"

9

▼▼▼▼▼▼▼▼▼▼▼▼▼▼▼▼▼▼▼▼▼▼▼▼▼▼▼▼▼▼

The Coming of Elvis

In 1955, Lloyd Tillman Binford could look back on a lifetime dedicated to keeping the moral fiber of Memphis as pure and lily-white as the cotton fiber traded by the city's Front Street brokers. The long-running head of the Memphis Board of Censorship, Binford enjoyed a national reputation earned in a half century of banning just about every piece of popular entertainment in sight — books, plays, and movies, all the way back to the early days of silent films. Compared to Binford's Memphis, bluenose Boston was Gomorrah-on-the-Charles.

But nothing lasts forever, even in Memphis. With the death of Boss Crump, the man from whom Binford had drawn power for fifty years, the censor's days were numbered. A few months after Crump died in the fall of 1954, Binford announced plans to retire. He remained the Baptist deacon's son from Duck Hill, Mississippi right to the end. In 1955, shortly before retiring, he told the *Press-Scimitar*, "In a sense all of us belong to the Devil, because he's trying to get us and plants wrong thoughts in our mind."

Binford's lifelong mission was to keep all wrong thoughts out of Memphis minds. And it wasn't only sexy scenes that drew his well-honed scissors: Like Boss Crump, Binford was dedicated to preserving the status quo of white supremacy. In 1914, he banned *Uncle Tom's Cabin*, citing its potential for creating racial tension (though he saw no such reason to ban D. W. Griffith's *Birth of a Nation*, which glorified the Ku Klux Klan and inspired its comeback, the following year). He later banned *Brewster's Millions*, featuring the popular black comedian Eddie "Rochester" Anderson, under the logic that "the picture promotes too much social equality and race mixing." Binford dismissed Charlie Chaplin as "that London guttersnipe," banning not only his comic films, but even movies he produced, including his version of the opera *Carmen*, in reaction to Chaplin's own support of social equality as one of Hollywood's first Communists. Binford also threatened to cut to ribbons the film *New Orleans*, which prominently featured such black stars as Louis Armstrong and Billie Holiday (in her only feature film role). Rather than fight Binford, the movie skipped Memphis. A theatrical production of *Annie Get Your Gun* was turned away because the cast included a black train conductor — a role that, in Binford's Old South, suggested too much authority. To his mind, the only black railroad men were Pullman porters; anything else was a "wrong thought."

His power lasted into the fifties, and if Binford's judgment seemed dull, even in his eighties his scissors remained sharp. He banned Marlon Brando's motorcycle gang classic, *The Wild One*, calling it "the most lawless picture I ever saw." But by 1955 he was nearing retirement, his power was waning, and when he tried to ban *The Blackboard Jungle* he failed. For many, the most radical part of that juvenile-delinquent drama was the song under the opening titles, Bill Haley and His Comets' "Rock Around the Clock." The rock revolution was already on; Dewey Phillips played the song over and over on *Red Hot & Blue*, tauntingly dedicating it to "Lloyd." His reign finally ended with his retirement in October 1955, but not before he tried, and failed, to keep one more movie out of Memphis — James Dean's *Rebel without a Cause*.

Even if he'd had his way, Memphis had long since figured out a simple way to get around Binford's bans. All it took was a short drive across the bridge to West Memphis, where the Sunset Drive-

In or more traditional "hardtop" movie theaters like the Joy did huge business showing films Binford had banned on the other side of the Mississippi. Binford used to boast that he was so beloved there were 135 babies named after him. Some, no doubt, were the offspring of grateful West Memphis theater owners.

With the forbidden delights of James Dean raising celluloid hell beckoning, Memphis teens flocked to *Rebel* and began imitating its star, from his halting speech to his heavy-lidded stare to his clothes. "I remember every kid came out the next week wearing a red jacket with the collar turned up," just like Dean, recalled George Klein.

One Memphis kid saw *Rebel* so many times that, along with Dean's look and attitude, he memorized the film's dialogue. A few years later, far away in Hollywood, he met *Rebel* director Nicholas Ray and shocked him by reciting whole scenes by heart.

By then, of course, everyone had heard of Elvis Presley. But in the days when Binford ruled, trying to keep Brando and Dean from bedeviling Memphis youth, Elvis was just another kid from the projects hungry for some recreational bedevilment. He spent his days struggling to get out of Humes High School. After school, along with a host of part-time jobs from movie usher to metal furniture factory worker, he struggled with his music. He was soaking up the sounds of his adopted hometown, slowly learning guitar hanging around the older guys in the Lauderdale Courts housing project just northeast of downtown, attending gospel concerts at Ellis Auditorium, and listening hard to the bluesmen Dewey Phillips played on *Red Hot & Blue*.

His life story has long since gained mythic status, but in the details, Elvis was remarkably typical of thousands of Memphis kids, black and white, who came before and after him. He was born dirt-poor in Tupelo, Mississippi, on January 8, 1935, in a shotgun shack his father Vernon had built for $180. His twin brother, Jesse Garon, was stillborn, an all too common occurrence in a state that still has one of the nation's highest infant mortality rates. It was a difficult labor, but when Elvis Aaron emerged a half hour later he was healthy. As if to realize his mother's fears, he'd soon become a sickly child, suffering whooping cough and measles as well as a near-fatal bout with tonsillitis. After nearly losing her only child, Gladys Presley became obsessively overprotective. Older than her husband, she was the true head of the household even when Vernon wasn't drinking. When Elvis was two, Vernon was arrested for forging a check. Jailed for six months before the trial, he was convicted and sentenced to three more years at Parchman Farm, the penal cotton plantation that had been temporary home to such Mississippi bluesmen as Booker T. Washington "Bukka" White, Son House, and Sonny Boy Williamson II.

The Presley family lived on welfare while Vernon was "away." He was released after only nine months, and things soon returned to normal. Vernon still couldn't keep a job, with his well-earned reputation for drinking and unreliability. World War II was a lucky break for Vernon and thousands of other Mississippians who took factory jobs in Memphis for the war effort, commuting back home on weekends. After the war, with few options, the small family joined the mass Mississippi migration north. Most continued on to Chicago; for the Presleys, Memphis was far enough.

The official story, according to Elvis's manager Colonel Tom Parker, says the Presleys arrived in Memphis in the fall of 1948. Presley boyhood friend Jimmy Denson claims Elvis and Gladys arrived shortly before Christmas, 1947, and he has spent most of his waking hours since Elvis's death telling his story to anyone who'll listen, believing the date change to be part of an overall Parker plot to rewrite Elvis's history. In the end, it doesn't really matter. Whenever they arrived, things didn't change much for the Presleys. Vernon had trouble finding and keeping jobs, and Gladys, fearful of the big city, had even more reason to keep her precious son close.

In 1949, the Presleys made the most important move in young Elvis's life. Their name came up on the waiting list for one of the 433 apartments in the Lauderdale Courts housing project. By the time they left their federally funded apartment early in 1954 (for a change, the oft-evicted family had to move because they were making too *much* money), Elvis was a new creature. He'd soaked up the lessons of his older musical neighbors and was well versed in the R & B hits on WDIA and Dewey Phillips's WHBQ show. In the summer of 1953, he had made that famous first record, paying Sam Phillips's assistant Marion Keisker four dollars at the Memphis Recording Service to cut a double-sided souvenir disc of "My Happiness" and "That's When Your Heartaches Begin" as a gift for his mother. Sam Phillips' assistant Marion Keisker would later tell how a shy Elvis had approached her about recording for "Mr. Phillips," but despite the often-told story, Sam insists it was he, not Marion, who recorded that first disc. "The truth of the matter is that I made the demo record of 'My Happiness' and 'That's When Your Heartaches Begin,' " he says. "I made the little record. He came in with his guitar; Marion was in front and I was in the control room." As further proof, he says that "I woudn't take anything away from Marion; I never had a better friend in my life. But Marion didn't know how to make an acetate record and she didn't try to." Elvis would soon return to the storefront studio on Union Avenue with more serious intent.

The Presleys left Lauderdale Courts on January 7, 1954, moving to an apartment nearby at 462 Alabama on the day before their son's nineteenth birthday. Elvis was ready to start a new life, and before the month was out, he was back at 706 Union Avenue. Along with his Memphis Recording Service business, which still kept him busy recording various religious and social events, Sam Phillips was pursuing his real love, recording blues artists for other labels. He had started his own Sun label in 1952, scoring a national hit the following year with Rufus Thomas's "Bear Cat," an answer song to Willie Mae "Big Mama" Thornton's popular "Hound Dog." It was a bit *too* close an answer, and Sam found himself facing a lawsuit by the publishers of "Hound Dog" and its composers Jerry Leiber and Mike Stoller. But it was also a hit, and Phillips had discovered his life's mission.

Along with Beale bluesmen and R & B singers, Phillips did some business recording the area's country acts, including Howard Seratt, Doug Poindexter & the Starlite Wranglers, and medicine show performer Harmonica Frank Floyd. Elvis, who'd been sitting in with such local country stars as Eddie Bond at outdoor appearances and honky-tonks like the Eagle's Nest, thought he could follow their lead and cut some records of his own.

Today, it all seems as inevitable and logical as the movement of the planets, part of some grand cosmic design. But in the context of the day it seems a little crazy: Why would this Memphis teenager, dressed in the latest Beale pimp-hipster threads and playing R & B hits he'd heard on *Red Hot & Blue*, think he could fit in with the Stetson-ed and cowboy-booted country folk on the Grand Ole Opry?

It makes more sense in light of country music's evolution in the late forties. Nothing changes pop culture faster than a war, and as the biggest of them all, World War II changed America top to bottom. Just as black vets returned from overseas with different attitudes, bigger dreams, and new tastes in clothes, food, entertainment, and most everything else, so did their rural white counterparts.

Music followed those social changes, splitting like an atom with equally explosive results. As the swing bands broke up, the countless R & B combos modeled on Louis Jordan's Tympany Five thrived, while other musicians explored the new, technically sophisticated jazz called bebop pioneered by Charlie Parker and Dizzy Gillespie. Blues singers, likewise, found themselves hewing to either the T-Bone Walker/Charles Brown supper club route or the Muddy-and-the-Wolf update of the raw Delta blues.

Country followed similar paths, and in large part took its lead from the big, influential Texas bands of Bob Wills and his followers. The term "western swing" didn't appear until the early fifties, when it was coined to describe the Hollywood-based big band led by Spade Cooley. While Cooley's and Bob Wills's big bands were the best known (Bing Crosby even covered Wills's "San Antonio

Rose"), smaller, harder-edged bands like Cliff Bruner's Texas Wanderers were far more common. After the war Wills followed their lead, forming smaller groups that plugged in, swung harder, and played an up-tempo bluesy style that would become known as hillbilly boogie. Wills's brother Johnnie Lee had a hit in 1941 with Kokomo Arnold's "Milk Cow Blues," and it was the Wills version that served as Elvis's model when he recorded it for Sun. In 1938, another Texas band, the New Orleans–influenced Roy Newman & His Boys, recorded "Everybody's Trying to Be My Baby," a song that Carl Perkins later cut at his March 1956 Sun session and which the Beatles, loyal Perkins disciples, revived again almost a decade later.

The blues had been an important part of country music since the days of Jimmie Rodgers and the Carter Family in the twenties, but in the late forties and early fifties it was making a strong comeback in the hands of such Wills-influenced honky-tonkers as Ernest Tubb & His Texas Troubadours, Hank Williams & His Drifting Cowboys, and Hank Thompson.

Hillbilly boogie, the most immediate precursor to rockabilly, had been topping the country charts since the end of World War II in such records as Red Foley's "Tennessee Saturday Night" and "Chattanooga Shoeshine Boy." Long before he became the "ol' pea-picker," Tennessee Ernie Ford rocked the house with "Shotgun Boogie." Bill Monroe forged his bluegrass sound mixing the music of his Scots-Irish heritage with the "old Southern blues" he learned from such roving guitarists as Arnold Schultz. In a country scene that included such rocking country hits as Hank Williams's "Move It On Over" and "Hey, Good Lookin'," it's no wonder that Elvis, with his mix of jumped-up Delta blues, bluegrass, and pop, felt like he'd fit right in.

Of course, by 1954, Phillips didn't want someone who fit in. He was looking for something really different, someone who could take the old Memphis music mix into the atomic age. In the early fifties, with no one else running a studio in Memphis, he had the field pretty much to himself when he started recording the wealth of local blues talent for northern labels like Modern and Chess. His monopoly didn't last long: Within a couple of years Modern Records had set up its own Memphis subsidiary, Meteor; Duke/Peacock was actively recording the new generation of Beale bluesmen; Sam's self-styled talent scout Ike Turner had left for St. Louis; his favorite artist, Howlin' Wolf, had loaded up his Cadillac and headed to "North Mississippi," Chicago's South Side. Sam Phillips had no choice but to look for something brand-new, something no one else was recording, something he could have all to himself.

Every Elvis fan can recite what happened next. Elvis returns to the studio, makes another "vanity" record ("Casual Love Affair"/ "I'll Never Stand in Your Way"); Phillips takes a fatherly interest in the boy, calls him back to cut a demo, teams him with two older musicians from Sun's country act, Doug Poindexter & the Starlite Wranglers. Guitarist Scotty Moore and bassist Bill Black give Elvis the benefit of their experience, and he infects them with some of his hormonal enthusiasm. Within a few weeks they work Arthur "Big Boy" Crudup's 1946 Victor Records release, "That's All Right (Mama)," which is exactly what Phillips is looking for. Dewey Phillips previews the disc on *Red Hot & Blue*, and it's a local smash. With a B side that's a rocked-up cover of Bill Monroe & the Bluegrass Boys' 1947 waltz "Blue Moon of Kentucky," Sun 209 is officially released on July 19, 1954.

"If I could find a white singer with the Negro sound and the Negro feel I could make a million dollars," are the famous words attributed to Phillips. In Elvis Presley, Mississippi-born and bred in the Southern Baptist church, weaned on the blues and R & B of Beale, WDIA and *Red Hot & Blue*, Phillips found what he was searching for — a modern essence distilled from the Memphis mojo of black-white cultural integration.

But what was new about Elvis? He recorded songs from the mid-forties; white blues singers were as old as Sophie Tucker or

Jimmie Rodgers. In the long-standing Memphis music mix, the blues was vital to such local country-and-western stars as the Swift Jewel Cowboys and harmonica player Lonnie Glosson, and it was integral to the styles of such transplants as the Delmore Brothers and the Louvin Brothers.

Elvis's tutoring in the projects came from slightly older, much more experienced musicians like Johnny and Dorsey Burnette and Jesse Lee Denson, guys familiar with the songs of Foley, Ford, and the Memphis country singers. But talented as those men were — and some of them would later make great records (about which more later) — only Elvis became the sort of teen idol he'd dreamed of being, sitting in the cool dark of those gilded Memphis movie palaces, watching Brando and Dean flicker across the screen.

Elvis connected with the teen audience like no one before him. When the other guys in the projects sang about cutting loose, getting wild and "Dixie Fried," it was totally believable. These were good old boys who'd been around, and it sounded like it.

Elvis, by contrast, had been so spoiled and overprotected that even though he was just a few years their junior he seemed far younger. He was an outcast even in the projects, surrounded by other families in similar financial straits. "Elvis, really, had very few friends," Sam Phillips remembers. Even after he had a record out, he remained the painfully shy kid Phillips once described to Elvis biographer Peter Guralnick as "the most introverted person that ever came into that studio. . . . He tried not to show it, but he felt so inferior."

Held back by his overprotective mother Gladys and social circumstances that branded him poor white trash to "decent" Memphis society, Elvis's sole outlet was to spill it all out in his music. His singing had an irresistible, yearning quality, the sound of unrequited lust for pleasures that seemed forever just out of reach. The teens responded to the same quality in Elvis that Sam Phillips had earlier homed in on with the bluesmen he recorded, "people laboring under very difficult personal circumstances, physically, but most especially, emotionally . . . having to live their lives within themselves to such a degree. I felt that these people must have something to say."

That duality, the tension between social circumstances and emotional expression, is at the very heart of Memphis music. If there's a single reason why Memphis became the most important city in the evolution of American popular music, it's the unique mix of strict social segregation combined with cultural integration. Although African Americans made up half the city's population and shaped the music, food, and other, less tangible aspects of everyday life in Memphis, they were forced to "live within themselves." Black Memphis had few outlets in which it was allowed to fully express itself, and music was an important one. From Monday through Friday, black Memphis was under control of its white bosses. But in Saturday night juke joints and Sunday morning church services, black Memphis could let loose.

Even as it made the rules, white Memphis was just as bound by them, tied up in its own knot of strict social standards. From the 1800s it was a Memphis tradition that when serious cutting loose was required, Beale could provide the means, no matter what your color. That's what kept the expensive, white-only whorehouses busy on Gayoso and what packed the Palace Theatre for Midnight Rambles. It's what turned Memphis barbecue from the rustic party food it once was into a symbol of the city, worshiped annually with Dionysian fervor by citizens of all social strata at the Memphis in May International Barbecue Contest.

Elvis was the first product of that environment to be sold nationally to that huge new market of white kids, teens who immediately identified with that subversive need to break down social barriers, at least for the duration of a three-minute record. For white Memphis, the forbidden pleasures of Beale Street had always come wrapped in the pulsing rhythms of the blues. Like W. C. Handy's compositions, George D. Hay's early Opry, and Sam Phillips's blues recording days, Elvis's country–R & B fusion offered those pleasures long familiar to Memphians to a new audience.

His timing was perfect. Those newly minted "teenagers," bored to death in thousands of comfy little suburbs, were waiting for someone just like him. Boys everywhere were soon slicking their hair back with pomade as their girlfriends teased theirs to impossible heights, everyone dancing the bop to the wild new sounds.

Rock and roll gave the teens' "cruising" culture a new spin. In 1954, the year Dewey Phillips sent the first Elvis record spinning onto the Memphis airwaves, traveling salesman Ray Kroc signed California's McDonald brothers to a franchise deal, bringing suburban America the fifteen-cent burger. Drive-ins in Memphis offered far more savory delights and more amenities, and any Memphis teen with a driver's license and access to Dad's sedan regularly headed to barbecue joints like Leonard's and the Little Pig. Staffed by black waiters offering curb service, the Q joints were favorite hangouts for teens, who took their pulled pork sandwiches with a side of *Red Hot & Blue*, as Dewey Phillips blared from every car radio.

As Kroc standardized road food, Memphian Kemmons Wilson standardized road rest. A builder who had once been the country's top Wurlitzer jukebox distributor (scratch *any* Memphian and there's music there somewhere), Wilson decided to build the sort of dependable family motels he'd always wished for when the Wilsons were on vacation. Like WHBQ's Lawhead, Wilson found his inspiration in the movies, naming his revolutionary chain of giant motels after the 1942 film starring Bing Crosby and Fred Astaire. In August 1952, he opened his first Holiday Inn on Summer Avenue in Memphis.

Though amorous Memphis teens might have preferred one of Wilson's rooms, young lovers made do with the area's drive-in movie theaters. But even as his first fans cruised Union Avenue in the summer of '54 with "That's All Right" blasting on the car radio, Elvis was no overnight sensation. He hit the road to promote his new record, but with the rock and roll concert business still a few years away, he was marketed as the latest hillbilly boogie act, providing a novel opener act for more legitimate country singers. On July 30, 1954, he played his first big concert, opening for falsetto-yodel king Slim Whitman at the Overton Shell on a bill that also included Wanda Jackson and the new Sun act, Johnny Cash & the Tennessee Two. The show was part of a series of country shows co-promoted by Presley's first real manager, Bob Neal, and John Novarese, a co-owner of the local Poplar Tunes. It was a departure for the bandshell in lush Overton Park, which was typically given over to events of a more refined nature — local theater, opera productions, and the like. The park, east of downtown in the Midtown section of Memphis, remains a cool, green magnet in the heat of summer, even in these days of universal air-conditioning. It was seen as so vital to the city that I-40 was built around the park. To this day, anyone driving through Memphis for the first time will probably find himself lost in the maze of roads and bypasses.

Bringing Elvis to Overton was business as usual for Novarese, who enjoyed pushing the envelope in the Memphis concert business. He had once booked Bill Haley & His Comets, riding high with "Rock Around the Clock," into the Ellis Auditorium downtown. Needing an opener at the last minute, Novarese booked Piano Red. Red happened to be a very light skinned black man, and no matter his shade, his appearance on the same show as Haley broke segregation laws. As the story goes, Memphis police threatened to stop the show, telling Novarese he couldn't have a "colored" opening act.

"Well, if y'all want us to stop the show, we'll do it," Novarese is said to have told the cop. "But just don't call him 'colored,' he's very sensitive." "What do you mean? He's colored isn't he?" asked the confused officer. "That man is Hawaiian and he's very proud of his heritage," came Novarese's reply. "Well if he's Hawaiian, that's different," the cop decided. So "Hawaiian" boogie king Piano Red opened for rock and roll star Haley and stole the show. And come Monday, Novarese's store sold a lot of Piano Red records.

Formal concerts like the one in Overton were still rare for Elvis, who was then expanding his regional audience on the country roadhouse circuit. By September, he was in Nashville to take his big shot in an audition for the Grand Ole Opry. But the Opry was no longer Hay's Beale-inspired brainchild. Elvis, unpolished and far too "black"-sounding, failed the audition. A few weeks later, in October 1954, he was given a chance on Shreveport's *Louisiana Hayride* radio show, the Opry's more open-minded farm team.

On October 14, just before his first *Louisiana Hayride* appearance, the *Commercial Appeal* predicted great things for "Elvis Presley, our homegrown hillbilly singer [who] is continuing his swift, steady stride toward national prominence in the rural rhythm field."

Two days later, Elvis made his *Hayride* debut, his turning point from local to national performer. That same night, E. H. "Boss" Crump, the eighty-year-old political leader who ruled Memphis for the first half of the twentieth century — manipulating the black vote while guaranteeing segregation to white supporters, guiding the city's eastern expansion away from the Mississippi and the black ghettoes — died in his sleep at his mansion on broad, tree-lined Peabody Avenue. Big changes were coming, and not just in Memphis. 1954 also saw the U.S. Supreme Court's landmark decision in *Brown vs. the Board of Education of Topeka, Kansas,* which declared unconstitutional 1896's "separate but equal" law, which had cleared the way for the Jim Crow legislation that followed.

Elvis's *Hayride* success, together with a concert in Jacksonville, Florida, drew the interest of veteran carnival promoter and country music manager Colonel Tom Parker. Parker, who managed country singers Eddy Arnold and Hank Snow, set about signing the kid making such a hit in Shreveport. On August 15, 1955, Parker visited the Presley's rented house at 1414 Getwell and, despite

Gladys's misgivings, Elvis signed an exclusive contract with him. Family friends say that was the beginning of the end for Gladys. Her life revolved around Elvis; now she was losing him.

Parker continued cutting Elvis's ties to Memphis; by November he'd arranged to sell Elvis's contract to RCA, earning himself an up-front payment of ten thousand dollars, in addition to the fifty-fifty split he had with his client. That one-sided arrangement held for the rest of their business dealings, continuing until Elvis's death twenty-two years and a day after they signed that first pact.

It can be argued that, like Handy and virtually every other Memphis musician, Presley's inspiration faded the further he got from his Memphis roots. For visceral power and electrifying emotion, he never bettered the records he cut at 706 Union Avenue between July 1954 and October 1955. He made some great rock and roll in the studios of New York and Nashville, but never anything so direct, so irresistible as "That's All Right."

For the last few months of his time at Sun, Presley pumped his hormonal energy into country, blues, and just about anything else he felt like. With Scotty Moore on the same type of electric hollow-body guitar favored by jazz and country swing players, and Bill Black playing the same upright bass he used on his country gigs, Elvis sang and beat out rhythm guitar on a worn 1943 Martin D-18. During Elvis's Sun tenure, drums and occasionally piano were added to his sound. But it was Phillips, creating modern record production at the same time Elvis was inventing rock and roll, who gave the band its really big beat, enlarging the group's sound electronically far beyond its three, four, or five instruments, adding echo and using distortion that made the records sound huge and fierce.

For the most part, those revolutionary early discs that set the style for rock and roll would be considered "unplugged" by today's standards. Elvis's guitar style was strictly country rhythm, open chords with ringing strings strummed with a straight pick. Those who say Elvis did nothing more than rip off black bluesmen need look no further than his guitar playing for proof to the contrary. No bluesman ever played rhythm like that. Black slapped his instrument, rhythmically striking the fingerboard between each pluck of the strings, creating a stuttering percussive effect akin to a snare drum. It was a common comedic technique in the country bands that he'd performed in, often in vaudevillian "rube" costume complete with blacked-out teeth. For his bass to produce maximum slap, Scotty Moore told me in Nashville in the summer of 1996, "Bill tuned the E [string] down and let it slap against the neck." Meanwhile, Moore played a bluesy, fingerpicking style drawn from the work of Kentuckian Merle Travis, tossing in some dissonant Memphis blues licks and jazzy chords.

Put all those parts together in Sun's tiny one-room studio and producer Phillips got an ensemble sound on record much fuller than three pieces had any right to be. Away from Sam, as the few surviving *Louisiana Hayride* recordings attest, Elvis, Scotty, and Bill's sound was much thinner, much "smaller."

The repertoire of those Sun records was just as remarkable as the sound. Along with the yin-yang of his Delta blues/Kentucky bluegrass first single, Presley crooned pop ("Harbor Lights," "Blue Moon"), belted out R & B ("Good Rockin' Tonight," the Roy Brown/Wynonie Harris), and mixed things up even more with western swing/blues ("Milkcow Blues Boogie") a straight blues by fellow Sun artist Little Junior Parker ("Mystery Train"), and even a country polka ("Just Because"). A Memphis musician in the classic W. C. Handy tradition, Presley was nothing if not versatile, and that would remain the single defining constant in his career, as he drew inspiration from a dizzying array of musical sources, from Dean Martin's cocktail seductions to Flatt & Scruggs rustic breakdowns and everything in between. He haunted the Home of the Blues record shop on Beale, and made Joe Cuoghi's Poplar Tunes store his second home, his new income enabling him to buy all the records he'd dreamed of owning for so long. A kid in a sonic candy store, he gobbled everything up, digested it, and turned it into pure Elvis.

But Elvis's days as a pioneer were numbered. Parker preferred the trite-and-true, saving his gambling for the roulette tables of Vegas. Taking no chances with his "boy," Parker controlled every aspect of his career. By the time he left Sun Elvis was a changed man onstage and off, the shy introverted mama's boy transformed into the bumping-and-grinding rockabilly cat. Some of his old friends say it was due at least in part to the effects of country music's drug of choice — amphetamines. In the fifties, when roads were poor and making a living in music meant overnight drives to the next gig, many country artists depended on those little white pills so readily available at truck stops and roadside cafés. "I'm taking little white pills and my eyes are open wide," Dave Dudley would sing a few years later in "Six Days on the Road." While truckers used speed as a more efficient substitute for caffeine, doctors would legally prescribe amphetamines for everything from sluggishness to weight gain. The then-fashionable "vitamin shots" were another source of the drug, and many physicians prescribed them without telling patients they included doses of speed. In the fifties, drugs — at least legal prescription drugs taken under a doctor's direction — were viewed by society as good things. It was, as the old ad slogan promised, the age of "better living through chemistry."

Whatever the reason, Elvis's newly confident music and moves caused a sensation on the early TV variety shows. Most homes in the South had yet to acquire the newfangled appliances, so the impact of his TV appearances, first with the Dorsey Brothers and later with Milton Berle, Ed Sullivan, and Steve Allen, was felt most heavily in the North. In the South, disc jockeys like Dewey Phillips in Memphis and the legendary John R (Richbourg) and Bill "Hoss" Allen at Nashville's powerful WLAC (heard coast to coast) broadcast the rock and roll gospel.

Elvis spread his new wealth around, buying his parents a new ranch-style house at 1034 Audubon Drive, near Audubon Park in East Memphis, paying forty thousand dollars cash. He'd been a star in Memphis for a couple of years, but for the rest of America 1956 was the Year of Elvis, and things were moving fast. January saw the release of his first RCA million-seller, "Heartbreak Hotel," which topped the country and pop charts and made it to No. 5 R & B, selling three hundred thousand copies in just three weeks. In August, he made his first movie, *Love Me Tender.*

Elvis returned to 706 Union Avenue once more. On December 4, 1956, he held court at the studio, jamming and chatting with his Sun successors Jerry Lee Lewis, Carl Perkins, and Johnny Cash. Bootlegged for years (and before that, according to local legend, held at a local pharmacy as collateral for Dewey Phillips's codeine cough medicine account), the recordings were legally released on CD in 1990. Along with its informal portrait of Elvis, who apparently didn't know there was a tape running, the disc provides insight into Presley's eclectic tastes, ranging from gospel to blues to Bill Monroe's bluegrass to Elvis's imitation of Jackie Wilson singing "Don't Be Cruel."

In retrospect, Sam Phillips's decision to sell Elvis's contract to RCA seems insane. But forty thousand dollars was an offer an independent record label owner simply couldn't refuse. With Elvis's success, other talented rockabillies were soon banging on the door at 706 Union, and like most independent labels Sun was chronically short of cash. Of the forty thousand dollars RCA paid for Presley's Sun contract, five thousand went to Elvis (and half of that to Colonel Parker) for back royalties. Sun was trapped in the catch-22 of the indie label — a flop was bad for business, but a hit could be fatal. As a rule, record distributors paid the small independent labels last; they were much lower on the pecking order than the dependable, hit-making major labels. And if the small, inevitably undercapitalized indie, having depleted its cash and credit in manufacturing all those hit records, went bankrupt waiting for its money, then the distributor never had to pay. The record industry, after all, has never been kind to the little guy. As Phillips complained in a 1958 interview, "The record business is so precarious, you can't get financial backing until you don't need it."

As a result, Sun, having paid for pressing, printing, and shipping, still had to fight to get paid. RCA's cash infusion helped keep Sun going, enabling Phillips to begin making stars of Carl Perkins, from nearby Jackson, Tennessee; Johnny Cash of Kingsland, Arkansas; and the Ferriday Flash, Jerry Lee Lewis, who came up from Louisiana confident that a piano player could win people over a lot quicker than all those guitar pickers.

Carl Perkins was a lot like the guys Elvis had idolized at Lauderdale Courts. He could moan the honky-tonk blues like a younger Hank Williams, but he was equally adept at writing rockers like "Blue Suede Shoes" and he could play the guitar like a-ringin' a bell. A couple of years older than the young King, he was also married and, with bad teeth and a receding hairline, no competition in the heartthrob department. Perhaps even more important, he was probably too "country" to have sustained a pop career, even if a car wreck hadn't sidelined him at the peak of his "Blue Suede" popularity.

Johnny Cash knew he was country as soup beans and corn bread, and never really tried to be anything else. As soon as he'd established himself at Sun with such classics as "Hey Porter," "Get Rhythm," Home of the Blues," "Folsom Prison Blues," and what may well have been the most insipid record to ever wear a Sun label, "Ballad of a Teenage Queen," Cash took the highway east to Nashville.

Jerry Lee Lewis, as he would be happy to tell you, was arguably the hottest rocker to come from Sun. For proof, just compare two versions of "Don't Be Cruel" — the original by Elvis, and the cover by Jerry Lee. Elvis is far and away the better singer, with a smoother sound and more confident phrasing. But while his version is a sweet-voiced plea, buoyed by the white gospel harmonies of the Jordanaires, Jerry Lee's is a stripped-down, angry warning, underscored by his pounding, ominous piano: "Don't Be Cruel or Else." What Elvis only promised, Jerry Lee delivered.

After Elvis and the rest of that Million Dollar Quartet, Sun would be home to dozens of other, lesser known rockers. Roy Orbison would become the best known of Sun's second wave. But his fame justly comes from his magnificent post-Sun ballads of the sixties, near-operatic productions that displayed one of the era's finest pop singers. Fresh out of Texas, Roy was a rocker at Sun. Sporting a Les Paul guitar and without his trademark Ray-Bans, Roy bopped it up with his classic "Ooby Dooby" and lesser lights like "Devil Doll." But he was still searching for his sound.

Billy Lee Riley remains the great Sun mystery. He was custom-made ideal rock star material — darkly handsome, stunningly versatile, and totally out of his mind. His "Flying Saucer Rock 'n' Roll" remains one of the most crazed recordings of all time, Riley's abandoned delivery matched by a wild young band featuring guitarist Roland Janes, whose twang-bar moves on his Stratocaster hinted at the thousands of surf bands to come. Christened the Little Green Men after Riley's "Flying Saucer" success, the band hit the road to capitalize on the record's success, wearing bright green suits, of course. Janes remembers that the only green material that Lansky's haberdashery could come up with fast enough was very thick pool-table felt. There was no time to wait — you toured while the record was hot. And hot they were. "That first night we got to playing," the former Little Green Man recalls his custom-cut green blanket with a laugh, "it got so hot in that suit I like to sweat to death."

Roland and the rest of the Little Green Men were much more comfortable back at Sun, where they also served as the house band, backing Jerry Lee Lewis and many others. Roland Janes still works for Sam today; he can usually be found behind the board, engineering at the "new" studio on Madison built in the early 1960s.

From Osceola, Arkansas, the same town that produced bluesman Luther Allison, and raised in the cotton fields, Riley was one of the best Sun rockers when it came to playing straight blues. Competent on several instruments, he blew blues harp and played fine guitar as well. But he had a reputation for drinking, and he became bitter when he failed to follow up "Flying Saucer" with another hit. He believed Sam Phillips wasn't promoting him enough, and one night, in the belief that Sam had pulled support of his "Red Hot" in order to promote Jerry Lee Lewis, Billy poured whiskey over all the recording equipment. It became a legend in the music business. More than thirty years later, when longtime Riley fan Bob Dylan met his hero, it was one of the first things he asked him, "Did you really . . ."

Nowadays, the archetypal rockabilly band remains Elvis, Scotty, and Bill, with the minimalist drummer D. J. Fontana adding a little snap to the proceedings. But the variations on that theme created by Sun's later rockabillies were many. Arkansan Sonny Burgess took a Dixieland slant, with a blaring trumpet competing with pumping piano and twanging guitar in his frantic 1956 hit "Red Headed Woman." With its blues form, call-and-response chorus, and kazoolike horn, the record sounds like a hopped-up, plugged-in Memphis Jug Band.

Charlie Feathers delivered some powerful straight-on rockabilly performances that never strayed far from his hard-country, honky-tonk roots. Malcolm Yelvington specialized in a souped-up honky-tonk style that was akin to the R & B–flavored western swing of Bob Wills's brother Billy Jack's band. Warren Smith played a rough and rocking type of rockabilly that revived Washboard Sam's classic put-down "Soap and Water" as "Miss Froggie." And while he may have been the best rocker, Jerry Lee Lewis wasn't the only Sun piano man. Carl Mann's time at the Sun upright piano yielded a series of rock conversions of ballads like "Mona Lisa."

About the only thing they all had in common was Sam Phillips. Even when Sam gave up engineering duties to Jack Clement, his philosophy remained in force. Sam had first bankrolled his Memphis Recording Service by recording events — weddings, graduations, and the like. And to Phillips, records were still events, musical snapshots of emotional outbursts — sloppy, out of control, even a little dangerous. If they captured a special moment, that was all he cared about.

Charlie Rich was, fittingly, the last Sun artist. He recorded his

"Lonely Weekends" in the fall of 1959 for the old label, but it wasn't released until January 1960, when Phillips put it on his new Phillips International label, the start of which coincided with his move out of the old twenty-by-thirty-five-foot one-room studio on Union to the plusher environs of Sam Phillips Studio. Released toward the end of Elvis's army hitch, Rich's song, with its Presley-esque vocal, caught on among the Elvis-starved pop audience. But Rich's heart was never in rock or pop music. A jazzman by nature, he chose as his idol Stan Kenton. But Rich and his wife and song-writing partner Margaret Ann prospered in pop, and Charlie wound up with one of the most diverse careers in Memphis music, successful in pop, rock, blues, and country, returning to his first love, jazz, for his final album.

He wrote several blues standards, including "Don't Put No Headstone on My Grave" and "Who Will the Next Fool Be," the latter a Top 10 R & B hit for Bobby "Blue" Bland in 1962, the same year Charlie left Sam's label. He briefly recorded for RCA/Groove before making a fine series of recordings for Smash that included the 1965 rock novelty hit "Mohair Sam." His biggest commercial success came in the early seventies, when another element of his many-faceted style — sophisticated, after-hours country balladry with a bluesy inflection — found favor on "countrypolitan" radio. But Charlie, a shy man whose soul yearned for something beyond the music that made him financially secure (helped along by an early, sizable investment in the Wendy's hamburger chain), remained deeply unhappy. He drank too much, often at exactly the wrong place at the wrong time, a habit that culminated in a famous episode at the 1975 Country Music Association Awards. As the previous entertainer of the year, the Silver Fox (so named for his prematurely gray hair) was to give John Denver the new award. Instead, Rich set the envelope on fire on national TV. As the seventies wore on, Rich made a few more dents in the country charts, but for the most part he and Margaret Ann stayed in their house in East Memphis. Charlie had a studio in back and held frequent jam sessions with local jazz and blues players. His final album,

1992's *Pictures and Paintings*, followed that model: a laid-back, late-night mix of jazz and blues standards and Rich originals, it revealed the real Charlie Rich at last. A master of easygoing jazz and blues, superb pianist and bandleader, intimate performer, Rich, sadly, was also a man who forgot one of show business's cardinal rules: Never get famous doing something you don't really love. Rich died in 1995 at sixty-two.

Not all the great Memphis rockabillies wound up at Sun. The older boys at Lauderdale Courts, who used to rehearse in the laundry room while the young Elvis watched, later made some great records. Johnny and Dorsey Burnette spent a little time picking on the mama's boy who always seemed to be hanging around, but by all accounts, the Burnettes would have picked on anyone handy. They relished their reputations for meanness so much they worked as bouncers in rough West Memphis joints like the Cotton Club just for fun. "They'd fight back to back and just clear a room," Jimmy Denson recalls. Both Burnettes were Golden Gloves boxers, as was the man who would be their lead guitarist in the Rock 'n' Roll Trio, Paul Burlison.

That group was formed around 1956. Maybe Johnny, Dorsey, and Paul were a little too close to Elvis, Scotty, and Bill, but for whatever reason, Sam Phillips turned them down when they auditioned for Sun. The trio took off for New York, where they earned a spot on TV's *Ted Mack Amateur Hour*. After winning three weeks straight, they were signed to the Decca subsidiary Coral Records in New York, and appeared in the 1956 movie *Rock Rock Rock*. Their version of jump blues bandleader Tiny Bradshaw's "Train Kept a Rollin' " remains among the greatest rockabilly records ever made.

But the raw rockabilly of the Burnettes was going out of style as quick as you could say "Be Bop a Lulu," and, though they remain rockabilly icons, none of the Rock 'n' Roll Trio's records followed Elvis up the charts. They broke up in 1957 and Johnny headed to Hollywood, hopping freights with a buddy.

When he got there, he picked up a tourist's map of the stars' homes, looking for Ozzie and Harriet's house. There, he sat on the front porch waiting for Ricky Nelson to come home. By then, the young TV star was already a teen idol and the first music-video rocker, performing his songs on *The Adventures of Ozzie and Harriet*. Nelson was a big fan of the Memphis sound, having started singing in response to a girlfriend's crush on Elvis. He also knew the Rock 'n' Roll Trio's records, so it wasn't hard for Johnny to convince him to do some of the brothers' material. As a team and individually, the Burnettes wrote some of Nelson's biggest hits, including "Waitin' in School" (1957), "Believe What You Say" (1958), and "It's Late" (1959).

Their old boxing skills also came in handy in the wild Hollywood scene. In Phillip Bashe's Nelson biography, *Teenage Idol*, he writes that Ricky, Johnny, and Dorsey and Eddie Cochran were visiting Cochran's girlfriend Sharon Sheeley's Hollywood apartment, "when a glassy-eyed stranger entered." Everyone figured he was someone else's friend, until he pulled a knife and said, "I came here to kill one of you." He didn't know he had two of the best bouncers in West Memphis to deal with first. "Dorsey picked this kid up and pitched him down three flights of stairs," Sharon told Bashe.

Their performing careers were showing far less impact — at least until 1960, when another pair of musical brothers, songwriters Bob and Dick Sherman (who later wrote "Supercalifragilistic-expialidocious," "It's a Small World," and other classic Disney fare) ran into Dorsey. Dick recalls paying the elder Burnette brother ten dollars or so to sing a demonstration record for a new Sherman song. In an odd twist, the demo wound up in Johnny's hands. He turned the Shermans' "You're Sixteen" into his comeback smash, launching his solo career in 1960 with a Top 10 pop hit and a gold record. In the end, both Burnettes' careers were cut short. Johnny died at thirty on August 14, 1964, in an evening boating accident on California's Clear Lake, when his small fishing boat was rammed by a cabin cruiser. Dorsey died at fifty-seven of a heart attack in 1979, the same year Johnny's son Rocky revived the family tradition, scoring a pop hit with the rockabilly-flavored "Tired of Toein' the Line." Dorsey's son Billy Burnette also made a name in modern rock, spending a few years fronting Fleetwood Mac in the late eighties after Lindsey Buckingham quit.

No one expected anything resembling long careers to come out of those early days of rock and roll. Just a few years after Elvis had first hit with "That's All Right (Mama)" the rock revolution began losing steam. In 1958, Elvis entered the army, reemerging in 1960 to make a few great records such as "Little Sister" and "(Marie's the Name of) His Latest Flame." Then he was off to Hollywood to star in what was probably the worst, most financially successful series of films of all time.

While their music lived on, time was not kind to the rockabillies themselves. Jerry Lee Lewis, after making such incendiary records as "Great Balls of Fire," "Whole Lotta Shaking Going On," "Breathless," "High School Confidential," and dozens of other great, if lesser-known, recordings, virtually lost his career in 1958 after he married his thirteen-year-old cousin Myra. Carl Perkins never recovered the momentum he lost in that 1956 car wreck and slipped into alcoholism, spending much of the sixties as a minor member of Johnny Cash's country troupe.

It was an incredibly volatile time in pop music. The gap between Elvis's first Sun single and his army induction was barely three years — a thousand days from shy Memphis kid to the dominant superstar in American music. In that light, Parker's game plan of moving Presley away from his teenage rock and roll audience makes some sense. The Colonel wasn't above hawking souvenir photos of Elvis at a dime apiece to screaming fans, but he saw rock and roll as that same sort of nickel-and-dime scam, a fad that would be over in a few months, if not a few weeks. It was a faddish decade, after all, with that other Tennessean, Davy Crockett, selling millions of coonskin caps after Walt Disney's 1954 TV series. Nineteen fifty-eight saw the sale of 100 million Hula Hoops. Make as much fast cash as you could, Colonel Tom thought, then get out of rock and roll. Get into a field where there was staying power and real money, like the movies. Even a few years later, the Beatles all figured they might be out of business within a year of their first records. In early interviews, they'd often talk about becoming shop-keepers when it all blew over; Ringo planned to open a beauty salon.

Of course, Parker was always a terrible gambler, and he folded his rock and roll cards a bit prematurely. He took Elvis out of the game long before the rock revolution of the sixties, when the Bea-tles, the Stones, Bob Dylan, and the Memphis soul movement would take the stage. But Parker believed that in order to survive Elvis needed to appeal to older audiences, much as his idol Dean Martin did. So Elvis headed west, where, except for the occasional decent film song, he would record almost nothing worthwhile until his 1968 NBC TV special and his subsequent return to Memphis and Chips Moman's American Studios.

At American, Moman was taking the Memphis sound and bringing it into pop music through such stars as Neil Diamond and Dusty Springfield as well as local rock bands like the Gentrys and the Box Tops. By then, it seemed, everyone wanted some of that Memphis magic; at John Lennon's insistence, even the Beat-les were planning to record their 1966 album *Revolver* at Stax, at least until local musicians' union demands made it cost-prohibitive. A year earlier, when the Yardbirds played Memphis, guitarist Jeff Beck tracked down Sam Phillips to record his band at Sun. By then the old Memphis Recording Service was closed, and Phillips was operating at 639 Madison; there the Yardbirds, under the watchful eye of Sam Phillips and his older son Knox, recorded "Train Kept a Rollin'," itself inspiring Aerosmith's version of a decade later.

But even if he set his sights too low, Colonel Parker got what he aimed for — a bankable movie star. Elvis churned out successful movies, surrounded by a crew of friends and hangers-on.

It didn't have to be that way, says Mike Stoller, half of Leiber &

Stoller, the songwriter team behind "Jailhouse Rock," "Hound Dog," "Charlie Brown," and dozens more seminal rock and R & B songs. The pair worked on a number of Elvis's early, best movies, notably *King Creole* and *Jailhouse Rock*. It was around that time that some very heavy Hollywood hitters took notice of Elvis's screen presence and came up with a serious project — a musical version of Nelson Algren's *A Walk on the Wild Side*. "Jerry had met a top agent in New York who had this idea and he wanted us to write the score for it and Budd Schulberg [Oscar-winning screen-writer of *On the Waterfront*] wanted to do the screenplay and [*On the Waterfront* director Elia] Kazan wanted to direct it."

Leiber & Stoller presented the idea to his contact with Parker, Jean Aberbach, who helped run Elvis's music publishing company. He told Stoller he'd speak to the Colonel about it.

"And the message came back, 'If you ever dare try to interfere in the career of Elvis Presley you'll never work in New York or Hollywood or any other town.' They just wanted to grind out what they knew they could do. [For them, Elvis was] the Golden Goose."

That's just one of the countless missed opportunities in Elvis's career, and some of the most intriguing were right in Elvis's Memphis backyard. What if RCA had been as forward-thinking as Atlantic was with Stax a few years later and, instead of merely "buying" Elvis, had signed Sun to a distribution deal? Sam Phillips could have remained Elvis's producer, while having the resources to develop and properly promote the rest of Sun's amazing stable of talent. What if the Colonel had allowed Elvis to remain contemporary in the sixties, perhaps teaming him with some of the songwriting greats from Stax Records: Otis Redding, Steve Cropper, Eddie Floyd, or the platinum team of David Porter and Isaac Hayes. Imagine Otis and Elvis in a duet on "Dreams to Remember," accompanied by Booker T. & the MGs and the Memphis Horns.

But Parker always chose the path of least resistance and easiest

money, and Elvis, who had apparently found the strong father figure he'd long been searching for, dutifully followed Parker's lead.
At his death at eighty-seven in 1997, Parker remained a highly
controversial figure. Country veteran Hank Snow, a former partner of Parker's and a key figure in bringing Elvis to national attention and getting him signed to Snow's label, RCA Records,
wrote disgustedly of Parker's business dealings in his 1994 autobiography. Snow called Parker "the most egotistical, obnoxious
human I have ever had dealings with." Dick Clark, the eternal
host of *American Bandstand*, shares that view, calling Parker's relationship with Elvis "the classic example of horrendous mis-
management."

By the late sixties, the rock revolution was raging at Graceland's
front door. While Elvis was playing at being a movie star out in
Hollywood, a new generation of Memphis musicians was coming
of age. As they did in the rest of the country, the Beatles inspired
dozens of young garage bands in East Memphis, Germantown,
and the Midtown area. The difference was that in Memphis, the
city's long musical tradition meant that everybody knew some musicians; good music teachers were easy to come by; the pawnshops
lining Beale were well stocked with used instruments; and small
recording studios owned by Sam Phillips wanna-bes began crop-
ping up like weeds in the sidewalk.

The mid-sixties saw a bumper crop of Memphis one-hit won-
ders. The Hombres scored with "Bottle of Wine"; the Gentrys,
fronted by the manic Larry Raspberry, topped the charts with the
very British Invasion–styled "Keep on Dancing." Former Sun session man Stan Kesler, who had played steel guitar in the Snearly
Ranch Boys, produced Sam the Sham & the Pharaohs' "Wooly
Bully." And when Chips Moman and his crack staff of American
Studios writers and producers turned their attention to sixteen-
year-old Alex Chilton and his band the Box Tops, the resulting
"The Letter" and "Cry Like a Baby" (the latter's hook provided by
an electric-sitar-wielding Reggie Young) topped the charts in 1967.

They were supported by local radio and by George Klein, who had continued Dewey Phillips's multimedia tradition with a local TV show and even hosted Saturday matinees at Goldsmith's department store downtown. Open to girls only (store owners wanted them to shop for clothes and makeup, not boys), the shows featured top local bands.

With kids from his hometown outshining him on the charts and the Beatles proclaimed as geniuses for *Sgt. Pepper's*, Elvis (who, by contrast, spent much of 1967 making the movies *Easy Come Easy Go*, *Double Trouble*, and *Clambake*) caught some of that fire. He briefly broke from Parker's iron grip to remind everybody just who had started the whole thing. After warming up with a few hot country singles, Elvis went back "home," getting back to his rockabilly roots on NBC TV's *Elvis* special. It aired on December 3, 1968, almost twelve years to the day after the Million Dollar Quartet sessions. Clad in black leather for an informal segment that was a precursor to MTV's *Unplugged*, surrounded by an audience just a few feet away, Elvis rocked with the old abandon. He was backed by his early rockabilly cohorts, Scotty Moore and drummer D. J. Fontana (bassist Bill Black had died of a brain tumor in 1965). Even the show's big production numbers couldn't smother that rock and roll flame.

Elvis was still burning a few months later when he returned to Memphis for the breakthrough sessions with Chips Moman at American Studios. It was a brave move: By January 1969, the King was in exile, a stranger in his own hometown, as he would sing in one of the best songs from those sessions. Moman's ace band had turned into a well-oiled hit machine. The music they'd been making with Neil Diamond and the rest had spent much more time at the top of the charts than anything Elvis had done in a long while.

Even so, he was still Elvis. Guitarist Reggie Young recalled the mood shortly before he and the rest of the American band, now dubbed the Memphis Boys, performed at B. B. King's Beale club in 1994. "The artists we had been cutting, they were all in the Top

10. So it was hard for us to be impressed by anybody that came in that back door at American. But one thing I'll definitely never forget, that's when he walked in. When the back door opened and he walked in, everybody backed up a step. It was, 'Wow! That's Elvis Presley.' I was amazed at the reaction that I had myself. We had been doing big-name artists, but I was in awe, like a fan, and we all had that same reaction."

From Elvis in Memphis was an album filled with promise, a record that found the King flexing muscles that hadn't been used for years. With a sound that owed as much to Stax and contemporary country as it did to his rock and roll roots, Elvis had finally made a real record again, one that didn't depend on a feeble film plot. Young remembered Moman showing little deference to Presley, even telling him when he was singing off-key. In addition, the sessions were closed to the Memphis Mafia, Elvis's paid crew of hangers-on. Free from distraction, Elvis thrived in the intensely musical atmosphere.

It should have been the beginning of another major phase in the thirty-four-year-old Presley's career. He could have cemented his comeback with a return to the rock circuit — Elvis headlining rock festivals, Elvis at the Fillmores East and West. Instead, RCA chose to diminish his momentum with a second Memphis album pulled together using lesser cuts from the same sessions. Within a year, the still-youthful King of Rock 'n' Roll found himself booked back into Colonel Parker's favorite Las Vegas pleasure domes. Elvis was in his prime — years younger than Bono, Michael Stipe, and the guys in Metallica are today — and twenty years younger than Mick Jagger was in 1997, as the Rolling Stones launched yet another worldwide stadium tour. But instead of new worlds to conquer, Elvis found himself beginning the final downward spiral of a career that never fulfilled its early promise.

In Vegas, Elvis played out his life in the big rooms, drawing huge crowds of middle-aged fans, frequently taking his lounge act on the road to hockey arenas around the country. His last concert was held in Indiana. On August 16, 1977, Elvis died in Memphis, his health weakened by years of prescription drug abuse. The cozy world of payrolled yes-men that had cocooned Elvis for almost twenty years had finally been his undoing.

Sales of Elvis records boomed following his death, as cynics joked that it had all been a smart career move. Since then, the enduring power of Elvis has amazed even the most devoted fans. From a stamp that almost single-handedly put the U.S. Post Office in the black (according to the U.S. Postal Service's chief operations officer William Henderson, sales of Presley stamps and related products such as T-shirts, jigsaw puzzles, etc., totaled more than $50 million, as of September 1994) to the huge success of Graceland, which annually draws almost seven hundred thousand, the Presley mystique grows stronger every year.

Even after the mountains of books about the Elvis phenomenon, the question remains: Why Elvis? It was a phenomenon whose impact an entire industry has tried tirelessly to re-create for more than forty years since, always falling short of the mark. In the end, Elvis was simply the right person at just the right moment in time. Superficially, he may have filled the alienated teen-idol void James Dean left vacant when his Porsche Spyder crashed on September 30, 1955, but there was more to it than that.

Like every other form of American popular music — jazz, blues, country, gospel — rock and roll could only have come from the South. And that first rock and roll star could only have come from Memphis, where the taboo of race mixing made his bumping-and-grinding R & B a very tasty piece of forbidden fruit. Earlier, the country music pendulum had swung from the pop of Jimmy Wakely to the hardcore honky-tonk of Hank Williams; in the blues, the crooners moved over for the harder Delta sounds of Howlin' Wolf and Muddy Waters. Pop, as usual, was last on board, but Elvis was the perfect antidote to Rosemary Clooney's novelty songs or Tony Bennett's bland covers of Hank Williams.

Memphis had been moving toward the creation of Elvis for

most of the twentieth century. By the twenties, there was already
a sizable white audience for the blues in Memphis; in the forties,
that audience had grown enough to make Dewey Phillips a major
radio star; by the fifties, a generation of white musicians came of
age making that music their own, doing it their own way. Elvis,
with his dark good looks and mama's-boy vulnerability, made that
sound accessible to mainstream (read "white") America, an America that wasn't quite ready for the real thing.

The next logical step was already on its way, as young white
rock and country musicians were beginning to work with black
R & B and jazz players to create the musical revolution known as
Memphis soul.

10

▼▼▼▼▼▼▼▼▼▼▼▼▼▼▼▼▼▼▼▼▼▼▼▼▼▼

Soulsville, U.S.A.

The club is packed so full you couldn't leave if you wanted to. The balcony throbs beneath the pounding feet of the crowd upstairs, while the tiny dance floor in front of the stage is shoulder to shoulder, swaying hip to swaying hip. Onstage, a four-piece band is working out on a deceptively simple blues riff. The drummer keeps perfect time, in that infectiously lazy, just-behind-the-beat Memphis mode; the bass player, his Fender Precision resting comfortably atop a paunch that can be blamed in part on the ever-present pair of Buds sitting atop his amplifier, plays a loping, unstoppable bass line that shakes even the most sedentary booty. The guitarist plays a Telecaster-style instrument, as basic an electric guitar as can be made — six strings attached to a neck screwed onto a flat hunk of wood with two single-coil pickups — in a style that's based on rhythm, not single-string fireworks. Off to the side, wearing a Buddha-like expression, the organist sits serenely behind his weathered Hammond B-3, effortlessly percolating along. There's a sense of dynamics here that's just about extinct in these modern digital times, an almost telepathic communication among the players that creates an unparalleled sense of tension and syncopation. In a pop music world of here today, gone tonight, where louder and flashier is the rule, Booker T. & the MGs remain the sanctified exception, sounding just as good in the nineties as they did in the sixties. And "Green Onions" fills dance floors just as fast in the era of Beavis & Butt-head as it did in the days of Abbott and Costello. Say amen.

The occasion is the MGs' Beale Street 1992 homecoming, a three-night stand at B. B. King's Blues Club. Sam Moore of Sam and Dave (Dave Prater died in a 1988 car crash) will sing, as will Eddie "Knock on Wood" Floyd. And many other local Stax veterans are on hand. The band behind Moore and Floyd includes Marvell Thomas, son of Rufus and brother of Carla, the first two Stax stars, and a longtime Stax musician in his own right; guitarist Michael Toles, another Stax sideman; and the Memphis Horns, saxophonist Andrew Love and trumpeter Wayne Jackson, the pair who have kept the Stax sound alive backing Elvis Presley, Rod Stewart, and seemingly everyone else in the music business. They're joined for the occasion by baritone saxman Floyd Newman, another Stax original who has returned to performing after retiring from teaching in the Memphis public schools. In the audience is Jim Stewart, cofounder of Stax, and such Stax alumni as J. Blackfoot, who fronted one of the last great Stax acts, the Soul Children.

It's another testament to the timelessness of Memphis music in general and soul in particular — as if one was needed. Just a few months before the B. B. King's gig, the MGs were Neil Young's band on a tour with Pearl Jam that was named *Rolling Stone's* Tour of the Year. In 1995, the MGs were the rhythm section chosen to back a Who's Who of rock and soul legends at the opening concert for the Rock and Roll Hall of Fame.

There were Stax stars before Booker T. & the MGs came along, but it was this band that gave Stax its trademark sound. Booker T. & the MGs is the Memphis sound boiled down to its purest essence. Unlike Motown, whose overproduced, tinny pop sound crossed over by whitewashing rhythm and blues, Stax stayed true to its funky southern roots. Little wonder Motown called itself "Hitsville, U.S.A." while Stax chose "Soulsville, U.S.A."

It would be an amazing story no matter when or where it happened, but as Stax founder Stewart said in 1992 when he inducted Booker T. & the MGs into the Rock and Roll Hall of Fame: "Black and white, working together in Memphis, Tennessee, in 1962, you were making more than just music history." The Stax recipe cooked up that Memphis stew of R & B, country, rock and roll, and the raw, emotional range of gospel, making it all seem like the easiest, simplest recipe in the world.

The Memphis music story, as we've seen, rings the same changes over and over, all the while introducing the variations that keep it interesting. W. C. Handy took the Mississippi blues (itself a mix of African and European musical traditions), smoothed some of its rough edges by adding popular-song touches, and arranged it for his legitimate brass band. George D. Hay countrified Beale Street vaudeville and created the Grand Ole Opry. Elvis and the other Memphis rockabillies took R & B out of the Beale clubs and black radio stations and put it on the pop charts, making southern blues part of the identity of just about every white teenager.

During the most explosive period of the civil rights movement, Stax took that musical integration even deeper. The heartbeat of Stax came from its half-black, half-white house band, its multiracial songwriting staff, and the songs themselves, which mixed down-home blues and R & B with more than a little country music. "Country music is white man's blues and the blues is black man's country music," goes the old musical saying, and nowhere was that truer than at Stax. Otis Redding, the biggest Stax star, was even nicknamed "Country."

But the catalyst that turned R & B into soul was gospel music, which brought the restrained power and cathartic release of Sunday morning to Saturday night, adding "churchy" harmonies and chord progressions. And like blues, jazz, and rock and roll, the roots of African American gospel run deep in Memphis.

Tennessee's Fisk Jubilee Singers had popularized choral spirituals after the Civil War, but the choir's stodgily formal arrangements were a far cry from the sounds that came pounding out of the Pentecostal and Holiness churches. There, much as they had been in Africa, prayer and singing were direct routes to the divine. The names of the divinities might have changed, but achieving trancelike states and speaking in tongues were still the goals of worshipers. Cultural anthropologists have cited the similarity between the Pentecostal services and the voodoo and Santeria rites still practiced by the descendants of slaves in Haiti, Cuba, and other tropical countries.

In 1907, the stage was set for gospel music to develop in Memphis when the Church of God in Christ (COGIC) was founded there by Baptist preacher Charles H. Mason. It would become the largest and most powerful African American religious sect.

But Memphis became a center for gospel music largely through the effort of one woman, Lucie E. Campbell. One of the two or three most important composers in the creation of modern gospel music, according to singer and gospel historian Berniece Reagon, Campbell wrote several of the most popular gospel songs of all time. "In the Upper Room" was a major success for Mahalia Jackson, who recorded it twice, while her "Jesus Gave Me Water" was recorded on March 1, 1951, by one of the most important and influential gospel quartets of all time, the Soul Stirrers. The occasion was the first session featuring the group's new twenty-year-old lead-singing phenomenon, Sam Cooke, born in Clarksdale, Mississippi. Before he crossed over to secular superstardom in 1957, the Soul Stirrers' charismatic front man drew an unprecedented young audience for gospel. Cooke remains one of the most important figures in the birth of soul.

While her influence on gospel continues today, Campbell's story begins in antebellum Mississippi. She was born in 1885 in Duck Hill, Mississippi, the granddaughter of a former slave once owned by Lloyd T. Binford — the father of the future censor of Memphis, Lloyd junior. She was born aboard a workers' train, her

mother, Isabella, having just delivered lunch to her father, Burrell.
It was a story she told often, as proof of her specialness. Educated
in Memphis, Campbell graduated from Kortrecht High School at
fourteen and was soon teaching school. But she gained fame as
musical director of the National Baptist Convention, a position
she held for more than forty years. There she set the standard for
religious music in the black Baptist Church and introduced such
gospel greats as the father of modern gospel, Thomas A. Dorsey
(the erstwhile Georgie Tom of "Tight Like That" fame). Dorsey
went on to create a thousand-song gospel catalog that included the
classics "Peace in the Valley" and "Precious Lord." But before he
could do that, he had to convince the faithful that his conversion
was sincere. In that, Dorsey was given a huge push by Campbell,
who gave him her stamp of approval, introducing him to the National Baptist Convention.

Another Campbell protégé was the Reverend William Herbert
Brewster of Memphis. Like Dorsey before him, Brewster received
his introduction to the National Baptist Convention courtesy of
Campbell. A true Memphis musician, Brewster put a bluesy spin
on his sacred music and wrote gospel music's first million-selling
records, "Move On Up a Little Higher," sung by Mahalia Jackson,
and the Clara Ward Singers' "Surely God is Able." After graduat-
ing college, Brewster came to Memphis in 1922 to take the position
of dean in a seminary the National Baptist Convention was to
build. The school was never built and Brewster settled for becoming pastor at a church in South Memphis. But once Brewster
started writing songs like "Move On Up" and "Surely God is Able,"
many of the biggest stars in gospel flocked to his modest East Trigg
Baptist Church for songs, among them Sister Rosetta Tharpe, Mahalia Jackson, the Clara Ward Singers, Sam Cooke, and Brewster's own star singer, Memphian Queen C. Anderson.

By the fifties, gospel was sounding a lot like secular R & B, due
in no small part to former Mississippian Cooke, whose trademark
"whoa-oh"s first turn up in his Soul Stirrers records. R & B was

meeting it halfway, as many of the new stars — most notably including Ray Charles, James Brown, and the Isley Brothers — began
folding gospel into their sound. Bobby "Blue" Bland was another
link in the change from R & B to soul. Bland got his start on record
at Duke, then still based in Memphis, singing with the Beale
Streeters, a recording unit that featured Bland, Johnny Ace, Roscoe
Gordon, and Earl Forrest. Bland's combination of southern blues
with the smoother stylings popularized by black crooners like Billy
Eckstine and Nat King Cole, and a good dose of "churchy" vo-
calizing tossed in, has stood him in good stead during a four-
decade career that has included induction into the Rock and Roll
Hall of Fame and, in 1997, a Grammy Lifetime Achievement
Award. Along with such fifties Duke classics as "Further Up the
Road" and "Stormy Monday," Bland, who makes his home in Germantown, an eastern suburb of Memphis, continues to enjoy hits
on Malaco Records.

By the mid-fifties, of course, the biggest thing in town was Elvis.
And along with dozens of Elvis wanna-bes around Memphis, all
the many would-be Sam Phillipses were looking for their break. It
seemed as if just about every radio buff or electronics hobbyist was
fiddling with recording equipment, dreaming of finding a new
Presley and becoming the next Memphis music mogul. In 1957,
Jim Stewart, a college-educated banker and part-time country fiddler whose country band had earlier been turned down by Phillips,
decided to take the plunge and launch his own label. And launch
it he did. In the era's space-race fever (and the local penchant for
naming record labels after celestial bodies — Sun, Moon, Meteor,
etc.), Stewart called his label Satellite. The first release was a country song Stewart had written called "Blue Roses." It was sung by
Fred Byler, a disc jockey for KWEM, a West Memphis station that
had helped start the careers of Howlin' Wolf and B. B. King and
that had once featured a young Elvis Presley on some of its open-
stage broadcasts. Stewart knew it was always a good idea to have a
disc jockey on your side.

Stewart's "Blue Roses" wilted on the charts, but it was a start. Stewart's country music background included stints with such Memphis bands as Clyde Leoppard and the Snearly Ranch Boys, a group that also included Scotty Moore and Stan Kesler and which played the Eagle's Nest honky-tonk back when Elvis was playing intermissions. But Satellite was not destined to compete with the booming Nashville recording scene. Stewart knew there was plenty of recordable talent around town, and he prevailed on his older sister, Estelle Axton, to loan him the money to improve his recording equipment. Unable to say no to her baby brother, she took a mortgage out on her home, the $2,500 she secured helping Satellite move out of Stewart's garage into a more legitimate studio.

As Sam Phillips had learned before him, the best way to start a Memphis record label is to record Rufus Thomas. Thomas has been an inescapable fixture on the Memphis music scene since he made his Beale stage debut at seven years of age, playing a frog in a Rabbit Foot Minstrels show. A pioneering disc jockey on WDIA, he hosted the amateur shows at the Beale Palace and provided Phillips with Sun's first hit when he recorded "Bear Cat" as an answer to Big Mama Thornton's "Hound Dog." For his Satellite debut, Thomas teamed with his seventeen-year-old daughter Carla on the duet "Cause I Love You." The song became a local hit and Carla followed it up with a song she'd written as a young teen, "Gee Whiz." It was a good time for ushering in new eras. Carla's sweet pop confection was released in November 1960, the same month that saw the election of the young, charismatic John Kennedy. The Memphis teenager's song crossed over to the pop charts to become Satellite's first major hit.

By then, Satellite had drawn the attention of Atlantic Records co-owner Jerry Wexler, a connection that was to spell the future of Stewart's operation. Wexler was then vice president of the New York–based independent label, having helped build Atlantic into one of the premier R & B and jazz labels when both those genres were enjoying something of a golden age. Atlantic's jazz roster featured John Coltrane, Ornette Coleman, and the Modern Jazz Quartet; its list of R & B artists included Ray Charles, the Clovers, the Drifters, Clyde McPhatter, Ruth Brown, and the company's hit franchise — the team of songwriter-producers Jerry Leiber and Mike Stoller and the group the Coasters.

By the end of the fifties, Wexler was disillusioned with the East Coast scene. When pressing plant operator Buster Williams told him about the regional success of "Cause I Love You," Wexler flew down to Memphis to check Satellite out for himself and wound up signing a distribution deal. When "Gee Whiz" broke out, Wexler was back to cut another deal. He found that things worked differently in the segregated South than in Manhattan. Unable to find an integrated restaurant where he could take Carla and Rufus for dinner, he had them up to his room at the Peabody, discreetly taking the freight elevator. Nonetheless, after the Thomases had left, Wexler was rousted by the local vice squad.

Even that couldn't sour him on the new sound he'd found in the city. "Despite the racist crap, the music in Memphis was a marvel," he later wrote in his autobiography, *The Rhythm and the Blues*. He was tired of New York, where, he wrote, "the arrangers were out of ideas, the songwriters out of material, the session players out of licks, and I was out of inspiration. Inspiration was on the boil at [Satellite]."

Much of that inspiration was due to Chips Moman, who played a key role in the early days of the label. The young guitarist came from LaGrange, Georgia, but had spent some time on the West Coast, where he had played with transplanted Memphians Johnny and Dorsey Burnette and rockabilly diehard Gene Vincent. He started out as a guitarist for some early Satellite sessions, but soon found his place on the other side of the studio window as a producer and arranger. It was Moman who found the Capitol, the old movie theater at 926 East McLemore that became the studio's permanent home in 1960. It was the unique, bass-heavy acoustics caused by the theater's sloping floor that gave the label its signature sound, many say. Moman also helped form the label's early session groups and is reputed to have named the house rhythm section the MGs after his British sports car, although the label's official promo says it stands for Memphis Group.

After Carla's "Gee Whiz," Satellite's next hit was "Last Night," an instrumental performed by an informal session band and attributed to the Mar-Keys, an Estelle Axton pun on the theater marquee in front of the studio. With Gilbert Caples playing the tenor sax solo and baritone saxophonist Floyd Newman moaning the vocal hook, "Ohhhh, last night," it was released in June 1961 and became the label's first genuine pop hit, hitting No. 3 on the pop charts (No. 2 on the R & B lists). Stewart was reluctant even to release it, but Estelle was adamant, largely because her son Packy played in the sax section and other members of his Messick High School band, the Royal Spades, also took part. Since the Mar-Keys didn't actually exist, the Royal Spades were recruited to be the Mar-Keys for road tours. The group included a crew of future Memphis music stars: MG-to-be Steve Cropper (who'd played piano on "Last Night"), Memphis Horn Wayne Jackson (the record's trumpeter), guitarist Charlie Freeman (who passed on to Cropper lessons he'd been taking from Memphis jazz guitarist Lynn Vernon), and baritone saxist Don Nix, who would later write the blues standard "Going Down" and play a key role in Atlantic signing Delaney & Bonnie.

In the middle of the Mar-Key's hit, when another Satellite Records started making noises about a lawsuit, Stewart took the "St" from his name and the "Ax" from Axton and redubbed the label Stax. And on the head of steam generated by "Last Night," Memphis soul was born.

The next Stax hit maker was William Bell, whose dignified presence and restrained vocal style put "You Don't Miss Your Water" on the charts in early 1962. Bell's high school group, the Del Rios, had been popular around Memphis, winning the Annual

Mid-South Talent Contest in 1956. They won a week's trip to Chicago and a one-record deal with Meteor, the Memphis label owned by Lester Bihari of the RPM/Modern Records Bihari family. They performed as the vocal group with Phineas Newborn Sr.'s R & B band at such spots as Cliff Miller's Flamingo Room at Hernando and Beale, and in West Memphis at the Plantation Inn. Bell left the group to go to college, but after a semester Phineas called with an offer to play New York, and Bell took a break from academia to accept. A year later he was back in Memphis waiting to be called up for the draft. While he was home he ran into Moman, who suggested he make a record for Stax. Bell had written "You Don't Miss Your Water" in New York, and Moman and Stewart both liked the song. By the spring of 1962 it had cracked the Top 100. More important, the song, with its southern lyric approach and laid-back groove, marked the beginning of the Stax sound. Today, the word "Stax" conjures a sound as distinctive as "Dixieland" or "reggae," but in its early days (as it would in its final days) the label threw anything against the wall, hoping something stuck. Just how scattered the label's early approach was can be readily heard on the nine-CD box, *The Complete Stax/Volt Singles 1959–1968*, as various R & B styles alternate with attempts at pop and rock. Stax even recorded Beale jug band legend Gus Cannon, then well into his seventies, in hopes of cashing in on the Rooftop Singers' 1963 hit version of his "Walk Right In."

Bell was "Stax's first real soul star," according to Memphis music historian Peter Guralnick's outstanding book, *Sweet Soul Music*, but it was the formation of Booker T. & the MGs that began the label's golden age. Booker T. Jones had earned a reputation as the boy genius of Booker T. Washington High School, breaking into the music business while barely a teenager, playing on Beale with Willie Mitchell's band at the Flamingo Room, across the street from where Mitchell's Beale club stands today. Adept at a variety of instruments, Jones found work playing various horns, electric bass, and keyboards, but was particularly fond of the electric organ.

The Hammond company had introduced the electronic organ way back in 1935, but unlike the electric standard guitar, which Gibson brought out the following year, it took a while for Hammond's instrument to catch on. At five hundred pounds, including the fan-driven Leslie speaker which provides its trademark quavering sound, the Hammond B-3 is a cumbersome dinosaur in today's digital, microchip age. But compared to the truly massive pipe organs that preceded it, it was downright petite. Former Louis Jordan band member Wild Bill Davis was the first R & B player to use the Hammond, but organist Bill Doggett would have the first major hit with it in 1955 with "Honky Tonk." In the late fifties, when jazzman Jimmy Smith emerged as a B-3 master, the organ trio — Hammond, guitar, and drums — became a mainstay of funky, hard-bobbing jazz.

Jones was on organ that fateful Sunday afternoon in the late spring of 1962 when Stewart called a jingle session at the studio. The teenager was on summer break before entering his junior year in high school. Estelle was in front of the studio, doing some paperwork in the Satellite record store, which she managed and which provided her the perfect vantage point for staying current with the black community's musical tastes. In the studio, Booker T. was at the Hammond, Steve Cropper of the Mar-Keys was on guitar, Al Jackson Jr. (whom many say was the group's de facto leader) was on drums, and Lewis Steinberg, of the prominent Memphis African American musical family (his father Milton had played with W. C. Handy) played bass. Accounts vary on whether the singer failed to appear, showed up drunk, or merely got through with the jingle quickly. Whatever the situation, there was time left over in the session, so the band started some instrumental jamming. Stewart recorded one piece that sounded pretty good and Axton recalls helping them come up with the title, "Behave Yourself." The B side was a blues groove that was so funky that Axton recalls with a chuckle that the musicians joked, "Oh that stinks. That really stinks." Axton, an avid gardener, came up with an idea inspired by the weed pulling she'd been doing in the sticky

Memphis heat. "Well, if it stinks," she remembers saying, "why don't you call it 'Green Onions'? Because *nothing* stinks as bad as green onions."

That sort of easy informality resulted in the most consistent hit-making machine Memphis has ever seen. The Atlantic people, from Wexler to producer-engineer Tom Dowd, were continually amazed and charmed by the seeming ease with which the Stax family turned out hits. Over and over again, Stax veterans tell similar stories of other classic sessions where a word or a phrase provided the seed of a hit record, or a chance meeting resulted in a lifetime partnership. "I admired what they were doing," says Dowd, who handled the first stereo Stax album, *Otis Blue*, in 1965, and who occasionally visited Memphis to repair and update Stax equipment throughout the label's deal with Atlantic. "They were doing much the same thing that we were doing in the late forties going into the fifties. They had a simple Ampex machine that was of moderately good quality. They had the simplest form of a mixer that Ampex made to match their machine."

Dowd still comes to Memphis, but nowadays it's to produce albums by Lynyrd Skynyrd or England's Primal Scream at the city's premier studio, Ardent. In 1993, taking a break from the Primal Scream sessions, he recalled his first trip to Stax, coming to town one weekend thirty years earlier when the label was experiencing lengthy production delays. He arrived in Memphis on a Friday night and Stewart took him straight from the airport to the studio. Dowd was familiar with the Ampex tape machine and knew which parts were needed, arranging them to be hand-carried to Memphis by a Delta Airlines stewardess the following day. By Saturday night the machine was fixed, and Booker T. & the MGs, which by then had replaced Steinberg with Royal Spade/Mar-Key bassist Donald "Duck" Dunn, were called into the studio on Sunday afternoon to see how things were really working.

"And Rufus came walking in," Dowd chuckled. "He was coming home from church and he saw the cars. And he said, 'You gotta be working.' And Duck and Steve said, 'Yeah, we're working.' So he said, 'I've got a song I want you to record,' and they said [to me], 'Hey, yeah, take this down.' " Still in his Sunday best, Rufus taught his new song to the band; Dowd, figuring it would just be a demo (a demonstration recording), decided to save a few bucks worth of tape, recording it at 7 1/2 inches per second rather than the standard 15. "And when I went home Monday morning," Dowd concludes with a chuckle, "I had 'Walkin' the Dog' under my arm." That impromptu after-church session became one of the biggest hits of Rufus's long career, reaching No. 5 on the R & B charts and No. 10 on the pop charts, later becoming a concert mainstay for the Rolling Stones, Aerosmith, and dozens of other rock and soul acts. Just another weekend in Memphis.

With Booker T. & the MGs serving as the house rhythm section, Stax had a distinctive sound for its records, but the label still lacked a superstar. That final piece of the Stax puzzle arrived in October 1962, a few months after the MGs hit with "Green Onions." The future Stax superstar arrived driving Johnny Jenkins & the Pinetoppers' rented station wagon from his hometown of Macon, Georgia. Otis Redding had been singing around Macon for years, and had even recorded a local single in 1960, but the visit to Stax turned out to be his big break when he wangled thirty minutes of leftover studio time at the end of Jenkins's session. He failed to make much of an impression with his sound, at the time a derivative mixture of Little Richard and Sam Cooke, but Stax was granted half of the publishing on Redding's first single to ensure the company's support. "Hey Hey Baby" failed to dent the charts — but Nashville disc jockey John R liked the flip side and he told Stewart he thought it could be a hit. In return John R was awarded the label's half of the publishing; not surprisingly, "These Arms of Mine" began appearing on his playlists with greater regularity. It took half a year, but the song finally became a hit, reaching No. 20 on the national R & B charts and No. 85 on the pop charts. It wasn't long before Redding was back at the studio on McLemore.

Chips Moman had angrily left the Stax organization just after the success of "Green Onions" and just before the arrival of Otis Redding, arguably the two most important events in the history of the label. Moman, who felt he wasn't getting his fair share of the company's growing profits, accepted a three-thousand-dollar settlement that he would later parlay into his American Studios. It was that recording facility that would take the Memphis sound full tilt into the pop world with sessions for Dusty Springfield, Neil Diamond, and the last great recordings of Elvis Presley.

MGs guitarist Steve Cropper and Otis eagerly took up Moman's slack. Cropper most directly filled Moman's shoes, playing guitar, producing sessions, and turning into the label's most consistent songwriter, writing, cowriting, or polishing dozens of Stax hits, including "Knock on Wood" and "Raise Your Hand" with Eddie Floyd, and "Mr. Pitiful," "Fa-Fa-Fa-Fa-Fa (Sad Song)," "The Happy Song," and "(Sitting on) The Dock of the Bay" with Otis Redding. Working with Eddie Floyd and Pickett on Pickett's first Atlantic sessions at Stax, Cropper cowrote "In the Midnight Hour," "634-5789," "Don't Fight It," and "Ninety Nine and a Half (Won't Do)." An amazing songbook, but Cropper's taut, concise lead guitar work shouldn't be overlooked: Echoes of Cropper can be heard in the work of thousands of guitarists. Listen to the Band, for example, and you'll hear just how much that group's ensemble sound was influenced by Booker T. & the MGs, and how much Robbie Robertson's lead guitar owes its bite to Cropper's playing.

If Cropper proved to be a masterful jack of all trades in the studio, Redding was the complete artist — singer, performer, songwriter, arranger, and inspirational leader. His list of self-written classics includes "These Arms of Mine," "I've Been Loving You Too Long (cowritten by Jerry Butler), "Respect," "Love Man," and "I've Got Dreams to Remember," as well as those he wrote with Steve Cropper.

The folks at Stax say Redding's energetic stage presence was no act. "Watching him in the studio was like watching a performance," recalls Carla Thomas, Redding's partner for a series of duets that included Lowell Fulsom's "Tramp." And he knew exactly what sound he wanted, she adds. "Even with the drums, although Al [Jackson Jr.] was perfect, he [Redding] would say, 'Ya know, I wish we could do a little . . . Here, let me show you.' We'd do a little joke when we couldn't get something going in the studio with other artists. We'd say, 'Be careful now. We're gonna call Otis on you.'"

Redding also contributed to Stax's signature horn section sound, a sound that trumpeter Wayne Jackson and saxophonist Andrew Love have kept alive for the three decades since. "We learned a lot from Otis," Jackson admits. "He was a natural horn arranger. Everything in his head was time and rhythm. He'd sing horn lines like he'd sing background."

While 1962 was the year it all came together for Stax, things were also coming together for four young rockers from Liverpool. Within a couple of years they were ready to bring their music, borrowed from such Americans as the Everly Brothers and Carl Perkins, back to its source. In February 1964, just as Stax was looking like pop music's next big thing, the Beatles arrived in the States for an appearance on Ed Sullivan. As Elvis had done eight years earlier, when there were far fewer television sets, the Beatles changed pop music overnight. It was the beginning of the British Invasion and while Top 40 radio still played everything from the Beatles to Otis Redding to Johnny Cash, every record label was signing anyone they could find with moptop hair and a British accent. Not coincidentally, Stax had a pretty rough 1964. The label's highest-charting single was Rufus Thomas's "Jump Back," which reached No. 49.

By 1965, things had calmed down a bit and Stax was back on track. That was the year that Sam & Dave first came to the studio and Otis Redding's "Respect" roared up the charts (only to be eclipsed by former Memphian Aretha Franklin's cover). Wexler, who had brought in Sam & Dave, also took the newly signed Wilson Pickett to the studio on McLemore in 1965, where the Stax team put together a complete package singers can only dream about. With backing by Booker T. & the MGs and the Mar-Key Horns, Pickett turned his soulful rasp to a set of soul classics-to-be: "In the Midnight Hour," "634-5789," "Don't Fight It," and "Ninety Nine and a Half (Won't Do)."

As if that weren't enough for a single year, in the fall of 1965, Alvertis Isbell arrived at the label to become national sales and promotion director. A former Washington, D.C., disc jockey, Al Bell was the label's first black executive and he became the owner of Stax in 1972. Despite the label's messy bankruptcy, Bell would come back in the nineties with his Bellmark label, the record company behind the phenomenally successful and absolutely ubiquitous "Daizy Dukes" and "Whoomp! There It Is" singles.

Bell, a Little Rock native and former disc jockey at WLOK in Memphis, the station that produces the annual Stone Soul Picnics in Tom Lee Park, brought Eddie Floyd with him to Memphis. Along with the hits Floyd cowrote for Pickett, he also collaborated with Cropper on his own huge hit, "Knock on Wood." Bell also brought a black consciousness and black presence to the leadership of the label. As Stax had put together an all-star team in the studio, Bell sought to do likewise in the office. Deanie Parker, former assistant executive director of the Memphis in May International Festival, was the publicity department (she also wrote songs, recorded for Volt, and wrote the liner notes for Albert King's classic LP, *Born Under a Bad Sign*). Bell did his job well. The year after he came to work at Stax, the label sold 8 million singles.

The momentum continued and 1967 looked to be the Year of Stax, as the little company in the abandoned movie theater took the Memphis sound further than anyone had thought possible.

By 1967, the Fab Four were no longer touring, spending their time hunkered down with George Martin working on their new album. With Beatlemania abated somewhat, the Stax Revue launched the Memphis Invasion, playing Europe in the spring, just a few weeks before the Beatles changed the pop music rules again, releasing *Sgt. Pepper's Lonely Hearts Club Band*. The Memphis musicians, who in the States were still regularly playing frat parties, found themselves doing sold-out concerts in venerable old theaters in London and Paris, where their music drew a hysterical audience response beyond their wildest dreams.

"That balcony was undulating about six inches, and [with] all the kids up there going and stomping, we expected it to collapse any minute," says producer-engineer Tom Dowd, who accompanied the tour at the request of the musicians both to record shows and provide performers with a familiar face who knew his way around the Continent. "You know how you're at a rock 'n' roll concert and after about ten or fifteen minutes, you play a certain song and ten thousand people come forward? They were amazed by the intensity of some of the crowds, overwhelmed."

But it was the Monterey Pop Festival in June 1967 that pointed the way to the future. Surprisingly, Redding, who was always ready to try something new, hadn't wanted to play the festival, according to his manager, Phil Walden, who later founded Capricorn Records. "Otis considered it a fairly strange request, to perform free for a large gathering of white people on the West Coast and they're going to give it to charity but they didn't say what charity. So he had a lot of questions about it." But Jerry Wexler convinced Redding of the importance of the festival and offered to pay expenses for Booker T. & the MGs and the Mar-Keys horns to back him up.

If the musicians had felt out of their element in Europe, when they landed in the middle of California's Summer of Love they seemed to be visiting another planet. Decked out in their sharpest Continental-style Memphis threads — bought at Lansky's on Beale, of course — they couldn't have looked more out of place among the tie-dyed crowd, recalls Wayne Jackson. "Everybody else was out there cool and laid-back with their long hair and their hippie stuff. And we came on with our little mohair suits and sweaters. It was cold that night, the wind was blowing down the stage. But we just went on and did our thing and they went crazy about it. Booker T. had gone on and then us, and when Otis hit the stage, it was all over for them. They didn't know what hit 'em."

Grateful Dead singer/rhythm guitarist Bob Weir was in the audience that night. Whether Weir'd been dipping into the electric Kool-Aid isn't certain, but the effect Redding's performance had on him was truly mind-blowing. "I was pretty sure I'd just seen God onstage," Weir said in an interview for Rhino Records' Monterey Pop boxed set. "Otis looked to be twelve or fourteen feet tall, stalking the lip of the stage like a caged tiger, just shooting lightning and sparks. He was amazing!"

Monterey was Redding's greatest triumph, and he was arguably the single greatest Stax artist; but the label's biggest hit makers were Sam Moore and Dave Prater. Sam & Dave had been trying for that elusive hit for years in their native Florida on Roulette Records, but it wasn't until Jerry Wexler signed the duo to Atlantic and took them to Stax for a dose of Memphis medicine that everything clicked. By then, David Porter had given up his day job bagging groceries at the Jones Big Star supermarket and was on the Stax staff, singing backup, doing some recording under his own name, and, most important for soul music history (and his future bank balance), writing songs. Porter wrote Sam & Dave's first single, "A Place Nobody Can Find," and cowrote the flip, "Goodnight Baby," with Steve Cropper. But it was the second single, "I Take What I Want," that aligned the planets. That song marked the first collaboration of Porter and Isaac Hayes. Hayes came out of Manassas High School, which had retained the pride, professionalism, and jazz tradition set forth in the twenties by the school's legendary band teacher Jimmie Lunceford. At Manassas, one of Hayes's bands had been the Missiles, a group that included Eddie Harrison, who went on to sing with Stax act the Premiers, and who can still be seen around Memphis fronting his group the Short Kuts.

As a keyboardist, Hayes had been working at local nightspots

Two genera-
tions of
Memphis
could-have-
beens: The
Burnettes'
Rock 'n' Roll
Trio (*above*),
their train
about to start
rollin', and
Alex Chilton's
Big Star—
theirs never
left the station
(*left*).

Jim Stewart (*above left*) of Stax and some members of his stable:

William Bell (*right*), "Stax's first real soul star," in the words of Peter Guralnick.

Below: Rufus Thomas (*left*), with children Carla, Vanesse, and Marvell.

Booker T. & the MGs: Donald "Duck" Dunn, Booker T. Jones,
Steve Cropper, and Al Jackson Jr.

Otis Redding, who electrified the Soulsville, U.S.A. studio.

Above: The ill-fated young Bar-Kays (*left to right*): Ben Cauley, Ronnie Caldwell, Carl Cunningham, Phalon Jones, Jimmie King, and James Alexander.

Cauley was the only survivor of the crash that also killed Otis Redding; Alexander was spared when he opted for a later flight.

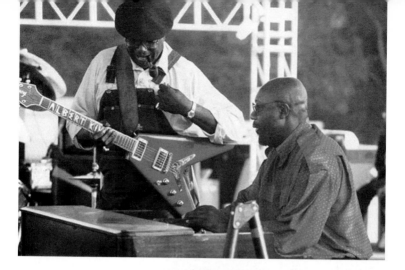

Above: Albert King (*left*) and Isaac Hayes: Stax soulmates, reunited in the 1990s for the Delta Blues Festival.

Full Gospel Tabernacle

787 Hale Road
Memphis, Tennessee
(901)396-9192
May 21, 1995

Reverend Al Green
Pastor and Founder

Above right: Al Green (*right*) with Hi producer Willie Mitchell and fright-wig comedienne Phyllis Diller; by the 1990s Reverend Green had reconciled gospel and soul in his own heart (*left*).

Passing on the music: Carl Perkins with Paul McCartney
(*top, facing page*), backstage at the 1993 Liberty Bowl show;
Jerry Lee Lewis (*bottom, facing page*) jams with Memphis Horns
Andrew Love and Wayne Jackson, and Ben Cauley of the Bar-
Kays; (*above*) Billy Lee Riley with Bob Dylan.

Junior Kimbrough—who, like Carl Perkins, passed on just as this book was going to press.

Isaac Tigrett and Gary Belz of the House of Blues, trying to help the music endure.

such as the Plantation Inn in West Memphis with baritone saxist Floyd Newman's band. When Newman was set for a Stax record session in the fall of 1963, Hayes and the band's drummer, Howard Grimes, who would go on to fame with the Hi Records rhythm section, wrote "Frog Stomp." Stewart liked Hayes's playing and offered him a regular studio gig, since Booker T. was off at college at the time.

In that, the Memphis music scene hadn't changed much since Elvis had rushed into the movies as soon as he got the chance. Music wasn't seen as the most reliable career, and a surprising number of Stax artists chose college over music, at least temporarily. Booker T., Carla Thomas, and William Bell were three who opted for the university, though Bell did later drop out to go to New York with Phineas Newborn Sr.

Writing for Sam & Dave, Hayes and Porter became one of the premier songwriting teams in soul music. "Soul Man," "You Don't Know Like I Know," "Hold On! I'm Comin' " (inspired, the story goes, by Porter's shout from the bathroom to an impatient Hayes), "You Got Me Hummin'," "When Something Is Wrong with My Baby," "I Thank You," and "Wrap It Up" were some of the songs created by Hayes and Porter for the duo.

Sam & Dave's records were released on Stax, which showed the Memphis label's growing clout, since it was Atlantic that had actually signed them. "Hold On! I'm Comin' " became Stax's first No. 1 R & B hit since "Green Onions." The Sam & Dave sound, a series of hook-filled songs with straining, emotional vocals, was as influential as it was popular, as thousands of young garage bands worked up their own versions of the duo's hits. Going to high school in Long Island, New York, the teenage Billy Joel would go to a record shop in the black section of Hempstead to buy the latest Stax/Volt singles. "The Hempstead bus station had all the really good 45s that you couldn't buy, like, at a Sam Goody," Joel recalls. "And we'd flip those records and learn the B sides and spring this on a suburban white audience and they would think, 'This is some great stuff we've never heard before.' " In the early sixties, the American pop business was pushing whitewashed singers like Fabian and Frankie Avalon, and Motown was presenting a lighter shade of soul, but Joel says, "The real stuff was coming out of places like Memphis by black artists. That was exciting and it was being covered by a lot of bands in Philadelphia, New Jersey, and New York, like the Rascals. That was what the scene was when I was in the Hassles" (his first professional band, whose major-label debut was a cover of one of those B sides, Sam & Dave's "You Got Me Hummin' ").

But just when Stax seemed unstoppable, tragedy struck. Redding's manager, Phil Walden, says Otis was a changed man after Monterey. He stayed in California, spending a week on a houseboat in Sausalito, listening to the weird new sounds on the Beatles' groundbreaking *Sgt. Pepper.* Out of that pensive period came a new direction for Redding, one that mixed his sweet southern soul with an introspective viewpoint that the "love crowd" could relate to. Back in Memphis in early December, Redding introduced his new sound, recording "(Sittin' on) The Dock of the Bay" with the MGs backing him up and Steve Cropper whistling a solo. Then Redding headed out to fulfill some college dates with his new backup band, the Bar-Kays.

•   •   •

The Bar-Kays had had a No. 17 pop hit in the spring of '67 with "Soul-Finger" and they were looking like heirs apparent to the MGs. The young members of the Bar-Kays had been hanging around the studio for years. "I remember when those little guys would first come around, especially little Carl Cunningham," recalls Carla Thomas. "He used to shine shoes outside [there was a barbershop next to the studio] and he would slip in and play on Al's drums when everybody would go to lunch. And one time Al caught him and he said, 'Look I'm going to teach you how to play.' And he was maybe twelve at the time." By the time he was thirteen, Carla, adds, he was already a good drummer.

All that promise went unfulfilled. The plane carrying Redding and the Bar-Kays to a college gig in Madison, Wisconsin, crashed into icy Lake Monoma in the middle of town. Of those aboard the small plane, only trumpeter Ben Cauley survived the crash. Bar-Kay bassist James Alexander was luckier still. It had been his turn to return the rental car the group was using, so he took a later commercial flight. He waited all night in the airport for the group to come get him before he heard the tragic news. Today, the fuselage of that plane is on display in the Rock and Roll Hall of Fame Museum.

Had Stax closed in 1967 with Redding's death, its place in music history would have been guaranteed. But though much of the heart and soul died with Redding and the Bar-Kays, Stax wasn't done yet. Sam & Dave kept churning out the hits; their next single, "I Thank You" b/w "Wrap It Up," came out on January 8, 1968, going to No. 9 on the pop charts. Eddie Floyd, William Bell, and Johnnie Taylor, the Arkansas native who had followed Sam Cooke as lead singer for the Soul Stirrers, helped keep the Stax soul man tradition alive after Redding was gone.

Some of the most innovative Stax sounds came from the label's most traditional artists. For years, musicians and record companies had been trying to update the blues. B. B. King did it in the early sixties by bringing in sophisticated big band arrangements. In the late sixties, Chess Records in Chicago tried to package Muddy Waters and Howlin' Wolf for the acid-rock generation with hilariously clumsy "psychedelic" albums (Muddy described his own *Electric Mud* as "dogshit"). But Albert King, backed by Booker T. & the MGs, often with Isaac Hayes on piano, finally brought the blues up-to-date and onto the soul charts at a time when the music seemed doomed to be preserved, like a fly in amber, at folk festivals and coffeehouses. With his ballsy, distorted electric guitar, King inspired everyone from Jimi Hendrix to Stevie Ray Vaughan. But it was the songwriting, such as "Born Under a Bad Sign," by William Bell and Booker T. Jones, and the funky, understated backup band that pointed a new direction

for the blues, one very different from Waters's electrified Delta
stylings or B. B. King's update of Louis Jordan and T-Bone Walker.
"It was the first blues-rock," says Steve Cropper. "Albert didn't
like it at first, but later, when we'd run into him on tour, say in Europe, he'd always say, 'When are we gonna make another album
together?' "

Along with King's progressive blues, Stax was producing the
bluesy R & B of Little Milton Campbell, who remains one of the
must-see acts of the black southern clubs known as the chittlin' circuit, and the dynamic gospel of the Staple Singers. Leader Roebuck "Pop" Staples had learned his craft in Mississippi, growing up
on Will Dockery's plantation, where some of the first live music he
remembers is Charley Patton playing Saturday afternoons at the
plantation store. It was after following the black exodus to Chicago,
however, that he added his distinctive tremolo guitar effect to the
mix. He first heard it played by the Crooms Brothers gospel group,
he recalls. "They came up with the tremolo," Pop says. "But they
didn't know what to do with it. I said, 'This is soul, this is deep, this
is something that nobody's heard and this is something I really
feel.' "

Along with putting new twists on traditional music, Stax was
breaking ground at the dawn of the funk era with the emergence
of Isaac Hayes as the label's first superstar of the seventies. Hayes's
sound track for *Shaft* earned him the distinction of being the first
African American composer to win an Oscar, as well as millions in
record sales, and paved the way for much of the seventies' funk and
disco.

The Soul Children, featuring future solo star J. Blackfoot, were
another success story from the twilight of Stax. The trio's backup
band Project Soul also found a second life after signing with Mercury as Con Funk Shun, scoring a No. 1 R & B hit in 1977 with
"Ffun."

Still, Stax never really regained its momentum after the deaths
of Otis and the original Bar-Kays. Just a few months later Memphis

became forever marked as the city in which Martin Luther King was assassinated. On April 4, 1968, standing on the balcony of the Lorraine Motel (a regular hangout for Stax musicians), King was shot down while chatting with some associates in the parking lot below. Just as the city was the scene of the first race riot after the Civil War, Memphis tragically lived up to its reputation as the epicenter of America's racial upheaval. In a bitter twist, just four days later, Stax released Redding's "The Happy Song," as the nation's cities were still smoldering from the riots that followed King's death.

Changes — cultural, political, racial, musical — were coming with dizzying speed in 1968. Bobby Kennedy was killed on June 5; a few weeks later, Chicago became the scene of police riots at the Democratic National Convention. In November, Richard Nixon was elected president, and the war in in Vietnam escalated. As though echoing the tougher rhetoric of the younger members of the civil rights movement, soul music was taking a grittier, more urban stance, leaving little room for the bittersweet, laid-back southern soul that had made Stax a success. When the label's distribution deal with Atlantic ran out, increasing differences between Stewart and Wexler made a renewed contract impossible. Instead, Stax signed new deals with Gulf-Western and Columbia based on quantity, not quality. The more product it generated, the more money the label received, and dozens of albums were churned out to little commercial or artistic effect. Stax, increasingly run by black entrepreneur Al Bell, proved it could still stay ahead of the times, releasing comedian Richard Pryor's groundbreaking comedy album *That Nigger's Crazy* on its Partee label. But then it seemed Stax was throwing everything against the wall to see what would stick. A 1974 ad for the label played on the label's finger-snapping logo, promising, "Music for the whole snapping world," listing every style the copywriter could come up with: "Blues, pop, soul, rock & roll, bluegrass, progressive, underground, contemporary, rhythm & blues, country, middle-of-the-road, jazz." Stax had lost its focus, ceasing to be the artistic and commercial entity it had been throughout the sixties long before finally closing its doors in 1976.

Saddened by the way the label had changed, William Bell finally left in 1971, a decade after he first hit the charts with "You Don't Miss Your Water." "I think one of the things that happened was that we turned into a big corporate structure. We started out basically as a mom-and-pop record company and there was a family kind of unit where everybody genuinely cared that every act had a hit record and was accountable. And it worked. If Sam & Dave was coming in or Otis Redding or Carla or Rufus was having a session, and they didn't have enough songs, then people like me and Isaac and David or Betty Crutcher or Homer Banks, the different writers, would really network and come up with songs for the acts. And then we became super successful and it was the age-old story. We turned into a big corporate structure and a lot of outside people were brought in and the acts became numbers in the computer."

Even so, Stax succeeded far beyond anyone's dreams, Bell is quick to add. "It was during the transitional period of integration and everything was in an uproar. But with Stax we kind of had the best of both worlds. The staff was about fifty-fifty [black and white], the creative people were fifty-fifty, and the key rhythm section was Booker T. & the MGs. And by that combination, the feel of the white side and the black side of music, by combining those two, I think we crossed over and touched a lot of people. I think we were instrumental in changing a lot of the attitudes about the black-white situation, not only in Memphis but around the world.

"I think that's the great thing about music and about Stax, we not only created the product but we kind of brought the healing process there during that same period Dr. King was assassinated."

By then, the Memphis sound had long since ceased to be the exclusive property of Stax. Other studios and labels were churning out their own versions of southern soul, but the Stax influence continued to spread in the seventies, shaping much of the decade's rock and roll in a style that Atlantic's Jerry Wexler would call "swamp."

▼▼▼▼▼▼▼▼▼▼▼▼▼▼▼▼▼▼▼▼▼▼▼▼▼▼

11

Spreading the "Swamp" Gospel

Drive down around the 900 block of East McLemore on any summer's afternoon and you'll probably spot a few tourists, cameras
around their necks, bewildered looks on their faces, searching for
the Stax building. It's not there. In a city that often leaves buildings
standing until they crumble to dust, the home of Soulsville,
U.S.A., was torn down in 1989, three years after the founding of the
Rock and Roll Hall of Fame and long after the tourism value of
preserving sites of musical interest was well known. The nominal
excuse was that a parking lot was needed for a nearby church, but
asphalt was never laid down, and many hinted at deeper, more sinister motives behind the demolishing of the site of the city's leading black music enterprise.

"That should have been a national monument," says Stax star
William Bell. "Everybody came through there — Janis Joplin, the
Monkees, Wilson Pickett, not to mention the European artists.
That should have been a national treasure. I think after the demise
of Stax, there was a kind of attitude among the powers that be, a
kind of an attitude of good riddance, and I couldn't understand
that. We brought so much to the city." But just as Elvis, Sun
Records, and the Beale club scene of the fifties inspired Stax, Stax
sowed seeds that continued blossoming well into the seventies,
eighties, and even today.

The late sixties were a heady time for Memphis music. In 1968, according to music historian Peter Guralnick, the Memphis music industry generated $30 million in revenue, an increase of $10 million from the previous year. Along with Stax, there was Chips Moman's American Studios hit machine at 827 Danny Thomas Boulevard (named for the entertainer who founded St. Jude's Children's Research Hospital). There, with a crack studio band that included guitarist Reggie Young, bassists Mike Leech and Tommy Cogbill, drummer Gene Chrisman, and keyboardists Bobby Emmons and Bobby Woods, Moman was producing Neil Diamond's longest-ever string of hits, as well as such classic albums as Dusty Springfield's *Dusty in Memphis* (perhaps the single best fusion of pop music and Memphis soul), Herbie Mann's *Memphis Underground,* and such homegrown soul men as James Carr, who assured his place in music history with his "Dark End of the Street." After Atlantic's relationship with Stax soured, Wexler began using American Studios and Muscle Shoals to produce his acts, later trying to reproduce that Memphis magic in Miami with the Dixie Flyers, a band that took its name from Flannery O'Connor's nickname for William Faulkner.

By the end of 1969, after his ties to Memphis had been pretty well severed, Wexler moved to Miami, bringing the Dixie Flyers — Jim Dickinson on keyboards, Tommy McClure on bass, Sammy Creason on drums, future Jimmy Buffett band member Mike Utley on keyboards, and on guitar former Royal Spade/ Mar-Key Charlie Freeman — to Criterion Studios. "In Miami, I sought to build my own little Stax, a clean soul machine that would turn out great music and hit records," Wexler says in his autobiography. It didn't turn out that way. Just as W. C. Handy had learned fifty years earlier, Wexler found that Memphis magic doesn't travel too easily. Still, the inspiration Wexler first found in the little movie theater on McLemore Avenue would fuel the rest of his career. Wexler's final production before retiring was Etta James's *The Right Time* album, recorded in 1992 at Muscle Shoals with a band that included Steve Cropper on guitar, with sax and horn arrangements by one time Memphian Hank Crawford, former bandleader-arranger for Ray Charles.

As the sixties drew to a close and Elvis returned from Tinseltown for his Memphis-based triumph, even old-time Beale was catching comeback fever; the folk-blues revival brought Furry Lewis, Bukka White, Gus Cannon, and Robert Wilkins back to recording studios and stages, including 1969's Memphis Blues Festival in Overton Park. All of those sounds would come together in various forms in the seventies, in a disparate movement that Wexler, writing in the seventy-fifth-anniversary issue of *Billboard* magazine in December 1969, described in a piece entitled, "What It Is — Is Swamp Music — Is What It Is."

Wexler's "swamp music" had other influences, from folk-rock to N'awlins funk, but what it mostly was, was Memphis music filtered through a dope-smoking hippie sensibility. It was plenty of Stax; especially in the person of ex–Mar-Key and perennial hipster Don Nix. And it also was Booker T. & the MGs and the MGs-inspired house bands of Chips Moman and Rick Hall's Muscle Shoals crew. Wexler's piece also cited "echoes of early Sun" and Elvis's "Suspicious Minds," Otis Redding, Tony Joe White, Clarence Carter, and the Rolling Stones, then in the deepest throes of their American roots–music phase.

Unlike "rhythm and blues," Wexler's earlier contribution to the pop lexicon, the "swamp" moniker never caught on. But a closer look at the music of the seventies reveals that Wexler was, as was so often the case, dead right. Take Eric Clapton, for example. After his stints with Cream and the so-called supergroup Blind Faith, Clapton turned his attention to American roots, joining Delaney & Bonnie as a sideman. In England, Clapton and the D&B rhythm section would back George Harrison on his first — and finest — solo album, *All Things Must Pass.* That band turned into Derek and the Dominoes, the first group in which Clapton was the primary lead singer and the band that really allowed him to explore his love affair with American music. Clapton still lacked confidence as a singer, and doubling his vocals was North Mississippian Bobby Whitlock. Clapton cited Delaney Bramlett, another Mississippi boy, as his most important vocal inspirtation, but outside of, say, the original "Layla," the mellow approach Clapton took on much of the Dominoes' stuff and his early solo material doesn't much resemble Bramlett's gospel-fueled intensity. A closer-sounding source is Dan Penn, the singer-songwriter who worked at Moman's American Studios and cowrote "Do Right Woman" and "Dark End of the Street" with Moman. Just listen to Penn's comeback album, *Do Right Man*, one of the best, most underappreciated albums of 1994, and you can hear where Clapton got his laid-back, blue-eyed soul man style. Joe Cocker was another Brit who benefited from the "Memphis thing," when Leon Russell took Delaney & Bonnie's Stax Revue-on-acid band to back Cocker on the infamous "Mad Dogs & Englishmen" tour.

Or take the Stones, who in the late sixties recorded Como, Mississippi, bluesman Fred McDowell's "You Got to Move," Robert Johnson's "Love in Vain," and Beale bluesman turned preacher Robert Wilkins's "Prodigal Son." The Stones even tried to record part of *Sticky Fingers* at Stax, but as had happened with the Beatles' *Revolver*, union problems got in the way. Unfazed, the Stones moved on to Muscle Shoals, where they recorded "Wild Horses" and "You Got to Move" with Memphian Jim Dickinson on piano. The Stones returned to Memphis on July 4, 1975, playing a concert at the Liberty Bowl Stadium that is still talked about today. In the grandiose, cocaine-fueled, decadent rock style of the day, the Stones' contract rider demanded elephants. The band wanted to ride onstage in honor of Independence Day, "when you took the colonies back from us," the Stones organization told Memphis promoter Bob Kelley. Kelley had had to battle city fathers to do the show at all, on July 4, just a year before the Bicentennial. But he still managed to find a circus troupe of pachyderms for the gig. Attempting to make the stage elephant-proof, Kelley wasted forty-five thousand dollars reinforcing ramps and risers. The elephants turned the stage to splinters every time. Kelley had to break the news to Jagger, who by then had lost interest. "I said, 'Mick, the elephant thing didn't work out. Nothing we can do will hold them.' And he just said, 'Oh, fuck it then. Where's me makeup man?' "

While the elephants never made it onstage, Furry Lewis did, by request of the band. He played for the crowd of more than fifty-one thousand people, the largest audience of his career. Paid one thousand dollars for his set (probably the biggest payday of his career as well), he just gave the money away to his neighbors in thanks for their watching out for him, recalls Sam Phillips's son Knox. The venerable Beale bluesman was also singularly unimpressed with the Stones. According to Phillips, who had driven Furry to the show, Lewis refused to stay, despite the pleas of his girlfriend, Fredonia. "Fredonia said, 'Don't you want to see the Rolling Stones? They're the biggest rock 'n' roll band in the world.' And he said, 'I don't care *nothin*' about it.' " The Stones gave Furry something else not to care much about: a fancy new guitar. Within a few weeks, it was hanging in a Beale pawnshop.

Wexler's swamp disciples also included the Band, former sidemen for Arkansas rockabilly Ronnie Hawkins, Delta bluesman Sonny Boy Williamson II, and Bob Dylan. Made up of four Canadians and Arkansas singer-drummer Levon Helm, the Band shared Dylan's austere songwriting approach in his *John Wesley Harding* phase. Their songs, most written by guitarist Robbie Robertson, meshed perfectly with the group's Booker T. & the MGs–style instrumental sparseness, creating one of the most compelling and influential sounds of the seventies.

Add to that list Ry Cooder, whose Memphis-flavored, Jim Dickinson–produced *Into the Purple Valley* remains the *Sgt. Pepper's* of American roots music. But the team who truly carried the ball the furthest for the Memphis sound in the seventies was the duo of saxophonist Andrew Love and trumpeter Wayne Jackson, better known as the Memphis Horns.

The Mutt and Jeff of Memphis music, they make an unlikely pair. Love, the tall, laid-back son of a preacher man, was raised in the congregation of the Mount Ebo Baptist Church. Jackson, a short, excitable, self-described redneck from West Memphis, was raised on cowboy music. Like the MGs, they remain the perfect symbol of the black-white, urban-rural alchemy that is the Memphis sound. And remain they do, as the longest-running partnership in the local music scene. After years of playing together in sessions and tours, they officially combined their talents in a self-contained horn section in 1967. That year they saw the power their music had over the European soul fans at the Stax/Volt Revue tour as well as the hippies at Otis Redding's Monterey pop show. Possessing one of the most instantly recognizable horn-section blends in popular music, Love and Jackson became the most readily available soul prescription during the back-to-basics trend of the early seventies. When Stephen Stills wanted some hot and sweaty horn sounds for his 1973 solo tour, he hired the Memphis Horns. So did Rod Stewart, Jimmy Buffet, and dozens of others. They remain as popular today as they were then. "They've got a real distinctive sound. . . . They're not this bombastic horn section. They sound like human voices crying," says producer Don Was, who used them on Bonnie Raitt's *Longing in Their Hearts* album and the *Rhythm, Country & Blues* set.

While British bands like Yes, Emerson, Lake and Palmer, and early Genesis were taking the lengthy improvisational jam as far as it could go, much of American music was going the other way, stripping down and getting back to basics. Just as the raw sounds of Muddy Waters and Hank Williams swung the music pendulum back from sweeter sounds in the late forties, the roots movement of the seventies pulled back from the psychedelic excesses of the sixties. And that roots movement seemed to lead straight to the muddy Mississippi bluffs of Memphis, Tennessee. Like any smart gambler, Memphis music had more than one card to play. As Memphis swamp spread around the world, back home there was the slick, wah-wah oozing funk of Isaac Hayes, the Bar-Kays, and the Soul Children's former backup band, which by mid-decade was calling itself Con-Funk-Shun and topping the charts with dance floor hits like "Ffun." Con-Funk-Shun bandleader Felton Pilate would go on to even greater success as the producer of MC Hammer, whose allegiance to seventies funk included borrowing Rick James's Superfreak riff for "U Can't Touch This").

Meanwhile, the biggest Memphis R & B success story of the seventies was being written by one of the city's oldest record labels. Hi Records had been founded as a rockabilly label in 1956 by Bill Cantrell, Quentin Claunch, and former Sun wildman Ray Harris, three country boys who'd worked for Sam Phillips. Harris had cut some of Sun's hardest-rocking 'billy, including the bopping "Come On Little Mama" (which included the line "Pull my britches straight to my knees, Mama, Mama, play house with me"). As Elvis shot into the pop star stratosphere, creating a rock-and-roll-crazed record industry, the trio wanted in on the action. But Hi didn't really take off until 1959, when Joe Cuoghi, owner of the city's largest record store, Poplar Tunes, took the reins and changed direction, moving the Hi sound toward R & B and concentrating on instrumentals made for juke boxes and teen dances.

Poplar Tunes had been a major player in the city's music scene since Cuoghi and Novarese opened the store in the late forties. The men had earlier tried wholesaling fruit, but when their first truckload of bananas turned out to be infested with tarantulas, they decided to go into something safer. Notwithstanding the comparable number of poisonous pests in the music business, a couple of months later the men opened a record shop.

When they hung their Poplar Tunes shingle, the postwar R & B business was booming. Dewey Phillips was broadening the market to include the white teens who listened religiously to his *Red Hot & Blue* show. The partners soon expanded, starting a jukebox business and opening a one-stop that supplied dozens of regional mom-and-pop record shops with everything from those newfan-

gled 45s to phonograph needles and display racks. In those pre—
Wal-Mart days, records were sold just about anywhere there was a
counter to stack them on — beauty shops, diners, grocery stores.
Supplying Tunica, Fort Smith, Helena, Blytheville, and other
towns dotting the region, Cuoghi and Novarese found their business exploding. All that vinyl meant power, as Poplar Tunes was
able to get records played and sold throughout the Mid-South.

In 1959, after Cuoghi signed Hi to a national distribution deal
with London Records, the label had its first major hit, "Smokie
Parts 1 and 2" by the Bill Black Combo (led by Elvis's former bass
player). The funky little tune reached No. 1 on the R & B charts
and cracked the pop Top 20, and Cuoghi had found his sound.
Over the next ten years the Bill Black Combo would enjoy eighteen more records in the Top 100, and played on the Beatles' first
American concert tour.

Hi released so many instrumentals that many assumed its name
stood for either Hit Instrumentals or House of Instrumentals. It was
Hi's unsung success that no doubt inspired the early emphasis on
instrumentals at Satellite Stax, during the "Last Night" period. By
1961, Hi's success had attracted the top Beale bandleader, trumpeter Willie Mitchell, whose Flamingo Room gigs frequently featured the teenage multi-instrumental prodigy Booker T. Jones.
Mitchell, whose bands also usually included the city's top drummer, future MG Al Jackson Jr., soon became part of the self-
contained Hi family of musicians, writers, and producers. That
communal aspect of Memphis music, a strategy that had worked
for Sun and would later work for Stax, is another recurring theme
in Memphis music's continuing story. Handy's Beale days, when
musicians gathered at Pee Wee's; Beale's country blues players
jammed at Church Park and Handy Park; the high school students that Jimmie Lunceford turned into a top Swing Era big
band; Duke Records' Beale Streeters and the bluesmen of B. B.
King's generation: The Sun, Stax, and Hi bands were carrying on
a tradition of community music that was almost a century old.

Today, in his mid-sixties, Mitchell is semiretired, producing groups only when the spirit moves him, still working at his Royal Recording Studio, the original Hi studio at 1329 South Lauderdale in South Memphis. Even more rarely, he'll unpack his trumpet and perform at his namesake Beale nightspot, just a few blocks east of the club of one of his first bosses, B. B. King. Back when he began his time at Hi, Mitchell seemed to be everywhere in Memphis, playing the blues on Beale and at the Plantation Inn in West Memphis, leading sweet big bands for the old-cotton-money society balls, writing arrangements and lead sheets for Sun and other local labels. He began making a national name in 1962 when his instrumental "Sunrise Serenade" dented the charts. In 1964 he did better, reaching No. 31 on the pop charts with "20-75," but Willie Mitchell the producer and the engineer joined first surfaced in 1968 with the crossover hit "Soul Serenade," a session Mitchell also engineered.

George Harrison once said that he believed the Beatles' energy was somehow transferred to the comedy group Monty Python's Flying Circus. That may sound a bit too cosmic for some, but the same idea may apply to Memphis music. As Sun's momentum was dissipating, Stax arrived to carry the torch; then, in 1968, as Stax floundered after the deaths of Otis Redding and the Bar-Kays and the loss of the label's Atlantic distribution deal, Mitchell was emerging as the driving force behind Hi.

Along with recording "Soul Serenade," Mitchell produced a young St. Louis singer that trumpeter Gene "Bowlegs" Miller had brought to him. Ann Peebles went on to record such soul classics as "I Can't Stand the Rain," written with her husband Don Bryant and local deejay Bernard Miller, and that ultimate triangle song "Feel Like Breaking Up Somebody's Home." When the hits stopped coming in the late seventies, she retired from music, running a school for handicapped children. She staged a comeback in 1992, releasing an album on Rounder/Bullseye that reunited her with many of her old Hi cronies. Soon after finding Peebles,

Mitchell discovered another Hi star in much the same way. He and his band were touring behind the success of "Soul Serenade" when a Midland, Texas, club date happened to feature a young singer as opening act. Mitchell liked Albert Greene's sound and excitedly called Cuoghi about his find. Born in Forrest City, Arkansas, but living in Flint, Michigan, the singer had already had a minor regional hit with "Backup Train." Working with Mitchell at Hi and changing his name to Al Green, he became the most successful Memphis soul star of them all.

In many ways Green was a throwback to the classic days of Stax — Otis Redding without the tragic edge. Mitchell's arrangements added a touch of refinement to the funky old Stax sound. It was a combination that found favor among the wider audience used to Motown-style sweetening. But Mitchell's polished sound was due more to his formal training and years as a bandleader than to any desire to mimic another style. "I came up playing jazz," Mitchell explains. So even when he played southern soul, "my chords were always different. They got a little more melody or harmony, but still had that laid-back rhythm underneath it."

The Mitchell-Green combination created an amazing string of hits, beginning with some chart rumblings in 1970 with "I Can't Get Next to You," a remake of the Temptations' 1969 hit (an arrangement the Rolling Stones copied on their "Voodoo Lounge" tour, crediting Green). Green was by then writing his own material, but he had a hard time convincing Mitchell to let him record any of it. "I was toting my song around in my pocket for days on end, saying, 'Hey I got a song.' And wasn't nobody listening to me. And finally, at the end of the session, I says, 'Well, I *still* got a song." And so Willie said, 'Al, what *is* your song?' " Mitchell grudgingly let Green record "Tired of Being Alone." The result was Green's first million-seller and the beginning of a new soul hit franchise. A few months later, Green collaborated with Mitchell and drummer Jackson for "Let's Stay Together." It went to No. 1 pop and R & B and began a string of fifteen Top 10 singles in just five years. In 1983, that song would find new life and revive the career of West Tennessee native Tina Turner, the former Annie Mae Bullock of Nutbush who had had such a difficult marriage to Sam Phillips's old talent scout Ike.

Meanwhile, Ann Peebles was regularly hitting the charts, while Syl Johnson was scoring Hi hits with "Coming Back for a Taste of Your Love" and a song that would become Al Green's trademark, "Take Me to the River."

Green seemed unstoppable — until 1974 when a fight with a girlfriend resulted in a violent, career-halting tragedy: He was scalded with a pot of boiling grits as he sat in the bathtub of his Memphis home; moments later, the woman shot herself. Devastated, Green began a move back to gospel music two years later. He had been considering such a move even before the grits incident, telling the *Commercial Appeal's Mid-South* magazine a few months earlier that his mother had told him, "Al, now the Lord has blessed you and you have been successful and you have made good money. Now it's time for you to start singing gospel again." Green had started his career with the Greene Brothers gospel group, but had been tossed out for listening to Jackie Wilson records. In 1980 he completed his return to the fold, declaring his allegiance to gospel and forsaking pop. He became one of gospel's most popular singers; then, a few years ago, he began singing his old secular hits — because, he says, the Lord told him to. "I prayed about it and was told, 'You sing *all* your songs. I gave you *all* your songs, *all* those good songs. They're about love and about people and they're about happy endings and life. Sing your songs.' So I started singing 'em."

As Hi was on the verge of revitalizing the Memphis soul sound, another Memphis studio was trying to get a handle on post–*Sgt. Pepper's* rock. John Fry had started his first studio in high school, setting up the equipment in his family's garage. He worked with a couple of buddies, John King and Fred Smith, but the trio broke up when Smith went off to Yale. When he returned Smith wasn't interested in the recording studio anymore; he'd fallen in love with a new idea for overnight package delivery all over the world, a project he'd outlined in a Yale term paper. He received a failing grade for the paper, but turned the idea into a start-up company he called Federal Express.

Fry, meanwhile, kept tinkering with his Ardent Studio, moving it from the family garage to 1457 National Street when his parents sold their house and then expanding again in 1971 into its present location at 2000 Madison Avenue. In the thriving Memphis recording scene of the late sixties and early seventies, Fry began picking up work from the more established but overbooked studios in town. He says he did sessions for just about every Stax artist except Otis Redding.

Ardent Records was to be Stax's rock label, though it didn't become the Sun of the seventies. But before it supernova-ed along with the rest of the Stax organization, Ardent managed to release two albums by one of the most influential bands of the decade. Big Star borrowed on the Memphis music tradition, but took it in entirely new directions. Instead of inner-city black musicians or poor country boys, these were white suburban kids. Led by Alex Chilton, who had tasted fame if not fortune with the Box Tops, Big Star helped lead the way to modern alternative rock. Jonathan Poneman, cofounder of Sub-Pop Records, the label that introduced Nirvana, Soundgarden, and Pearl Jam, calls Big Star "the sound track of my youth." The Seattle bands regularly cite Big Star as a major inspiration, as do Paul Westerberg, R.E.M., Teenage Fanclub, Freedy Johnston, the Gin Blossoms, and dozens more.

By 1971, Chilton, having quit the Box Tops and spent a year hanging out in New York's underground rock scene, was back in Memphis. Broke and disillusioned with rock stardom, he was looking for something to do, something over which he could have a little more control. Chilton, whose parents ran a local art gallery, consciously viewed his music as "art," rather than the commercial venture that Moman had built the Box Tops into. Rather than start a band from scratch, Chilton approached Icewater, a local trio made up of middle-class guys like himself. He told them about his plans for a four-piece band that would combine a bit of the old Memphis soul and R & B with Beatle-esque pop rock and some seventies decadence. Singer-guitarist Chris Bell, drummer Jody Stephens, and bassist Andy Hummel thought that sounded pretty cool. The group was soon working up material at Ardent.

They still needed a name. "When the studio was located on National there was a Big Star [supermarket] located right across the street," recalls Stephens. "And it actually came from Alex and Chris sitting on the Ardent stoop one evening and looking up and seeing this big neon star, the store's logo, and they said, "That's great. We'll take on this name that has all these different kind of connotations, the pretentiousness of it all. And the next thing you know, the first record was called *No. 1 Record*. It was all part of this positive attitude that we had, at least at the outset."

The first album was critically acclaimed (*Rolling Stone* called it "exceptionally good" and "one of the sleepers of 1972"), but by then Stax was in serious disarray. Distribution of its Ardent subsidiary was nil. Chris Bell, disillusioned and frustrated at having to compete with Chilton in fronting what had once been *his* band, decided to quit. Chilton, Stephens, and Hummel managed to make a follow-up album, *Radio City*. Big Star followed up all its good press by playing an Ardent Records showcase at a 1973 rock writers convention in Memphis. Released in 1974 to yet more raves, *Radio City* somehow managed to receive even less distribution than the band's debut. By the time Big Star returned to the studio for the third album, Hummel too had jumped ship. With Jim Dickinson producing, musical support was enlisted from the Memphis ranks, including Steve Cropper on guitar and Stephens's brother Jimmy on bass. By the time Chilton and Stephens completed the album in 1974, Stax and Ardent Records were barely breathing. The album wasn't released until 1978, when a limited run appeared in Europe.

By then, Chilton recalls, the Big Star cult was already growing. "I guess I first realized that we had had some effect in 1977, when I went up to New York to play a gig and the place was packed. I didn't expect there to be quite so many people there, and I realized instantly that the Big Star records were what these people were responding to." The longer the band was gone, the bigger the cult grew. Big Star had all the ingredients of a world-class rock and roll legend, including mysterious death: Bell was killed in a 1978 auto accident that may have been a suicide. For those searching for hidden meanings, Chilton's edgy, druggy songs were the perfect mix of pop sensibility, self-absorbed adolescent musing, and open-to-interpretation dark lyrics. "We walked into the studio and made the most depressing album of the seventies." Stephens says of the third album with a shrug. "Which was perfectly desirable."

The *Trouser Press Record Guide* calls *Third/Sister Lovers*, as the album's 1992 rerelease was called, "a brilliant job of balancing madness and genius . . . some of the most chillingly beautiful music ever produced in the pop medium."

In 1993, Chilton and Stephens reunited for what was planned as a one-time-only Big Star reunion. Big Star disciples Jon Auer and Ken Stringfellow of Seattle's Posies were recruited. "I don't think anybody in the world could do it better," Chilton said of his new Big Star-lets in a rare complimentary moment. The pair had declared their allegiance with a Posies release of Chris Bell's "I Am the Cosmos." Big Star played a free concert at the University of Missouri, recording a live album for Zoo. That one-time-only reunion grew into tours of Europe and Japan and selected domestic dates, including a homecoming show at the New Daisy Theatre on Beale and a *Tonight Show* appearance — the latter a return engagement for Chilton, who had done the show with the Box Tops twenty-five years earlier. Chilton also found himself back on his old label, re-signing with Ardent twenty years after recording *Third/Sister Lovers.* His first Ardent release was *Cliches*, a solo set of pop standards on acoustic guitar.

Chilton's return to Ardent, where Stephens was A and R director, brought the Big Star story full circle, as the remaining members worked side by side with the latest generation of their band's disciples. Modern rock bands continue to come to Ardent to record where Big Star made those legendary albums that never sold. It started with the Replacements, who recorded 1987's *Pleased to Meet Me* at Ardent with Jim Dickinson producing. More recently the Gin Blossoms' multiplatinum *New Miserable Experience* and its follow-up, *Congratulations I'm Sorry*, came out of Ardent, the first creating a new hot producer in John Hampton. The Afghan Whigs, Primal Scream, and All are just three of the bands that have stopped in at Ardent for some of that "Memphis thing." As 1997 began, the latest version of the all-star, part-time band Golden Smog was in Ardent's main studio, with Jody Stephens playing drums.

Around the time the remnants of the group were piecing together the *Big Star Third/Sister Lovers* sessions, a very different band was finding a home at Ardent. ZZ Top had done part of its *Tres Hombres* album at the Memphis studio, and the combination of the city's musical heritage and Ardent's up-to-date equipment won over Texas diehards Billy Gibbons, Dusty Hill, and Frank Beard. Former ZZ Top roadie and Gibbons high school chum David Blayney recounted the effect Ardent had on ZZ Top in his 1994 book, *Sharp Dressed Men*. "Talk about a step up! Compared with the studio in Tyler, [Texas], Ardent Studios was the Taj Mahal . . . ZZ Top's days of being strapped for cash were behind, and it showed in this place. With the pressure off, now the boys could enjoy some of the finer things in life and do some experimenting with their music."

For Gibbons, the Memphis vibe was just as big a draw as Ardent's high-tech toys. "Dan Penn said, 'Memphis is the kind of place, the air that's been breathed in and out affects everyone who comes through town,' " Gibbons says. "And when you think about it, you say, 'Gee whiz, yeah. I'm breathing in some of the air that was part of this whole musical heritage.' It can't help but ignite those musical sensibilities."

The seventies also saw the emergence of the Memphis singer-songwriter movement, performers inspired as much by the southern literary tradition as the city's musical heritage. Jesse Winchester drew well-deserved critical attention with his 1970 self-titled debut for the short-lived Ampex label. Featuring backing by Robbie Robertson, who got him his record deal, as well as other members of the Band, the disc remains a classic. Winchester's assured, austere southern songcraft shone on "The Brand New Tennessee Waltz," "Yankee Lady," and "Biloxi." Winchester, justly acclaimed as a major new talent, was unable to translate all his good press into record sales. A conscientious objector, he had been living in Montreal since 1967 to avoid the Vietnam draft. He couldn't tour the States until the Carter amnesty in 1977, but Winchester made a few more albums, notably *Talk Memphis*, produced by Willie Mitchell. Nowadays, his recorded appearances are far too rare. His most recent album, 1988's *Humour Me*, is a brilliant showcase of his undiminished talents. One of his biggest boosters remains Jimmy Buffett, the Pascagoula, Mississippi, beach boy who has recorded Winchester's "Biloxi" and "Defying Gravity." Wynonna Judd recorded two more Winchester songs on her *Tell Me Why* album, "Just Like New," which combines the Elvis myth with Robert Johnson's Faustian legend, and the gospel of "Let's Make a Baby King." Chris Smither leads off his latest album, *Small Revelations*, with Winchester's "Thanks to You." All that may help pay the bills, but he's sorely missed, especially at a time when anyone with an acoustic guitar and a rhyming dictionary is called a singer-songwriter.

Another Buffett-Memphis connection from back in the late seventies is Keith Sykes, composer of one of the Head Parrot's favorite songs, "Coast of Marseilles," and cowriter with Buffet on the concert favorite "Volcano." His name regularly turns up in the songwriting credits of contemporary country records, and he has been known to organize songwriter guitar-pulls at local clubs.

The seventies also saw a bit of a Sun revival unexpectedly blending with the singer-songwriter movement. Sykes's pal John

Prine, who had recorded his first album in Memphis, returned to
cut his *Pink Cadillac* LP at Sam Phillips Studio. Knox and Jerry
Phillips produced, with a special appearance by Sam. Knox also
produced the debut album for the Amazing Rhythm Aces, a way-
ahead-of-its-time band that featured the songwriting of Russell
Smith, who today combines Memphis soul and bluegrass in the
novelty act Run C & W. The Aces' big hit, "Third Rate Romance,"
again topped the country charts in 1994 in a version by Sammy
Kershaw. The country-rock sound of the Aces still sounds up-to-
date in today's Nashville, but the band failed to find a niche in the
days when longhairs and country music went together about as
well as Buddhists and barbecue.

Like the music of Big Star, most of the Memphis sounds of the
late seventies were far more influential than they were commercially successful. As the decade drew to a close, times were getting
harder for Memphis musicians, at least those who stayed in town.
Record labels shuttered their Memphis offices, musicians left town
in droves, Reggie Young and the rest of the American Studios
crowd headed for Nashville, where they became first-call session
players. Booker T. Jones moved to Los Angeles to become a producer whose credits would include Willie Nelson's country-pop
classic, *Stardust*.

Of course, Memphis music's most earth-shattering event of the
decade took place on August 16, 1977, when Elvis Aaron Presley,
forty-two, died on the floor of his upstairs bathroom at Graceland.
His career had continued the downward slide that had been in-
terrupted briefly in 1968 and 1969 with his TV special and subsequent Memphis recordings, but the outpouring of emotion that
followed his death left no doubt that he remained the King. NBC
news anchor David Brinkley, a man not known for hyperbole and
admittedly no Elvis fan, expressed Presley's impact: "Elvis Presley
was one of the few people in our lifetime who changed things. You
hear Mantovani in every elevator, but so what? Elvis changed our
hairstyles, dress styles, our attitudes toward sex, all the musical
taste."

Those were dark times in Memphis music. As Elvis was buried in back of Graceland, Beale was at its burned-out bleakest, its glory days growing ever dimmer in the fading memories of a few old men and women. But just as things looked their worst, the Home of the Blues was on the verge of yet another revival.

The eighties would see a reclamation of the city's musical past. There had been talk of a Beale revival as far back as the 1950s, as city fathers took note of the success New Orleans was enjoying with Bourbon Street. Danny Thomas, who was spending a lot of time in town raising funds for the city's St. Jude's Children's Research Hospital, became involved in what became a prolonged skirmish over the name of Beale Street, when the city decided that as an east-west thoroughfare it should properly be called Beale Avenue. Thomas was a Beale Streeter, even writing a song to protest the city's position. Beale remained a street, but early attempts at Bourbonizing Beale came to naught. Beale revival talk died out completely by the late sixties, and after the riots that followed Martin Luther King's assassination in the nearby Lorraine Motel the city bulldozed much of Beale and the surrounding neighborhoods, ostensibly in the name of urban renewal.

In the early eighties, though, Beale revival talk returned in earnest. More than sixty years after Handy had decamped for New York, complaining that Beale "was losing something essential to its former character," the street had just about no character left. It had become a burned-out shell of its former self. The blocks of bustling nightclubs, theaters, restaurants, and barbecue joints celebrated in story and song had slowly degenerated into boarded-up, ruined storefronts, beer-by-the-quart carryouts, and pawnshops. After much struggle and debate, Beale launched its revival in 1983 with a $14.2 million grant from the city government. The revival, ironically, was slowed by the city's earlier decision to demolish the surrounding neighborhood; unlike New Orleans's French Quarter around Bourbon Street, Beale had no nearby buildings to be renovated into apartments, shops, or artists' studios, which would have created both additional rental income and greater tourist draw.

At first the Beale revival seemed almost cursed. The contractor hired to lay fresh bricks on the street cut corners and laid them in sand rather than concrete, resulting in a massive shift of all three hundred thousand bricks. Every single one had to be removed and relaid in concrete, at a cost of one dollar per brick. Even when the street finally reopened, it took a long time to get things going. " 'We're not going to pour any more money down that rathole,' " developer John Elkington recalls one city councilman telling him early on. In addition, even after some clubs got up and running, the street virtually shut down once the weather cooled in the fall. Odd, since it doesn't really get "cold" in Memphis until January, when the average temperature is a relatively balmy forty-three degrees, a fact lost on tourists; even today the city hasn't done much to advertise the mildness of Memphis winters.

The first music club to really make a go of it on the revived Beale was the Rum Boogie Cafe, at 182 Beale. With blues-rocker Don McMinn leading the house band, the Rum Boogie anchored the east side of the street, standing at the corner of Beale and Third. Third Street, as it heads south to Mississippi, becomes the legendary blues highway U.S. 61, a connection to the Delta blues heritage the club played up. There's some nice Stax memorabilia in the west side of the building, but the real Rum Boogie trademark hangs all over the place — dozens of cheap guitars autographed by everyone from Stevie Ray Vaughan to the New Kids on the Block.

For the most part, Beale struggled through the early days of the revival, and clubs opened and closed at a dizzying pace. That finally changed in 1991, when, within a couple of months, both B. B. King's Blues Club and Doe's Eat Place opened at the west end of the historic district at Beale and Second. The street had turned the corner, reporting its first million-dollar sales month in May 1991. Nowadays Beale averages more than a million dollars every month, and $2 million months are common.

At the same time, Beale's authenticity has been called into

question. Jim Dickinson, self-appointed keeper of the Memphis flame, has called Beale "a city-run liquor mall." But like other historic cultural attractions everywhere, Beale needs to find that balance between profitability, historical authenticity, and the need to serve the community that made it important in the first place. For the most part, Beale is slowly becoming the modern Home of the Blues. Though the revival began largely as a white tourist attraction presenting mostly blues-rock bands, today the clubs bring in some of the best black blues artists, including Luther Allison, Sam Myers, and the Black Top Records Blues Revue. Today, with young blacks rediscovering their cultural roots, Beale has become an important stop for many, as African American organizations such as Memphis's Heritage Tours offer musical jaunts along with visits to Underground Railroad houses and the National Civil Rights Museum.

Around the same time the city was first trying to resuscitate Beale as a tourist attraction, some musicians and fans set about reclaiming the city's blues heritage. In 1977, a group of Memphians, led by blues scholar Harry Godwin and including the great blues pianist Peter "Memphis Slim" Chatman, petitioned the U.S. Congress to have Memphis officially designated the Home of the Blues. In a rare case of congressional aptitude, this was done, though it's hard to tell. You won't find it on the official "Welcome to Memphis" signs; they tout the city as "America's Distribution Center," yet another example of the ongoing Memphis identity crisis.

In 1980 bar owner and blues lover Paul Savarin conceived of an organization that would present awards to blues musicians at ceremonies in Memphis that would be the equivalent of the Grammys. Savarin started the Blues Foundation and began signing up blues societies, those clubs of blues fans that had begun springing up around the country in the late seventies. His timing was right, as the first stirrings of yet another blues revival were being felt. In 1979, Eric Clapton toured the country's arenas with the Muddy

Waters Band opening his shows. Each evening, Clapton would close the concert with an encore featuring Muddy and his harmonica player, Jerry Portnoy. In 1978, the Blues Brothers, John Belushi and Dan Aykroyd, debuted with their *Briefcase Full of Blues* album, followed two years later by the first *Saturday Night Live* spin-off film, *The Blues Brothers*. In between car crashes, the movie featured performances by John Lee Hooker, Cab Calloway, Ray Charles, Aretha Franklin, and a backup band that included Memphians Steve Cropper, Duck Dunn, and blues guitarist Matt Murphy. Covering Sam & Dave's Stax/Volt hits and a handful of blues standards, "Elmore Blues" Aykroyd (who as a teenager first heard Memphis soul coming out of a roadhouse jukebox in the tiny Canadian town of Kazabazua) and "Jake Blues" Belushi might not have been the most authentic blues performers, but they kept people laughing and developing a taste for real music while Top 40 radio blared "My Sharona."

The Fabulous Thunderbirds came out of Austin in 1979 with a series of fine albums (some of them recorded in Memphis), and in 1983 Stevie Ray Vaughan, younger brother of T-Birds guitarist Jimmie Vaughan, released his debut album. Stevie Ray's *Texas Flood* had all the makings of a coronation. It was produced by John Hammond, A and R man for Bessie Smith's last session and Billie Holiday's first, and the "discoverer" of Dylan, Springsteen, and the pioneer electric jazz guitarist Charlie Christian. The album lived up to the hype, loosing the floodgates for a blues revival that continues today. The Texan was the latest white blues-rocker to go to the Albert King well for inspiration; King's steely tone and backward string bends were a big part of Vaughan's sound. He wasn't alone, as Eric Clapton, Gary Moore, and countless other blues-rock players looked to the former Stax star as the king of hard-edged contemporary blues, his Memphis records providing what many blues critics consider the only successful updating of the blues style in the sixties.

Along with Stevie Ray's debut, 1983 also saw the introduction of the compact disc, an invention that, like a musical time machine, would help bring back much of Memphis music's past glories, as a huge reissuing trend began. Today everything from W. C. Handy's dance orchestra to the Memphis Jug Band to B. B. King's first recording, Elvis Presley's complete Sun and American sessions, the entire Stax catalog of singles, all the Big Star albums, and hundreds more Memphis recordings by musicians famous and obscure are available in crisply remastered digital discs.

Live Memphis music also made a comeback in the eighties — not that it ever really went away. The Beale Street Music Festival began informally in 1977 with free shows in the fields behind Beale Street, featuring such locals as Alex Chilton, Billy Lee Riley, and Furry Lewis. The festival grew throughout the eighties along with its sponsor, the Memphis in May International Festival; in 1990 it moved to the much larger environs of Tom Lee Park. Today the festival is becoming a destination point for eclectic music lovers, as the show mixes nationally recognized local performers like Keith Sykes and Little Jimmy King with headliners like Bob Dylan and James Brown and national performers with strong Memphis roots like "Memphis" Charlie Musselwhite and Al Green.

The eighties also saw some veteran rockers make the Memphis pilgrimage to recharge their musical batteries. Tommy Boyce, cowriter of many of the Monkees' biggest records, became a common sight on Beale in the middle of the decade, sitting in with any band that would have him; people still talk about his punked-up versions of Monkees hits. Eagles guitarist Joe Walsh became even more of a musical presence in town when, between musical projects, he settled in Memphis for a while. "I wasn't getting much done in Los Angeles at the time," Walsh said during the Eagles' "Hell Freezes Over" reunion tour. "And Memphis was and still is a real center of undiscovered talent and, just, tradition." While in town, Walsh worked with Gary Belz, whose family renovated and reopened the Peabody Hotel in 1981, to open the Kiva Recording Studio. The studio went on to record Stevie Ray Vaughan, Albert King, Luther Vandross, Anita Baker, and others.

For Walsh it was a refreshing change from LA. "I met a cross section of the music community and I really loved it," he recalled. "It really expanded my awareness. It was a real kick in the pants playing with some of the folks downtown . . . to get back in a club situation," Walsh said. "It was great to get down to the roots again. . . . There's nothing like going back to the basics to get headed off in a new direction. It really brought me around to basic blues and stuff when I was probably trying to overintellectualize or overorchestrate. Sometimes less is more, y'know?"

One of those folks downtown was Albert King, who after following the Mississippi up to St. Louis and Chicago returned home to Memphis in the eighties. When King died in late 1992, Walsh flew back for the funeral, paying tribute at the memorial services at Mississippi Boulevard Baptist Church playing a heartfelt "Amazing Grace" on slide guitar.

Paul McCartney also came back for a dose of Memphis on his 1993 world tour, playing the Liberty Bowl and warming up backstage by jamming with his old friend Carl Perkins. McCartney's tour also helped bring the Stax legacy full circle: His drummer was Blair Cunningham, the youngest brother of Carl Cunningham, the original drummer for the Bar-Kays, who was killed in the Otis Redding plane crash. Blair's older brother Kelly started the Cunningham drumming dynasty; just about all the Cunningham kids — and there are more than a dozen — played drums, which couldn't have made them popular with their neighbors in Orange Mound. During his Memphis days in the mid-seventies Blair had recorded with such regional mainstays as Don McMinn and Denise LaSalle, and was part of an Ardent Studios house rhythm section with Marvell Thomas, Michael Toles, Ray Griffin, and Lester Snell in yet another Memphis attempt to replicate Booker T. & the MGs. But in the late seventies, disco, not soul music, was the sound, and the Memphis scene fell on hard times. "All of the record companies started going out west and east and all of a sudden there was nothing, it just went dead," Blair recalls.

Back then, Target, the Memphis version of the era's hard-rocking arena bands, seemed like the most likely local candidate for stardom. Despite the powerful vocals of Jimi Jamison and the blues-tinged lead guitar of Buddy Davis (whose father John occasionally played trumpet on Stax sessions), Target's two A&M LPs missed the commercial mark. The label dropped them before the third could be released (shades of Big Star). Blair, meanwhile, headed for England, where he'd been told good drummers were at a premium, and soon became one of the busiest drummers in the exploding new wave scene, playing with everyone from the Pretenders to Echo & the Bunnymen.

For Blair, who worshiped his big brother Carl, his Memphis homecoming to play the biggest room in town with the biggest tour of 1993 was a bit eerie. "I always feel like I kind of replaced him in another life," Blair said. "It's kind of weird, 'cause I'll look at these old Otis Redding [videos] . . . and he's sitting up there on his [drum] riser. And I'll say, 'That looks like me.' We kind of look alike. It's really weird; it's frightening, in a way. I'll think, 'Well, maybe I'm reliving his life.' "

Blair's conscious re-creation of Ringo's drum parts on the tour, the first in which McCartney purposely tried to recapture the Beatles' sound was part of a continuing musical trend as we head toward the millennium — rock and roll's acceptance of its past.

Elvis felt his music had to mature and move away from rock; Mick Jagger had talked about how ridiculous it would be to perform at age forty. But by the mid-eighties rock and roll wasn't necessarily just for the young and the sixties generation was heading into middle age still rocking. Rock and roll began at last to be accepted as another American musical tradition, one in which younger players learned from older ones in the oral tradition familiar to folklorists. Perhaps it was due in part to the aging of the baby boom, but it was a welcome, inevitable change from the adolescent, "hope-I-die-before-I-get-old" attitude. In 1986, a Rock and Roll Hall of Fame was announced by an alliance between Atlantic Records founder Ahmet Ertegun and *Rolling Stone* publisher Jann

Wenner. Several cities vied to house the hall of fame, Memphis among them. With no firm financial support and a weak proposal that didn't go much further than "This is where it belongs," the city lost the museum to Cleveland.

But an undeniable Memphis cast was given to the Hall of Fame by its early inductees, most of whom hailed from Memphis and its environs. The first year's honorees included Elvis, Jerry Lee Lewis, Clarksdale-born Sam Cooke, Western Kentucky's Everly Brothers, Sun Records founder Sam Phillips, Delta bluesman Robert Johnson, and country pioneer Jimmie Rodgers. And the trend has continued: In 1992, for example, the diversity of the region's music was paid tribute at New York's Waldorf-Astoria, and Rock and Roll Hall of Fame inductions became a virtual Memphis night, including the Stax house band, Booker T. & the MGs, and the label's biggest hit makers, Sam & Dave, along with Delta bluesman Elmore James, Beale R & B great Bobby "Blue" Bland, and Sun rockabilly Johnny Cash. The only thing missing were Peabody ducks in the Waldorf fountain. In 1995, the year the Rock and Roll Hall of Fame itself finally opened, the post-Stax era of Memphis music was honored, as Al Green was inducted in his first year of eligibility.

Memphis music had survived decades of changing tastes and changing styles; but even as the rest of the world recognized the enduring power and beauty of the many sounds that came out of this resilient, unrepentant river town, a question remained: When would Memphis begin recognizing it?

12

Modern Memphis

I had mixed feelings about moving to Memphis in the fall of 1991. I'd loved the music from there for as long as I could remember, so becoming the music critic/reporter for the city's sole daily newspaper, the *Commercial Appeal*, looked like a dream job. Still, I couldn't help wondering if Memphis was just the colonial Williamsburg of rock and soul, more relic than real-life.

But I found plenty of life in the Home of the Blues. B. B. King's Blues Club and Doe's Eat Place had just opened a few months earlier on Beale, turning the summer into the street's busiest tourism season since the revival began. The twenty-thousand-seat, state-of-the-art Pyramid Arena was set to open in a matter of weeks. The Beale Street Music Festival, part of the Memphis in May International Festival, was getting bigger every year. Young alternative bands were playing the Antenna and other local clubs. Major-label acts were recording at Ardent. And there was still plenty of blues and R & B to be found off the beaten tourist path.

Though born in New York, I was no stranger to Southern culture, having traveled throughout the South with a succession of bluegrass bands since the late seventies. But nothing prepared me for Memphis, for both the good and bad I would find there. For the most part, the races seemed to get along, although there was so little daily black-white interaction that it almost seemed as if there were two completely different cities there; Memphis was like a science fiction story in which two worlds in different dimensions occupy one space. And the poverty on the black side was often shocking, people living in the sort of shacks and ruined housing projects that one might expect to see in São Paulo, Brazil, but not modern America.

Music often seemed to be the only thing that brought people together, and this was especially true of the musicians, who for the most part continue to be immune to the city's racial divisions. It's hard to hate people while loving their music and trying to play it as hard as you can. Of course, when the music stops playing, it's often a different story, especially for the audiences.

Nathan Bedford Forrest could admire his slaves' musical talents, but mostly because those talents made them that much more profitable as merchandise. The white folks who crowded W. C. Handy's dances or the Palace's Midnight Rambles didn't emerge with markedly more liberal racial attitudes from the experience. In the sixties it was believed that Motown and Stax helped bring about integration. But today, when soul, now called "urban-contemporary" music, is more popular than ever, the races are hardly less polarized than during the 1960s. It takes more than music to break down the barriers, a truth borne witness to by generations of Memphians.

Say it again: The Memphis music story is the same story over and over, in a city that changes little beyond the surface.

In Memphis, music has always tended to emerge from community rather than industry. Even when it does have a major impact on the music business, the people involved tend to be far better visionaries than businessmen. Sam Phillips had Elvis, Jerry Lee Lewis, Carl Perkins, Johnny Cash, and plenty of others. He revolutionized the world's popular music. But he couldn't turn that once-in-a-lifetime stable of talent into a viable record label for more than half a dozen years. Jim Stewart built Stax, an even larger stable of Memphis talent, but failed to check his contract with Atlantic, an oversight that gave the larger label ownership of his catalog. In the Memphis music business there's always been more music than business.

Along with the city's other contrasts — black and white, rich and poor, rural and urban — Memphis has always been a very big small town. When I covered the MIM festival, phone lines wouldn't work, volunteers in golf carts hijacked performers to show off to their friends, and dozens of other moments of comedy transpired; I joked with promoter Bob Kelley about it being "Memphis in Mayberry." Yet the city's small-town nature is a big part of why Memphis has managed to be the nation's musical flashpoint for so long.

Before I moved there, I always took the stories of Elvis hanging out on Beale, or rockabilly guitarist Paul Burlison sitting in with Howlin' Wolf, to be Memphis folk legends. But even today, all the musicians seem to know each other. In the fifties and earlier, when there were far fewer musicians, it would have been even more likely that Elvis would see the Phineas Newborn Sr. Band, or that Charley Pride would audition for Sam Phillips, or that Dewey Phillips could talk himself from a store counter into a radio studio.

As in most small towns, there's also plenty of jealousy and gossip; everyone seems to know everyone else's business, and sharing information is a popular pastime. But there's also a genuinely affectionate attitude, and musical ideas are swapped as freely as stories. With so little industry pressure the communal feeling of the brass-band scene Handy experienced at Pee Wee's, or that sixties kids found hanging out at Estelle Axton's Satellite Record Shop, is free to thrive.

That family feeling is still alive at events like the various neighborhood festivals, such as the one held each September in Cooper-Young or at the far bigger Center for Southern Folklore's annual Heritage Festival. Every July, on stages throughout downtown Memphis appear several generations of the area's best musicians, from octogenarian blues pianist Mose Vinson to young alternative

rock–R & B–rap band Big Ass Truck; rockabillies like Billy Lee
Riley, Sonny Burgess, the Sun Rhythm Section, rockin' grandma
Cordell Jackson, and Jerry Lee's piano-pumping little sister Linda
Gail Lewis have all become part of it. The free festival draws
serious music fans from around the world, even while attracting
surprisingly few Memphians.

Which was perhaps the single biggest surprise I found in
Memphis — local apathy toward the city's single most outstanding
resource. Once you got out of Midtown, people didn't seem to
know or care much about Memphis music. The signs outside the
airport welcoming visitors to "America's Distribution Center" only
added insult to injury.

As a music columnist for the city, I took as my not-so-hidden
agenda to share my passion for local music and show the citizens
of Memphis just what people worldwide thought of their city's
music. Everyone read the *Commercial Appeal,* and while I was
flattered when Sam Phillips would quote from my articles at music
industry events, I felt my more important audience was people
like the woman who called to complain about a Michael Bolton
review, but who didn't know that Otis Redding had originally
recorded "(Sittin' on) The Dock of the Bay" in Memphis.

But taking music for granted is just another longstanding Memphis tradition. Perhaps because of its racial origins, it's always been
considered lower class, something the help provided for parties
when they weren't serving dinner or cleaning up. At best, it was
merely an accompaniment to drinking and dancing. To this day,
Memphis audiences remain some of the world's toughest: Ask performers who've played there and they'll tell you about crowds that
never quiet down, from the first song to the encore. Memphis musicians say that's part of their inspiration, making them want to
play and sing something so good, so powerful that they'll finally get
that crowd to sit up and take notice. And just like the absence of a
local music industry infrastructure, audience apathy helps take
the pressure off musicians ("They're going to ignore me no matter

what I do"), allowing for an informal, what-the-heck onstage attitude perfect for experimentation and chance taking.

And, as in any small town, informality is the order of the day.
Everyone knows everyone else, so nobody's allowed to put on airs,
to "get above their raising." In the summer of '92, you could have
seen Albert King hanging out on Beale on any given Saturday
night, pipe clenched in his teeth, wearing his trademark overalls,
just watching the crowd go by. And to this day Rufus Thomas still
walks along Beale, his trademark foxtail key chain in hand and his
name right there in the phone book along with everyone else's.
Show up at a local music-industry event and you'll find yourself
rubbing shoulders with Sam Phillips himself, or Estelle Axton of
Stax, or Isaac Hayes's song writing partner David Porter, or Jim
Dickinson, or the Memphis Horns.

You never knew who you might run into. Working the music
beat on a daily basis I got used to that, but there were still days that
made my head spin. One afternoon, I was going home from the
newspaper office at 495 Union and stopped in at Sun, just a couple of blocks away. There, a crew was shooting an Elvis TV special
in the tiny studio with Carl Perkins, Scotty Moore, and a band
that included Carl's sons and drummer D. J. Fontana. Scotty
hadn't been in Sun since the last Elvis sessions almost forty years
earlier. "Hell, you got to do something with this damned recession," he cracked when asked what brought him back. After an
hour of watching the men jam and chat, I drove the few blocks to
Sam Phillips Studio to find Billy Lee Riley recording a brand-new
album for Hightone, *Blue Collar Blues*. Roland Janes, Riley's guitarist from the Little Green Men, was engineering. Riley's old
drummer, J. M. Van Eaton, was visiting, and the guitarist for the
session was Travis Wammack, whose instrumental hit "Scratchy"
remains a cult classic. That's a whole lot of living rock and roll history to pack into a couple of hours and a couple of blocks on a
Thursday afternoon.

If the hometown folks were a tough sell, it seemed the rest of the world couldn't get enough. I covered such bizarre stories as the one about the picturesque Italian resort town of Porretta Terme, which, like a soulful Brigadoon, comes to life as a mini-Memphis every year during the third week in July. That's when Graziano Uliani holds his Sweet Soul Music Festival in Rufus Thomas Park. Uliani, who convinced the town fathers to dedicate the park to the Memphis soul man, has been producing the annual event since 1988, the year after he came to the States to attend the twentieth-anniversary memorial for Otis Redding and the Bar-Kays. Ever since, each year he has brought over as many Memphis soul stars as he can afford, augmenting better-known names like the park's namesake and Sam Moore of Sam & Dave with more obscure Memphis singers such as James Carr, who had the classic cut on "Dark End of the Street," or the late Muscle Shoals session man Eddie Hinton. "For me, soul music is Memphis sound, no Motown, no Detroit sound. Memphis is the roots of all modern music," Uliani told me. Uliani may be more fanatical than most (he also had the town rename his street "Via Otis Redding"), but he's certainly not the only true believer, as I found out working for the *Commercial Appeal*. Phone interviews with bored rock stars are trying chores for any music writer, but it was never hard to get my subjects excited and out of their interview rut. Even if they'd been on the phone all day rattling on about their new album or tour, I could always get them to "talk Memphis." No matter who I interviewed, whether Bonnie Raitt, Billy Joel, Robert Plant, Etta James, or Soul Asylum's Dave Pirner, some kind of music from Memphis had moved them.

In the last few years, Memphis music has been as inspiring for filmmakers as for musicians. Perhaps the best example was 1991's *The Commitments*, about a young Irish band infatuated with the Stax sound. The Stax brand of soul continues to be featured on dozens of film sound tracks, as varied as 1994's sports movie for kids, *Little Big League*, which included new recordings by the re-united Booker T. & the MGs, and Quentin Tarantino's *Pulp Fiction*. The sound track to the much-copied independent film relied on Memphis music, notably Dusty Springfield's "Son of a Preacher Man," recorded at Chips Moman's American Studios, and Al Green's "Let's Stay Together." Tarantino even says the John Travolta–Uma Thurman scene in which "Preacher Man" appears was written around the song. "I can't even imagine it without 'Son of a Preacher Man,' " he said after the film was released. "I probably would have cut it out if I couldn't get 'Son of a Preacher Man.' "

For those who like their Memphis music served with a side of slapstick, Dan Aykroyd stars in *Blues Brothers 2000*, a sequel he made with John Landis, director of the first film. Aykroyd again performs with the Blues Brothers band, which, along with former Memphians Steve Cropper, Duck Dunn, and Matt "Guitar" Murphy, features ace Memphis session drummer Steve Potts. Aykroyd and company have been opening Isaac Tigrett's growing House of Blues chain of clubs around the world and the actor/comedian/singer, a partner in the venture, has also been heavily involved in the HOB TV and radio productions.

House of Blues, with its unique mix of blues, folk art, southern culture, and pantheistic spirituality, is the latest and most universal vision of Mid-South music created by Tigrett. In the 1970s, Tigrett, a Jackson, Tennessee, native and scion of one of the area's wealthier families, became something of the Walt Disney of rock and roll, packaging American rock culture for the world with his Hard Rock Cafe restaurant-bars. Started in London in 1971, the restaurants served up hamburgers and rock memorabilia, spreading to dozens of cities across the globe. When Tigrett cashed in in the eighties he sold his portion of the business for a reported $100 million.

For his next project, Tigrett, who fondly recalls his younger days in Memphis driving Furry Lewis to gigs, dug deeper into his West Tennessee roots, opening his first House of Blues in 1993 on Harvard Square in Cambridge, Massachusetts. Presenting live blues and other roots music and decorated with folk art and artifacts from Memphis and the Delta, the flagship proved hugely successful and the chain has since expanded to New Orleans, Los

Angeles, and New York in increasingly larger and ever more elaborate clubs. The L.A. HOB even features a hydraulic bar which folds back into the walls, opening the second-floor restaurant to the first-floor stage.

With HOB, Tigrett hopes to bring the blues into the mainstream and into the twenty-first century. "It never has been mainstream and every time it's come close to notoriety, it soars every time," Tigrett explained just before the opening of his New Orleans club, leaning against the French Quarter nightspot's Blues Brothers Bar. "Those two," he said, gesturing to a huge blowup of a Blues Brothers photo. "John and Dan, in 1979, on the cover of *Rolling Stone*. It's the coolest thing happening in America. A whole generation is focused on them and they [Belushi and Aykroyd] are saying this music is where it's at. . . . When you can raise the consciousness to the music, the music sells itself."

Tigrett has been a somewhat controversial head of HOB, responding bluntly to charges that a white southerner born into old money is the wrong person to be coming to the "rescue" of the blues. "I think that's a bunch of racial nonsense," he said. "Only a white liberal from Jackson, Tennessee, could even walk this goddamn tightrope, could even know how to. . . . You do not exploit this genre. You have to earn the right to represent it and you have to do it every day."

Tigrett has won few friends among blues purists. After all, the Blues Brothers are hardly a serious blues act, and his bigger clubs book more rock than blues. More to the point is the fear that HOB will become the blues Wal-Mart, running the little guys out of business, the smaller clubs that steadfastly kept the blues flame alive when the music wasn't a hot ticket. But whether Tigrett is more Sam Phillips or Sam Walton, he's here to stay. And selling the blues to mainstream America is what started the whole Memphis music thing in the first place.

Thus far Tigrett has avoided bringing an HOB club to Memphis, citing the city's lack of support for its music community. But a studio is another thing. Apathy is bad for club business but good for music, and Tigrett believes there's still magic in Memphis. That's why he and his boyhood friend Gary Belz have converted Kiva Studios into the first House of Blues Records complex. "I think Memphis has been overlooked for the last twenty years," he says, citing the last major hit to come from the city — "Disco Duck." "We believe that the timing is finally here. The city's perceptions of its assets are growing, the talent is here. That's why we're here. We didn't go there to get California people to come and record there. I think there are artists in Memphis who are wonderful who need a break. . . . I believe in Memphis."

Nowadays, it seems that everyone wants a piece of the Memphis thing. While crowds in New York, Nashville, New Orleans, and L.A. line up for the sounds served up at HOBs, other southern cities have begun renovating their own blues streets with Beale as the model. Jackson, Tennessee, eighty miles east of Memphis, is trying to revive Shannon Street, a stomping ground for the likes of John Lee Williamson, the original Sonny Boy, who wrote the classic "Good Morning Little Schoolgirl" and who was a key figure in the evolution from the Beale Street jug bands to the electric postwar groups. Clarksdale is trying to bring back its Issaquena Street in the same manner, hoping to increase the tourism that already comes to visit the city's Mississippi Delta Blues Museum. The museum has become a regular stop for some of the bigger names in rock, who regularly make the trip down U.S. 61 when making a Memphis concert appearance. Robert Plant is one who never fails to make the trip, part of his lifelong search for "the vibe," a quest that has also taken him to "power points" in Cornwall and Morocco. "You don't find it on a map," he explains. "I think there's a lot of spent emotion down there. It just feels quite sad. I think there's a lot of absolutely beautiful one-, two- and three-lined eloquence [in the blues] that sums up how much misery and how much hope can be put into life."

Others keep searching for that vibe, whether it's one-hit-wonder Marc Cohn in his "Walking in Memphis" or John Hiatt singing "Let's go to Memphis in the meantime." The same inspirational

power that W. C. Handy found here a century ago still hangs over
the city like a blue haze. "Even just pulling into Memphis makes
me soooo . . . ," says Bonnie Raitt. "It's just the whole history. . . .
Tradition just hangs in the air, like some sort of great elixir that just
sort of starts seeping into my pores as I get closer and closer. . . . I
never know whether it's real or if it's just something I project. But
it doesn't matter, because all I know is that I'm imbued with it
when I'm there."

Nowadays it seems the locals may finally be catching on, although it's surprising the city and county mayors didn't do something long ago. Memphis mayor W. W. Herenton went to school
with Booker T. Jones and David Porter, Shelby County mayor Jim
Rout with Steve Cropper and Duck Dunn. But for years, both
politicians treated music as just something to mention in public
appearances for a bit of easy applause for "our great heritage of
Memphis music."

A Grammy museum is in the works for the Pyramid, planned
as a high-tech attraction that would showcase American popular
music and include a Grammy Hall of Fame. That broad perspective leaves open the possibility of other attractions of a more distinctively "Memphis" focus. Meanwhile, Gibson guitars is
planning an archtop guitar factory south of the Beale historic district that will include a guitar museum.

But just as those Beale bricks had to be relaid at a greater cost
after the fact, Memphis has the uncanny ability to overlook those
all-important minor details. When the Pyramid opened in November 1991, after years of delays, no one had thought to check the
plumbing. At the Judds' opening concert, toilets backed up in bib-
lical proportions, flooding half of the arena floor. A more serious
problem was the unusual shape of the arena, which made for
equally quirky acoustics. It took tens of thousands of dollars to create an acoustic baffling system to correct the problems.

Even B. B. King's Blues Club seems to have turned into another story of promise unfulfilled. Unlike the glitzier HOB chain,

the Beale B. B.'s is just touristy enough to satisfy casual visitors, while taking care of serious blues business at the same time. It has professional sound, lights, and staging, and while the club features such top acts as James Cotton, Rod Piazza, and Joe Louis Walker, cover charges are a bargain, ranging from five to seven dollars. But the club's ownership decided to expand too soon and built a glitzier, far more expensive version of the club on the Universal Citywalk in Burbank, California. When I visited there in 1994 it was obvious what was wrong. Tourists come to Hollywood for glitz; Citywalk is not the place for a down-home juke joint. To make matters worse, the club was forced to take the only spot left, tucked away on the second floor, above the traffic flow. Transplanted to L.A., Beale's top success story was bleeding millions of dollars a year. Expansion plans were halted and the licensing deal with the club's namesake is in jeopardy. The L.A. club closed and a nearly completed Nashville club never opened. Today, the only B. B. King's Blues Club is on Beale Street.

Even as the street's clubs post record sales, Beale's expansion has pretty much stalled since B. B.'s opened in 1991. Clubs open and close with regularity. Jerry Lee Lewis briefly had a namesake club, but the Killer rarely played there, and with no other major attraction the place didn't last a year. Willie Mitchell's Rhythm & Blues Club is now in that spot. It's having a hard time as well. Mitchell is a certified legend in the music industry, but the producer is little known among the general public. Developer John Elkington managed to bring Beale back from the dead, but the question is, "What now?"

As so often is the case in Memphis, the answer to that question may be "Elvis." Elvis Presley's Memphis, the first nightclub venture by EP Enterprises, opened in 1997 in the old Lansky's building at the northwest corner of Second and Beale, to tremendous fanfare. B. B. brought Beale all the way back. Can Elvis take it to the next level?

The Beale revival has been criticized by the music purists as a

Blues Disneyland, or, in Jim Dickinson's phrase, "a city-owned liquor mall." But the street has proven its relevance, providing work for veteran musicians and producing fine younger bluesmen like Little Jimmy King and Preston Shannon. Shannon is a Beale success story in the classic tradition: In the eighties, he was a factory worker dreaming of a musical career, playing in his spare time, occasionally sitting in on Beale. He landed a steady gig on the southern black club circuit with R & B singer Shirley Brown, and quit his day job; after leaving her band, he found work on the occasional off-night on Beale, sharpening his skills with low-pressure weeknight gigs and eventually working up to weekends at the Rum Boogie. In 1993, he won the Long Beach Blues Contest's Memphis preliminary, going on to take the national title in California. Two critically acclaimed albums for Bullseye Blues followed and today Shannon tours internationally, a modern Beale bluesman.

While the lack of a music industry has its benefits in the local scene's ambience, it can be frustrating for those struggling to earn a living. Many local musicians left in the seventies when the labels did, but many remained. The Memphis Horns, David Porter, Rufus Thomas, and his daughter Carla all continue to be part of the scene, along with dozens of former Stax musicians still performing around the city's hotels and clubs. Marvell Thomas, eldest of Rufus's musical offspring, has been a mainstay of the scene since he was playing piano and subbing for Booker T. Jones on organ when Jones was off at college. Thomas coproduced Hayes's revolutionary *Hot Buttered Soul* album and has continued playing sessions, Stax reunion shows, and even easy-listening jazz for the hotel-lounge set. He has fought most of his life to get Memphis music recognized by the city.

"Memphis has a pretty severe identity crisis, as far as I'm concerned," Thomas asserts. "It doesn't really know what it is. What Memphis is known for internationally . . . is its music, and a whole large part of that music happens to be black music. And that's something I don't think this town wants to be publicly acknowledged, even if it knows it. I look at places like New Orleans, which not only acknowledges its musical heritage and history, it trumpets it, pushes it, exploits it, makes money off it. . . . Even if it happens here only so somebody can make some money, that's fine. As long as it gets done."

Memphis talent also continues to have an impact on the national industry. Recent local acts with national record contracts include guitarist Shawn Lane, who as a fourteen-year-old guitar prodigy was already playing with Black Oak Arkansas and who, fifteen years later, records instrumental albums for Warner Brothers in a highly evolved guitar style that blends blues, rock, jazz, and classical touches. Eric Gales, another Memphis guitar wunderkind, recorded his Elektra Records debut at sixteen, reaching the Top 20. After Eric played blues-inflected hard rock with his brother Eugene in the Eric Gales Band, the brothers signed a deal for a bluesier album with East/West and recorded a Gales Brothers album for House of Blues that also featured their brother Little Jimmy King, born Manuel Gales. Wendy Moten continues the Memphis soul tradition, but her EMI debut smothered her raw soul with Whitney Houston–style pop production, obscuring the spectacular voice she developed under legendary music teacher Lulah Hedgman at Overton High School. Todd Snider is one of the newest Memphis names on the charts. A singer-songwriter and protégé of Keith Sykes, Snider released his debut album, *Songs for the Daily Planet*, on Jimmy Buffett's Margaritaville/MCA label. The album, named after the Memphis bar Snider played every Thursday, included his national radio hit, "Talkin' Seattle Grunge Rock Blues." In alternative rock, the two Memphis bands to watch are the Grifters, whose Sub Pop releases have earned the guitar-driven band national attention, and Big Ass Truck. BAT takes a lighter-hearted tack, adding hip-hop and funk into their rock mix, sporting a record-scratching deejay onstage. The group is fronted by Steve Selvidge, a second-generation Memphis musician whose folk-singing father, Sid, records under his own name and was a member of the group Mud Boy & the Neutrons. Sid also produces *Beale Street Caravan* for National Public Radio, a blues program hosts that has featured Memphis Horns Andrew Love and Wayne Jackson and Sam 'The Sham' Samudio and Joyce Cobb as the hosts.

Beale Street Caravan is produced by the Blues Foundation, whose executive director as of March 1997 was Howard Stovall, a Yale-educated descendant of the Stovall family who owned the plantation where Muddy Waters grew up. Stovall also plays blues keyboards in regional blues bands, as fitting a symbol of the New South as can be imagined.

There's been a movement in the past few years to unite some of the Delta's blues stops — Beale, Clarksdale, Greenville, Greenwood, and Helena, Arkansas — into an organized tourism area, a sort of United States of the Delta, cutting across state lines and governments. Not surprisingly, those state governments have been slow in supporting the idea. "Mississippi keeps saying, 'Why does Tennessee have to be involved?' And Memphis government asks why Mississippi has to be part of it," complained Beale developer John Elkington, organizer of the first Delta Heritage conference in 1994. Despite the problems, it's an idea whose time has come, as the Delta casinos, combined with the growing blues revival, are reaching critical mass in attracting tourists from around the world.

Certainly, for musicians, the Delta has always been a single region, as itinerant bluesmen such as Robert Johnson made the rounds in Helena, Clarksdale, Greenwood, Robinsonville, and on up into Memphis to enjoy the pleasures of the big city.

That tradition lives on in events like the Mississippi Delta Blues Festival in Greenville. Held in mid-September, it draws tens of thousands of fans each year, with a lineup that ranges from acoustic players like Eugene "Sonny Boy" Powell and Eddie Cusic to uptown R & B revues. At the 1994 event, headliner B. B. King and R & B great Ruth Brown took part in ceremonies issuing the blues stamps honoring Johnson, Muddy Waters, and Howlin' Wolf, along with vaudeville blues singers Bessie Smith and Ma

Rainey and swing singers Billie Holiday, Mildred Bailey, and Jimmy Rushing.

Few events in recent memory have better illustrated the changes in American culture than that stamp issue. Born black and poor in the Mississippi Delta, the best that Johnson, Waters, and Wolf could have hoped for was a lifetime spent sharecropping from "can to can't," predawn to total darkness. In those desperate circumstances, hopping a freight train with a battered guitar was upward mobility. Despite odds that make Delta casinos seem like easy money, those men's music forever changed the world.

That Delta tradition plays a major role in the Memphis in May Beale Street Music Festival, which in 1996 drew a record crowd of more than sixty thousand. Along with a blues tent highlighted by an incendiary appearance by Luther Allison, who grew up not far from Memphis, the 1996 festival introduced a long-overdue stage presenting gospel music and local Memphis artists from Rufus Thomas to Alex Chilton to Big Ass Truck; among the other sensations were the Riverbluff Clan, a unique group that mixes progressive bluegrass and that old Memphis beat, featuring singer-songwriter Jimmy Davis and virtuoso multi-instrumentalist Tommy Burroughs. Standing room only at its debut, that stage is now being expanded.

The Elvis faithful continue to fill Graceland, as seven hundred thousand fans wander annually though Elvis's house. Sun Studio is another important stop on any Presley pilgrimage, the storefront at 706 Union providing a refreshingly low-key yet moving historical experience. The studio tour makes a point of presenting the entire Sun story, including the lesser-known bluesmen and rockers along with the superstars. In addition, the studio has started a label, 706 Records, producing CDs of neo-rockabilly Billy Swan, Cincinnati blues-rocker Sonny Moorman, and veteran Sun country-swinger Malcolm Yelvington, who made his first records there more than forty years ago. And just like the day I ran into Carl Perkins and Scotty Moore, you never know who'll show up there.

Another must-see is antique collector John Montague's Memphis Music Hall of Fame on Second Street across from the Peabody. The museum features everything from Gus Cannon's original jug to a pair of Isaac Hayes's equilibrium-challenging platform shoes.

But as yet another local axiom goes, "Memphis music endures," and just as Elvis seems very much with us today, so does much of the rest of Memphis music history. The nineties have seen many of the old conflicts resolved. Jerry Lee Lewis, whose unrepentant hell-raising attitude hasn't changed much since the days he was setting fire to pianos onstage and burning out his insides with whiskey and pills, celebrated his sixtieth birthday on Beale on September 27, 1995. I'd seen the Killer in action backstage in the early eighties, less than a year after much of his stomach had been removed in an operation that had barely saved his life. He was holding court in his dressing room at Cincinnati Gardens, a run-down arena near the city's industrial west side. Sitting in the center of the room in a straight-back chair with a half-empty whiskey bottle between his legs, he reminisced at full speed about his Sun glory days.

But twelve years later, at the party given by his daughter Phoebe (from Lewis's ill-fated marriage to thirteen-year-old Cousin Myra), the birthday boy was happy, mellow, and genuinely moved. Sitting in the back of the Blues City Band Box bar (formerly Doe's) with Sam Phillips, the legendary hell-raiser acted like a polite teenager. He drank nothing stronger than the white wine Phillips had ordered, and gave his former Sun boss "Mr. Phillips" credit for his career. Lewis later took the stage for ferocious performances of his first two Sun singles, "Crazy Arms" and "Whole Lotta Shakin' Going On." Completing the eerie time-warp effect, his backup included his original bassist, J. W. Brown — Phoebe's grandfather and Lewis's ex–father-in-law. It had been a big year for Lewis, including the release of his *Youngblood* album and his show-stealing appearance at the opening concert of the Rock and Roll Hall of Fame.

Lewis's main competition at that Cleveland Stadium show was Al Green, in the biggest year of his career. Winning his first pop Grammy, inducted into the Rock and Roll Hall of Fame in his first year of eligibility, Green released his first secular album in almost twenty years and saw it top many critics' best-of-1995 lists, a quarter century after he started making hits with Willie Mitchell at Hi Records. Since then, his recorded-in-Cleveland performance has received a Grammy nomination and the Right Stuff has released a three-CD boxed set of his classic Hi sides. Nonetheless, in a city where so much and yet so little ever changes, the Reverend Al can still be found Sunday mornings tending the flock at his Full Gospel Tabernacle on Hale Road, just south of Graceland in Whitehaven.

Despite his conflicts with his namesake club, B. B. King remains a loyal part-time Memphian. He recorded his all-star Grammy-winning 1993 album *Blues Summit* at Ardent and in 1995 was honored on his seventieth birthday with a concert at the Orpheum. Pop Staples returned to Memphis to record his two albums for Pointblank Records, and Memphis studios also saw the final recordings of the great bluesmen Albert King, who died in Memphis on December 21, 1992, and Albert Collins, who died just a year later.

Even as Memphis music faces the twenty-first century, what's most amazing is just how little has changed here. You can still see Little Milton, Clarence Carter, Denise LaSalle, or J. Blackfoot at the old Club Paradise — after you're frisked at the door for weapons, of course. Rufus Thomas still holds court on Beale, showing up at various nightspots or visiting the Center for Southern Folklore, now located at Hernando and Beale. New young bands work the local clubs, recording for indie labels and hoping to be the next big thing to come out of Memphis.

In a particularly surreal event, the biggest thing to come out of Memphis was honored on October 7, 1994, in the biggest room in town, as *Elvis Aaron Presley: The Tribute* was beamed by pay-per-view TV to more than forty countries from the twenty-thousand-seat Pyramid arena. The concert brought together country stars like Dwight Yoakam, rockers like Bryan Adams, Iggy Pop, and Melissa Etheridge, pop stars like Michael Bolton, such legends as Tony Bennett and Chet Atkins, and Sun survivors like Carl Perkins, Jerry Lee Lewis, and Scotty Moore. The concert also drew Lisa Marie Presley, who attended with her then-new husband Michael Jackson, ensuring a heavy tabloid presence at the event. But while the event presented a dizzyingly diverse package of performers, producers failed to deliver the promised superstars. There was no U2, no Springsteen, not even a Billy Joel. Although it was a fund-raiser for St. Jude's Children's Medical Center, the organizers, including EP Enterprises, were taking a piece of the action. Bono, Bruce, and Billy prefer charity events to be genuine charity events. Although it featured superb performances by Dwight Yoakam, Etheridge, the Mavericks, and Chris Isaak, the resulting album had little long-term impact and sank after almost no promotion. But as usual the Memphis folks knew how to throw a party: The night-before bash at Graceland was a wild one, as every performer showed up at Elvis's house. In the party tent Michael Hutchence and George Klein debated lyric variations in "Baby, Let's Play House," as Aaron Neville compared biceps with Eddie Rabbitt. Inside the house, Sam Phillips took a tour. He said it was the first time that he'd been inside since Elvis's funeral. In the Jungle Room, his son Knox pointed out the waterfall, saying that Elvis had gotten the idea from Sam's house. Downstairs in the garish yellow TV room, Sun disciple Dwight Yoakam noticed the charismatic Phillips and hesitantly approached. "You left your fingerprints on all of us," the visibly moved Yoakam told him.

Despite the apathy, the business hassles and bankruptcies, the racial tensions, the personal problems, petty jealousies, paranoia, and parochial gossip, the music of Memphis survives. Today it doesn't really matter how much Michelangelo was paid for painting the Sistine Chapel, how much Beethoven drank, or what

Leonardo da Vinci's sexual preferences were. What remains is the work, the art. And a century after W. C. Handy was first awakened by the blues in that Delta train station, the power of that music continues to move us. Four decades after those first Sun sides, Elvis still has the power to inspire young musicians with his newness, his sexuality, and his ecstatic abandon. B. B. King's juke joint days are long gone, but he continues traveling the world, defending his title as King of the Blues. You can walk into a record store and buy three full boxed sets — twenty-eight discs in all — of the complete Stax/Volt singles, as well as boxed sets of Sun Records and Hi Records and dozens of individual albums of Memphis music. Pianist James Williams continues to preach the jazz gospel according to Phineas, hosting annual jazz awards in his name; George Coleman and Hank Crawford remain among the most admired sax players in jazz. New books are published extolling the genius of gospel pioneers Lucie Campbell and Herbert Brewster, while O'Landa Draper makes brand-new powerhouse gospel for the hip-hop generation. And even as we look back to the past to see how we got here, young Memphians like Todd Snider, Eric Gales, and Big Ass Truck point to where we're going. And you can bet there's a young musician somewhere in Whitehaven or Orange Mound getting ready to take the Memphis sound into the twenty-first century.

In pop music's endless search for the next big thing, one of the biggest recent trends has been regional scenes, whether it's Seattle, Chapel Hill, Cincinnati, or Athens, Georgia. Memphis remains the daddy of them all, with each generation of musicians inspiring the next. There are echoes of the Old Testament here: Just as Handy begat Lil Hardin, Buster Bailey, and the twenties Beale blues scene, those early Beale bluesmen and -women begat the first generation of electric players, who begat Sun, which begat Stax, which begat American Studios and Ardent, and on and on. Even as outside influences come into play, from the Beatles to MTV, the blues continues to run through Memphis music, inescapable as the city's origins as an untamed river town, unstoppable as the Mississippi itself.

That it has endured is a tribute to the musicians. Underpaid, or paid not at all, with little respect from record producers, concert promoters, or club owners — let alone the city's powers that be — black and white musicians in Memphis have mixed the primary colors of American music into a force that continues to change and shape people's lives the world over. There's something here, something that's still alive in that old Mississippi mud, something that continues to move with the lazy rhythms of the river — just a little bit in back of the beat, just far enough behind to be ahead of everyone else.

Epilogue

It's almost dark down at Junior's juke joint, outside Holly Springs near the Chulahoma crossroads in north Mississippi, close enough to Memphis to see those big-city lights reflected against the hazy sky. A crowd is gathering in the dirt parking lot outside the ramshackle wood-frame building. They still play the old Mississippi hill country blues here, and Sunday nights, as the sun goes down on the dusty, kudzu-covered countryside, the locals gather to hear Junior Kimbrough.

He's usually backed by a couple of his sons, David junior and Kenny, part of Kimbrough's living blues legacy. There's no talk of a blues revival here, no earnest young musicologists debating the merits of one scratchy old 78 record over another. Here the blues is a living thing, walking like a man, and within the colorfully painted walls Kimbrough and his boys plug in their guitars and get the crowd up and dancing. Most are Kimbrough's young black neighbors in their twenties and thirties, along with a smattering of college kids from the University of Mississippi in nearby Oxford, and occasionally some European or Japanese blues fans.

The center of all this attention is singularly unimpressed by the recent fame that has come to him through the Robert Mugge/Robert Palmer film *Deep Blues* and his resultant exposure on the international blues circuit. "I'm thinkin' of quittin'," he says nonchalantly between drags on a Kool. "I done got too old to play now." In his mid-sixties, despite a stroke, Kimbrough seems to have a few good years left. "Pull your clothes off, baby," he shouts jauntily into the microphone, his lips curling into a leer beneath his dapper, pencil-thin mustache.

"It's a family thing," says one of Kimbrough's sons, Larry Washington, who helps run the bar. "We're all like one big family." The extended clan includes the Burnsides, the children of Kimbrough's *Deep Blues* partner and longtime friend R. L. Burnside. Gary Burnside, seventeen, plays bass with both his father and Kimbrough. "I like rap, but I'm mostly into blues," he says with a grin. For this evening's gig, the bass chair is held by David junior, who, when he fronts his own band, calls himself "David Malone," so as not to be confused with the older Junior.

Young Kimbrough/Malone has already lived a bluesman's life, spending seven years in Parchman Farm State Prison on drug and burglary charges. He has a solo album, *I've Got the Dog in Me*, on the same label as his father, Oxford-based Fat Possum. David's proud to bear his father's legacy. "I respect my dad," he says solemnly. "He de man. But I'm the son. My father's old, but with him we've got a backbone in the family. If my father passes on, we've got people who can carry it on, my brothers and myself."

Carry it on they do. The music Junior plays is the rawest Mississippi blues, often just a single chord, played over and over with a throbbing, trance-inducing rhythm that probably isn't far removed from the whining slide guitar W. C. Handy heard in that Delta train station so long ago. As the evening wears on and Junior wears down, he passes his beat-up Gibson guitar on to Duwayne Burnside, while a young blonde Ole Miss kid sporting a spanking new Strat slides in to play rhythm. David junior anchors the band on bass as Duwayne starts a song in a single-string style more modern than Junior's. It's a different sound, but the beat goes on, and the changes don't matter a bit to the churning, dancing crowd, as the room gets hotter and sweatier, and the blues just keep rolling on into the north Mississippi night.

BIBLIOGRAPHY

Albertson, Chris. *Bessie*. New York: Stein and Day, 1972.

Barlow, William, and Cheryl Finley. *From Swing to Soul*. Washington, D.C.: Elliott and Clark, 1994.

Bashe, Philip. *Teenage Idol: The Complete Biography of Rick Nelson*. New York: Hyperion, 1992.

Bile, Roger. *Memphis in the Great Depression*. Knoxville: University of Tennessee Press, 1986.

Blayney, David. *Sharp Dressed Men: ZZ Top behind the Scenes*. New York: Hyperion, 1994.

Buckman, Peter. *Let's Dance: Social Ballroom and Folk Dancing*. Paddington Press, 1978.

Cantor, Louis. *Wheeling on Beale*. Fort Wayne, Ind.: Pharos Books, 1992.

Capers, Gerald M., Jr. *The Biography of a River Town*. New Orleans: Tulane University Press, 1966.

Charters, Sam. *The Legacy of the Blues*. New York: Da Capo, 1977.

Cohn, Larry, ed. *Nothing but the Blues*. New York: Abbeville, 1993.

Coppock, Paul. *Memphis Sketches.* Memphis: Friends of Memphis and Shelby County Libraries, 1976.

Deffaa, Chip. *Swing Legacy.* New Brunswick: Rutgers University Press, 1989.

Dixon, Robert, and John Godrich. *Recording the Blues.* New York: Stein and Day, 1970.

Escot, Colin, with Martin Hawkins. *Good Rockin' Tonight: Sun Records and the Birth of Rock and Roll.* New York: St. Martin's Press, 1991.

Feather, Leonard. *The Encyclopedia of Jazz.* New York: Bonanza, 1960.

Flippo, Chet. *Everybody Was Kung Fu Dancing.* New York: St. Martin's Press, 1991.

Foster, Pops, as told to Tom Stoddard. *Pops Foster: New Orleans Jazzman.* Berkeley: University of California Press, 1971.

Garon, Paul and Beth. *Woman with Guitar: Memphis Minnie's Blues.* New York: Da Capo, 1992.

George, Nelson. *The Death of Rhythm and Blues.* New York: Plume, 1988.

Gillett, Charlie. *The Sound of the City.* New York: Dell, 1972.

Guralnick, Peter. *Last Train to Memphis: The Rise of Elvis Presley.* Boston: Little, Brown, 1994.

——. *Lost Highway.* New York: Harper Perennial, 1989.

——. *Sweet Soul Music.* New York: Harper Perennial, 1989.

Handy, W. C. *Father of the Blues.* New York: Da Capo, 1985. Originally published 1941.

Harkins, John E. *Metropolis of the American Nile.* Guild Bindery Press, 1991.

Hasse, John. *Ragtime: Its History, Composers, and Music.* New York: Schirmer, 1985.

Hershey, Gerri. *Nowhere to Run.* New York: Times Books, 1984.

Kennedy, Rick. *Jelly Roll, Bix, and Hoagy.* Bloomington: Indiana University Press, 1994.

Kimball, Robert, and William Bolcom. *Reminiscing with Sissle and Blake.* New York: Viking Press, 1973.

Lanier, Robert. *Memphis in the Twenties.* Zenda, 1979.

Leadbitter, Mike. *Nothing but the Blues.* London /New York: Oak, 1971.

——, and Neil Slaven. *Blues Records.* London/New York: Oak, 1968.

Lehman, Nicholas. *The Promised Land.* New York: Vintage, 1991.

Lomax, Alan. *The Land Where the Blues Began.* New York: Pantheon, 1993.

Lyons, Len, and Don Perlow. *Jazz Portraits.* New York: Morrow, 1989.

Magness, Perre. *Past Times: Stories of Early Memphis.* Memphis: Parkway Press, 1994.

Malone, Bill. *Country Music U.S.A.* Austin: University of Texas Press, 1973.

Malone, Bill C. *Southern Music American Music.* Lexington: University of Kentucky Press, 1979.

Marcus, Greil. *Mystery Train.* New York: Dutton Obelisk, 1990.

McCarthy, Albert. *Big Band Jazz.* New York: Berkley Windhover, 1974.

McIlwaine, Shields. *Memphis Down in Dixie.* Colonial Press, 1948.

McKee, Margaret, and Fred Chisenhall. *Beale Black and Blue.* Baton Rouge: Louisiana University Press, 1981.

Morgan, Thomas L., and William Barlow. *From Cakewalks to Concert Halls.* Washington, D.C.: Elliott and Clarke, 1992.

Morton, David C., with Charles K. Wolfe. *DeFord Bailey: A Black Star in Early Country Music.* Knoxville: University of Tennessee Press, 1991.

Oakley, Giles. *The Devil's Music.* Taplinger, 1976.

Olsson, Bengt. *Memphis Blues.* London: Studio Vista, 1970.

Pleasant, Henry. *The Great American Popular Singers.* New York: Simon and Schuster, 1974.

Porterfield, Nolan. *Jimmie Rodgers.* Champaign: University of Illinois Press, 1992.

Pride, Charley, with Jim Henderson. *Pride: The Charley Pride Story.* New York: Morrow, 1994.

Quain, Kevin, ed. *The Elvis Reader.* New York: St. Martin's Press, 1992.

Reagon, Berniece Johnson. *We'll Understand It Better By and By.* Washington, D.C.: Smithsonian Institution Press, 1992.

Rogozinski, Jan. *A Brief History of the Caribbean.* New York: Signet Meridian, 1994.

Rowe, Mike. *Chicago Breakdown.* London: Edison, 1973.

Russell, Tony. *Blacks Whites and Blues.* New York: Stein and Day, 1970.

Santelli, Robert. *Sixties Rock: A Listener's Guide.* Chicago: Contemporary, 1985.

Schuller, Gunther. *The Swing Era.* New York: Oxford University Press, 1989.

Shapiro, Harry. *Waiting for the Man: The Story of Drugs and Popular Music.* New York: Morrow, 1988.

Shapiro, Nat, and Nat Hentoff, eds. *Hear Me Talkin' to Ya.* New York / Toronto: Rinehart and Company, 1955.

Shaw, Arnold. *Honkers and Shouters.* New York: Collier, 1978.

Snow, Hank, with Jack Ownbey and Bob Burris. *The Hank Snow Story.* Champaign: University of Illinois Press, 1994.

Tosches, Nick. *Country: The Biggest Music in America.* New York: Dell, 1977.

Trelease, Allen W. *White Terror: The Ku Klux Klan Conspiracy and Southern Reconstruction.* New York: Harper and Row, 1971.

Weeks, Linton. *Memphis: A Folk History.* Parkhurst, 1982.

Welding, Pete, and Toby Byron, eds. *Bluesland.* New York: Dutton, 1991.

Wexler, Jerry, and David Ritz. *Rhythm and Blues.* New York: Knopf, 1993.

Whitcomb, Ian. *After the Ball.* Harmondsworth: Penguin, 1974.

SELECTED LISTENING

This list isn't meant to be exhaustive by any means. There are hundreds more rock, pop, gospel, rap, funk, jazz, blues, and folk CDs of great Memphis music out there and it seems more arrive daily. The entire history of Memphis music can now be heard on disc or tape, from Handy's earliest recordings to underground cassettes of the latest local rapper being sold at South Memphis auto parts stores. Needless to say, there isn't room to list everything, but here's a look at some of what's currently available. This list is subject to change at a moment's notice.

Roots

Altamont: Black String Bands (Rounder) is a vibrant, exciting document of rural African-American fiddle and banjo music collected by the Library of Congress.

A Treasury of Library of Congress Recordings (Rounder) features more, though not exclusively, early black string music.

Brukdon in Belize (Rounder/Corason) showcases an intriguing offshoot of Anglo-Afro-Celtic-American dance music.

The Retrospective (Columbia/Legacy) is a broad-ranging four-CD collection of black string music, ragtime, and blues, along with various hillbilly, white blues, and Cajun recordings.

Before the Blues (Yazoo). All three volumes of this series released to date are worthwhile, covering early black string band music and pre-blues songs, from the mandolin-led ragtime of the Dallas String Band to the fiddle music of Taylor's Kentucky Boys.

From Where I Stand: The Black Experience in Country Music (Warner Bros.). Slated for release in February 1998, this three-CD collection documents African-American country music, from such pioneers as DeFord Bailey and the Memphis Sheiks to the Staple Singers, Charley Pride, and O. B. McClinton.

61 Highway Mississippi (Rounder) is the third volume of Alan Lomax's Southern Journeys series and includes the first recordings of bluesman Fred McDowell, as well as prison work songs and the archaic fife and drum sounds of Sid Hemphill and Lucius Smith.

Handy and the Jazz Era

The Complete Recordings—Lieut. Jim Europe's 369th U.S. Infantry Hell Fighter's Band (Memphis Archives). Includes Europe's arrangement of "The Memphis Blues" that the Castles found so irresistibly danceable.

W. C. Handy's Memphis Blues Band (Memphis Archives). When Jelly Roll Morton said Handy couldn't play jazz, he may well have had these stodgy, un-swinging recordings in mind. Interesting only from a historical perspective.

Animule Dance (Rounder). Jelly Roll Morton's Library of Congress recordings include his version of "Benny Frenchy's Tune."

Bessie Smith (Columbia/Legacy). Her complete recordings are available in five volumes, featuring Buster Bailey as a frequent accompanist, including "Jazzbo Brown from Memphis Town" (Vol. 3).

Louis Armstrong—Portrait of the Artist as a Young Man 1923–1934 (Columbia/Legacy). This boxed set is also a portrait of the artist's young wife, Lil Hardin, featured as pianist with his Hot Fives and Hot Sevens and as writer and arranger of many of Louis's early tunes including "Struttin' with Some Barbecue."

A *Study in Frustration: The Fletcher Henderson Story: Thesaurus of Classic Jazz* (Columbia/Legacy) features Pace & Handy's former house pianist as leader of the legendary big band that included Louis Armstrong, Coleman Hawkins, and Memphian Buster Bailey.

Mary's Idea (Decca/GRP) Andy Kirk and Mary Lou Williams. The star here is pianist Mary Lou Williams, arranger of the Kirk band's material. Her husband and the band's alto sax player is Memphian John Williams. A few years earlier they were playing on Beale as the Chickasaw Syncopators.

Stomp It Off and *For Dancers Only* (both on Decca/GRP). Jimmie Lunceford, Manassas High School's former gym teacher, and his band of former students had come a long way when they made the classic swing sides that comprise these two excellent CD reissues.

Fantasy has five CDs of Phineas Newborn Jr.'s music in trio settings, from *A World of Piano!* (1962) through the 1976 set *Look Out!—Phineas Is Back.* In both cases, the copywriter's love of exclamation points was warranted. This is amazing playing, a mix of jaw-dropping virtuosity and deep blues feeling. His later sessions found him in the company of the equally daunting rhythm section of bassist Ray Brown and drummer Elvin Jones.

The Key Players (Columbia) The Contemporary Piano Ensemble. After Phineas, this is the ultimate Memphis piano set, featuring four of the best Phineas followers—James Williams, Mulgrew Miller, Donald Brown, Harold Mabern—plus honorary Memphian Geoff Keezer and the killer rhythm section of bassist Christian McBride and drummer Tony Reedus (Williams's nephew).

Memphis Convention (DIW). James Williams organized this set (released only in Japan) featuring a lineup of world-renowned players and local best-kept secrets. Includes the four Memphis players from the Contemporary Piano Ensemble, plus guitarist Calvin Newborn, pianist Charles Thomas, saxophonists George Coleman, Bill Easley, Lewis Keel, and Herman Green, trumpeter Bill Mobley, bassist Jamil Nasser and drummer Tony Reedus.

In a more contemporary vein, Kirk Whalum is the reigning smooth jazz saxophonist in Memphis. His album *Cache* (Columbia) is in the urban-contemporary mode; *In This Life* (Columbia) is more adventuresome, mixing country stylings and Nashville songwriter Mike Reid with some down-home soul.

Heart and Soul (Rhino) Hank Crawford. *The* finest Memphis soul-jazz saxophonist has had his Atlantic albums individually reissued by Rhino. This two-CD anthology is the best single package of his work featuring his sessions as leader, his work with the Ray Charles Orchestra, and backing such stars as B. B. King and Etta James.

Berlin, 1962 (Pablo) Ray Charles. Hank Crawford is featured on alto in this live concert set.

Blues + Jazz (Rhino) Ray Charles. More Hank Crawford, playing both alto and baritone, on this sweet and soulful collection of classic Ray Charles.

My Horns of Plenty (Verve/Birdology). George Coleman on alto, tenor, and soprano, working through a set of standards with a band, featuring Harold Mabern on piano.

James Williams Meets the Saxophone Masters (Columbia). Like the title says, the Memphis jazz standard-bearer in company with his old neighbor George Coleman and two other hot tenors—Joe Henderson and Billy Pierce.

Prewar Memphis Blues

Wild About My Lovin': Beale Street Blues 1928–1930 (RCA/Bluebird) features four songs each by Jim Jackson and Frank Stokes and five songs apiece by the Memphis Jug Band and Cannon's Jug Stompers, the latter including "Walk Right In" and the song that "inspired" the Lovin' Spoonful's "Younger Girl," "Prison Wall Blues." A good one-CD overview of the 1920s Beale scene.

Four Women Blues (RCA). A twenty-three-song collection dominated by Memphis Minnie's thirteen sides. The real find here is the early recording of her "Bumble Bee Blues," which would be a hit a few years later. Here it's done with the Memphis Jug Band backing her and may just be the first recorded example of that lazy, loping Memphis Beat.

I Can't Be Satisfied — Early American Women Blues Singers Vol. 1 (Yazoo). This twenty-three-song set is heavy on Memphis and Mississippi singers (and players, such as the innovative Geeshie Wiley). A superb collection of very rare recordings.

Memphis Masters (Yazoo). A twenty-song collection of classics, featuring a wide range of artists, from less-knowns like Will Batts, Tom Dickson, and Mooch Richardson to the usual Beale suspects — Furry Lewis, Memphis Jug Band, Memphis Minnie, Frank Stokes, and Gus Cannon.

Hoodoo Lady (Columbia/Legacy). Twenty songs by the first lady of Memphis blues, Memphis Minnie.

I Ain't Gonna Be Worried No More 1929–1941 — Sleepy John Estes (Yazoo). A superb twenty-three-song collection that includes his early sides with mandolinist Yank Rachell. Some of the most eerie, influential ensemble blues recordings ever made.

Memphis Jug Band (Yazoo). The best American CD collection, it will satisfy the casual collector. Serious MJB fans should seek out the British label JSP's series of reissues — an exhaustively complete collection featuring obsessively clear sound.

In His Prime 1927–1928 (Yazoo). The first recordings of the Furry Lewis canon.

The Complete Works (Yazoo). Cannon's Jug Stompers. Two dozen songs featuring good sound from the most rural of the Beale jug bands.

Stop and Listen (Yazoo) Mississippi Sheiks. Twenty songs by the finest black string band.

Good Time Tonight (Columbia/Legacy). Big Bill Broonzy was one of the first Mississippi bluesmen to make an impact in Chicago; he helped create the "Bluebird beat" and gave Muddy Waters his start. This twenty-song set features his great early recordings, including the classic "Long Tall Mama" as well as his "Too Many Drivers," modern Chicago blues before its time.

King of the Delta Blues Singers (Yazoo) Charley Patton. This collects the works of the powerful, influential singer and guitarist.

The Complete Plantation Recordings (MCA) Muddy Waters. This collects the Lomax/Muddy Waters sessions on Stovall's Plantation, ranging from Robert Johnson covers to black string band music.

Negro Blues and Hollers (Rounder). A dozen performances from the Lomax Library of Congress Delta field trips, ranging from the sophisticated blues guitar of William Brown to Son House's grittier approach to religious music from a couple of Delta churches.

Delta Blues (Biograph) Son House. Features the Delta great on fifteen recordings made for the Library of Congress, ranging from string band blues to solo pieces.

Father of the Delta Blues (Columbia/Legacy). Son House after his "rediscovery" in a powerful set of 1965 recordings.

The Complete Bukka White (Columbia/Legacy). The label has been a bit too quick to slap "complete" on its album titles, but this disc does contain the great early recordings of one of the last of the great Delta acoustic slide players. Featuring Washboard Sam on his namesake percussion instrument.

The Bluebird Recordings 1937–1938 (RCA/Bluebird) features Sonny Boy Williamson I, the Jackson, Tennessee, Sonny Boy. Two dozen songs, including the classic original recording of his "Good Morning Little Schoolgirl." These acoustic sides pointed the way to the modern electric blues band.

The Bluebird Recordings 1938 (RCA/Bluebird). The second volume of Sonny Boy I, this set has eighteen more West Tennessee blues classics, including Williamson's tribute to his hometown's version of Beale, "Shannon Street."

The Complete Recordings (Columbia/Legacy) Robert Johnson. The last of the prewar Delta bluesmen in forty-one recordings that crystallized the country blues sound and opened the door to the electric revolution to come.

Rockin' My Blues Away (RCA/Bluebird). Washboard Sam backed by his half-brother Big Bill Broonzy in a set of proto Rhythm & Blues. This is where jump blues began.

That's All Right Mama (RCA/Bluebird) Arthur "Big Boy" Crudup. These twenty-two tracks, recorded between 1941 and 1954, include Arthur "Big Boy" Crudup's contributions to rock 'n' roll history, the title song and "Mean Ol' Frisco." But there's lots more good stuff in these raw 'n' rockin' electric Delta blues sides.

Memphis Country

The Essential Jimmie Rodgers (RCA) is as good a single-disc collection as is available. The twenty tracks show the range of his repertoire, from heart songs to his famed blue yodels, including "Memphis Yodel." Completists should get the Rounder series.

Okeh Western Swing (Columbia). The Swift Jewel Cowboys have a song here, a bit of gospel hi-de-ho in "When I Put On My Long White Robe." Unfortunately, Western Swing, despite being frequently reissued throughout the 1970s (by such labels as Western, Texas Rose, and others), hasn't quite made the jump to CD.

Tragic Songs of Life (Capitol)/Vintage). The Louvin Brothers honed their skills in Memphis, inspiring the young rockers to come. This is their finest LP, a collection of the old-time duets they used to sing in their Memphis days.

A *Tribute to the Delmore Brothers* (Capitol Vintage). The Louvins are at their best in this set of twelve songs popularized by the duo who preceded them in Memphis. It's as fine a mix of country and blues as you can find. The photo of the Delmores included on the album dates from the brothers' time broadcasting over Memphis's WMC.

Defrost Your Heart—Sun Country Vol. 1 (AVI) features five

songs by Charlie Feathers and a couple by swinging honky-tonker Malcolm Yelvington.

Drink Up and Go Home—Sun Country Vol. 2 (AVI) includes another couple of dozen country sides, ranging from Carl Perkins and Johnny Cash to Charlie Feathers and a bluegrass band featuring a young Norman Blake on dobro.

The Sun Years (Rhino) Johnny Cash. An excellent collection, including "Home of the Blues," which inexplicably was left off Columbia's otherwise fine boxed set.

Feel Like Goin' Home—The Essential Charlie Rich (Columbia/Legacy) is Peter Guralnick's superlative two-disc portrait of the complete Charlie Rich. From "Lonely Weekends" through cuts from his final album, a laid-back jazz set, it touches on all facets of this complex man's complex career.

The Complete Smash Sessions (Mercury). The post-Sun phase of Charlie Rich's career, less country, more R&B, but still years away from his pop-country success of his Epic years.

Killer Country (Mercury). Jerry Lee Lewis recorded country back in his Sun days, but he hit his stride in the 1960s and this twenty-song set has some of his best, including "Another Place, Another Time" and the devastating "She Even Woke Me Up to Say Goodbye."

Dewey Phillips

Red Hot & Blue (Memphis Archives). A complete CD of Dewey Phillips in full rave. A must-have for any Memphis collection.

Sun Blues

Blue Flames (Rhino) is a solid eighteen-song overview, including the first Sun single, "Driving Slow," by alto saxophonist Johnny London, as well as sides by B. B. King, Howlin' Wolf, Rosco Gordon, Junior Parker, Little Milton, and that "first" rock 'n' roll song, "Rocket 88," by Jackie Brenston & his Delta Cats (Ike Turner's band).

Mystery Train (Rounder) showcases nine blues songs by Junior Parker, three by James Cotton, and two by guitarist Pat Hare, the last including the powerful "I'm Gonna Murder My Baby."

Harmonica Classics (Rounder) collects fourteen more Sun blues sides from the likes of Big Walter Horton, Doctor Ross, Hot Shot Love, and Joe Hill Louis.

More Early Electric Memphis Blues

Juke Joint Blues (Flair/Virgin) is a great set of twenty-two raw recordings from such electric Memphis and Delta pioneers as B. B. King, Howlin' Wolf, Jimmy Reed, Joe Hill Louis, Walter Horton, and the duo of Bobby Bland & Junior Parker.

Howling Wolf Rides Again (Flair/Virgin) features eighteen of the Wolf's earliest Memphis recordings, powerful stuff indeed.

Cadillac Daddy Memphis Recordings 1952 (Rounder). A dozen great Wolf sides, including "Oh Red," complete with "Ornithology" sax quote.

Johnny Shines and Robert Lockwood (Paula). Ten songs apiece by the Memphis/Delta/Chicago blues greats.

I Like Ike — The Best of Ike Turner (Rhino). Eighteen Tina-less recordings, most showcasing his underrated guitar work. Thanks to the movie *What's Love Got to Do with It*, Ike seems doomed to be remembered as an untalented wife-beater. Untalented he has never been, as these sides show, ranging from "Rocket 88" to his legendary Icke Renrut instrumentals.

Early B. B. King

B. B. King still delivers a great, sweat-soaked live show, but it's been a long time since he raised a sweat on record. So long, in fact, that most modern blues fans will be surprised by the intensity of these early recordings. All are worthwhile, and all are on the Virgin/Flair label.

Singin' the Blues/The Blues—His First Two Original Albums on One CD. This is the must-have of the batch, a solid mix of early hits ("3 O'Clock Blues," "Sweet Little Angel") and a lot of rocking jump blues ("She's Dynamite").

Heart & Soul. Subtitled "a collection of blues ballads," this is the mellower side of the young blues king.

Spotlight on Lucille is the instrumental side of the Beale Blues Boy.

Do the Boogie—Early '50s Classics. Another twenty-song collection, some repetition with the other CDs.

The Best of B. B. King Vol. 1. A twenty-song set of his most popular early records.

Live at the Regal (MCA) is one of the great live albums, showcasing the 1960s B. B. King, a man far more in command than he was on his early records. But that showmanship comes at the cost of his early recordings' more intense blues edge.

King of the Blues (MCA) is a varied four-CD collection that includes his earliest recordings, done in after-hours sessions at the studios of WDIA. Shows his evolution from young guitarslinger to blues ambassador.

Blues Collections

Chess Blues (MCA). This four-CD collection shows why Chicago was called "North Mississippi." The bluesmen and women here are almost exclusively from Memphis and its Delta environs, from Memphis Minnie and Koko Taylor to Muddy Waters, Walter Horton, Howlin' Wolf, Elmore James, Albert King, Robert Nighthawk, Jimmy Rogers, Memphis Slim, Johnny Shines, Willie Dixon, John Lee Hooker, and Sonny Boy Williamson.

The Cobra Records Story (Capricorn) is a two-CD set of electric Delta blues from Magic Sam, Ike Turner's Kings of Rhythm, Sunnyland Slim, Walter Horton, and includes the classic sides by Otis Rush.

Duke/Peacock

Duke began as a Memphis label and its best bluesmen continued to hail from the Mid-South long after the company's move to Houston.

The Best of Duke/Peacock (Duke-Peacock/MCA) is an eighteen-song collection that includes Beale Streeters Earl Forest, Johnny Ace, Rosco Gordon, and Bobby Bland as well as Junior Parker, Memphis Slim, and Larry Davis.

Duke/Peacock's Greatest Hits (Duke-Peacock/MCA) includes Johnny Ace's "The Clock," Junior Parker's "The Next Time You See Me," and Bobby Bland's "Farther Up the Road."

I Pity the Fool—The Duke Recordings Vol. 1 (Duke-Peacock/MCA). The classic early recordings from one of the unsung pioneers of soul, this two-CD set features the best of Bobby "Blue" Bland's early recordings.

Turn On Your Lovelight (Duke-Peacock/MCA) is another two CD collection—fifty songs of prime Bobby "Blue" Bland.

Junior's Blues (Duke-Peacock/MCA). Another criminally neglected Memphis great, Junior Parker walked the line between down-home blues and jumping R&B with unmatched grace, as these eighteen songs attest.

Sun Rocks

Sun's Greatest Hits (RCA). There's simply no way one CD can live up to that title, but RCA tries anyway: four by Elvis, three each by Carl Perkins, Johnny Cash, Jerry Lee Lewis, and one apiece by Roy Orbison, Bill Justis, Carl Mann, and Charlie Rich.

The King of Rock 'n' Roll—the Complete '50s Masters (RCA) includes all of Elvis's issued Sun recordings, as well as the rest of his classic rockers. The essential Elvis box.

All Killer, No Filler (Rhino). Jerry Lee Lewis's wide-ranging career is summed up as neatly as possible in this two-CD box.

To date, there's no comprehensive collection of Carl Perkins available domestically. Rhino has a good Sun hits CD and Columbia issued a good collection of his post-Sun rockers a few years back. Ironically, his death in January, 1997, will no doubt result in a definitive boxed set.

Let's Bop—Sun Rockabilly Vol. 1 (AVI). Twenty-four Sun sides that didn't change the world, but rocked like crazy anyway. Includes Ray Harris's manic "Come On Little Mama."

Rock Baby, Rock It— Sun Rockabilly Vol. 2 (AVI). Twenty-four more rockabilly sides, many originally unissued, including Sun mainstay Malcolm Yelvington's "Rockin' with My Baby."

Rock Boppin' Baby— Sun Rockabilly Vol. 3 (AVI) includes the future stars who didn't make it on Sun, such as Conway Twitty when he was still Harold Jenkins, Gene Simmons before he found his "Haunted House," a pre-Ray • Ban Roy Orbison, plus future country boys Dicky Lee and Ed Bruce.

Hittin' That Jug—The Best of Sonny Burgess (AVI). Great stuff by one of the must durable Sun men, a disc packed with obscure rockers, alternate takes, and the seminal 'billy sides "We Wanna Boogie" and "Red Headed Woman."

Red Hot—the Best of Billy Lee Riley (AVI). Two dozen tracks featuring the versatile Mr. Riley showing off his chops from manic rock to down-home blues. No artist better shows the fickle nature of the music business. This guy had it all.

Uranium Rock—the Best of Warren Smith (AVI) is more proof of just how deep the Sun talent pool went. Warren Smith had lots more great songs than he did hits, and they're all here.

Lonely Weekends—Best of the Sun Years (AVI). Charlie Rich never had a hit on Sun. The title song was released on Phillips International. Like Roy Orbison, his biggest successes would come later. But these sides showed his talents as a singer, pianist, and songwriter, including his blues standard-to-be, "Don't Put No Headstone on My Grave."

The Million Dollar Quartet (RCA) is an aural snapshot of Elvis, Carl Perkins, and Jerry Lee Lewis (and briefly Johnny Cash) hanging around Sun Studio one December day in 1956. Bluegrass, R&B, gospel, country, a little bit of Jelly Roll Morton, and even some rock 'n' roll. A must-have, informal look at the young King away from the spotlight, and away from the Colonel.

Stax

The Complete Stax/Volt Singles Vol. 1 (Atlantic). By far the best of the three exhaustive collections, this details the birth of the label through its golden age, ending shortly after the death of Otis Redding (and, more to the point from the business standpoint, the end of Stax's distribution deal with Atlantic). This nine-CD set features the biggest hits for Stax's biggest stars, including all of Otis Redding's Stax singles, plus Carla and Rufus Thomas, Sam & Dave, Booker T. & the MGs, Johnnie Taylor, Eddie Floyd, Albert King, William Bell, the Mar-Keys, and the Bar-Keys and such lesser known Stax artists as Deanie Parker, Mabel John, and dozens more.

The Complete Stax/Volt Soul Singles Vol. 2 (Fantasy). There was still plenty of life left in the label, as this nine-CD box reveals with great music by the Staple Singers and the Soul Children, as well as Stax songwriter/producer-turned-superstar Isaac Hayes.

The Complete Stax/Volt Soul Singles Vol. 3 (Fantasy). The final box, this has the most CDs (ten) but the least worthwhile music. Rufus Thomas still effortlessly spun out dance records; Albert King still played great progressive blues; the revamped Bar-Kays worked on adding the new funk sounds to that Memphis backbeat; but the old Stax sound was giving way to more derivative, less original styles.

Just about every original Stax/Volt LP is available on CD, but those on a limited budget will want to stick to the excellent best-of collections available through Rhino. There's a superb four-CD Otis Redding box on Rhino, as well as equally must-have two-CD collections by Albert King and Sam & Dave. Rhino also has fine single CD collections by Otis Redding, Carla Thomas, Rufus Thomas, and Booker T. & the MGs.

Fantasy has taken up the Stax banner, owning the post-Atlantic recordings and seemingly dedicated to putting every last one of them out. Such rarities as David Porter's soul opera, *Victim of the Joke*, is available, as is *Presenting Isaac Hayes*, the debut of the future Oscar winner, and albums featuring Mabel John and Ruby Johnson, two of Stax's lesser known queens of soul.

Fantasy also has an album of Otis Redding rarities, *Remember Me*, and a third volume of unreleased recordings culled from the legendary 1967 Stax/Volt Revue's European tour (the first two previously released volumes are available on Atlantic CDs). Serious Stax fans will want to get a copy of the Fantasy catalog, listing the label's complete reissues. It's available by mail from:

Fantasy Records

10th and Porter

Oakland, CA

In addition to Stax, Fantasy owns the Specialty and Prestige labels, among others, and has reissued everything from the Soul Stirrers, featuring Sam Cooke, to Phineas Newborn Jr.'s classic jazz piano albums to the two original blues albums by Memphis Willie B. to Big Star's first two Ardent LPs (the last reissued on one CD). It's a catalog any Memphis music fan should have in his or her reference library.

Hi Records

Capitol is the current owner of the Hi masters and in 1995 released the excellent sixty-eight-track overview *Hi Times: The Hi Records R&B Years* on its Right Stuff subsidiary. A four-CD Al Green box is also available, but completists will want to pick up all the original Al Green Hi albums, available individually on bargain-priced CDs, as well as an expanded greatest hits collection.

In addition, there are excellent single CD collections of Hi's second and third biggest hitmakers, Ann Peebles and Syl Johnson, respectively, as well as Otis Clay.

More "Memphis Sound"

The Essential James Carr (Razor & Tie) collects the best songs by the unfairly obscure Memphis soul great. It was Carr, a grits 'n' gravel-voiced singer in the Otis Redding tradition, who delivered the seminal Memphis soul classic, "Dark End of the Street." That's here, along with nineteen other fine songs, including "Pouring Water on a Drowning Man."

Dusty in Memphis (Rhino/Atlantic). Dusty Springfield's Chips Moman-produced pop-soul classic.

Queen of Soul: The Atlantic Recordings (Rhino/Atlantic). Aretha Franklin may not have spent much time in Memphis as an infant, but she was a Memphis soul singer; even if she didn't record at Stax, that was the sound she and her producers went for, as this four-CD set testifies.

The Best of Wilson Pickett (Atlantic). The Wicked Pickett did start his hit streak at Stax, although his records came out on Atlantic. All the good stuff is here, raw soul records so elemental it's hard to imagine them actually being written and recorded. They sound like they've always existed.

Contemporary Memphis Blues

A broad section of the area's modern blues scene is available on CD. Hightone Records recently began reissuing Dave Evans High-water label, featuring such popular North Mississippi performers as Jessie Mae Hemphill. Fat Possum covers the modern scene represented by such juke joint vets as Junior Kimbrough and

R. L. Burnside. This is the one popularized by the late Robert Palmer's movie *Deep Blues.* Favoring droning, one-chord, trance-stomps, at its best this is blues from another dimension. At its worst, though, it can be so defiantly un-slick that it goes too far. After all, playing in tune isn't necessarily "selling out."

At the other end of the spectrum are the discs being released by modern-day Beale bluesmen Preston Shannon and Little Jimmy King. Both men record for Rounder/Bullseye, Shannon coming out of a soul-blues bag, King coming out of the Albert King/Stevie Ray Vaughan guitarslinger mode. King also made a pretty good record for House of Blues with his fellow southpaw brothers Eric and Eugene Gales, *Memphis Left Hand Brand.* Big Star's Alex Chilton has had most of his solo album rereleased on Razor & Tie. His Box Tops recordings are available on *Soul Deep* (Arista). Along with Fantasy's two-fer Big Star set, Rykodisc has the complete *Third/Sister Lovers* set, as well as a live Big Star CD and a collection of Chris Bell's solo recordings. All are must-have for the self-respecting Memphis collection. Big Star drummer Jody Stephens is finishing a Big Star tribute album as this is written, featuring contributions from such acolytes as the Gin Blossoms, Whiskeytown, and Kelly Willis. Jody also is the current drummer with the all-star alt-rock band Golden Smog.

The singer-songwriter scene remains pretty vital. Keith Sykes released a fine album on John Prine's Oh Boy label a few years back, *It's About Time.* His earlier stuff can be heard on *I'm Not Strange I'm Just Like You* (Keith Sykes Music). His protégé Todd Snider has two excellent CDs on Margaritaville Records, *Songs for the Daily Planet* and *Step Right Up.* Garrison Starr is the latest guitar-strumming Memphian on a major label, with her *Eighteen over Me* (Geffen).

The alt-rock banner in Memphis continues to be carried by the Grifters, who record for Sub-Pop, and Big Ass Truck, who tour relentlessly (check your local listings) and have a couple fine albums on Rounder/Upstart.

Index

▼▼▼▼▼▼▼▼▼▼▼▼▼▼▼▼▼▼▼▼▼▼▼▼▼▼